The Embodiment of Characters

University of Pennsylvania Press
NEW CULTURAL STUDIES
Joan DeJean, Carroll Smith-Rosenberg, and Peter Stallybrass, Editors

A complete listing of the books in this series appears at the back of this volume

The Embodiment of Characters

The Representation of
Physical Experience
on Stage and in Print,
1728–1749

Jones DeRitter

University of Pennsylvania Press

Philadelphia

Library of Congress Cataloging-in-Publication Data
DeRitter, Jones.
    The embodiment of characters: the representation of physical experience on stage and
in print, 1728–1749 / Jones DeRitter.
        p.   cm. — (New cultural studies)
    Based on the author's dissertation.
    Includes bibliographical references and index.
    ISBN 0-8122-3265-8 (alk. paper)
        1. English literature—18th century—History and criticism.
    2. Characters and characteristics in literature.   3. Body, Human, in literature.   4. Sex
role in literature.   I. Title.   II. Series.
    PR448.B63D47   1994
    820.9′27′09033—dc20
                                                                            94-16539
                                                                            CIP

This book is dedicated to

LESLIE GOSSAGE

my best critic and my best friend

Contents

Acknowledgments

Much of the primary research for this study was conducted at the Huntington Library in San Marino, California, during the summer of 1983; I am grateful to the staff of that institution for their hospitality and kindness. My research was funded by a grant from the Forstmann Foundation, which was awarded under the auspices of the Society of Fellows at the University of Virginia. My membership in the Society was sponsored by J. C. Levenson, who also helped me throughout my years in graduate school by employing me as a research assistant for his edition of *The Letters of Henry Adams*. I learned a great deal about literary and historical research methods under the tutelage of Mr. Levenson and his associate editor, Viola Hopkins Winner. Without this preparation, my own efforts in this area would have been much more difficult and much less productive.

The project itself began as a dissertation under the direction of Martin Battestin. I am grateful to Mr. Battestin for his support, advice, and encouragement; more particularly, I am keenly aware that his judicious criticisms of my early drafts helped to broaden and deepen my knowledge of the literature of the period, and that his counsel on stylistic matters has, I hope, stayed with me through several later versions of this study. Some of the changes that I incorporated into the second and third drafts of the project were inspired by other teachers at Virginia, most especially Benjamin Bennett, who allowed me to attend his seminar meetings on theater and performance theory in the spring of 1988.

Among the many longtime friends whom I first met at Virginia, three deserve special thanks. Over the past few years, Pat Gill has alerted me to a variety of primary and secondary sources that I might otherwise have missed, and introduced me to a number of colleagues whose works and conversations have further enriched my study. Peter Burgard and Sylvia Schmitz-Burgard listened patiently to my early attempts to construct parts of this argument and offered me timely advice on both substantive and technical issues that arose as I proceeded.

At various stages of this project, I have sought advice and commentary from Ann Ardis, Rick Barr, Al Filreis, Diane Freedman, Michael Friedman, Kevin Railey, Stephen Whittaker, and David Wyatt. Each of these individuals gave generously of his or her time and expertise, and my gratitude goes out to one and all. I would also like to thank Jerry Singerman, the acquisitions editor at the University of Pennsylvania Press, and my two outside readers for the pains they took with my manuscript and for the valuable suggestions they provided.

Finally, I am grateful for the generous support provided by the University of Scranton, which awarded me release time so that I could work on my writing and research funding so that I could afford to devote my undivided attention to the project during its final stages.

Parts of this manuscript have appeared in print before. An earlier and much different version of my second chapter was published in *Comparative Drama* in January 1988. The material which is carried over from that earlier version is reprinted by kind permission of the editors of that journal. A small part of Chapter 5 was included in *English Language Notes* in 1989; it is reprinted here with the editor's permission. Finally, an abbreviated version of Chapter 3 will appear in *Genders* in the spring of 1994. It is reprinted here by permission of the New York University Press.

I would also like to thank the British Library for permission to use the engraved portrait of Charlotte Charke which was adapted for use in my cover illustration.

All this assistance notwithstanding, any errors of fact or judgment in the following pages should be considered my own.

Scranton, Pennsylvania
November 1993

Abbreviations

Page references for specific citations are included in my text. In the case of multiple works by the same author, I have used abbreviations to indicate which work is being cited; those abbreviations are explained below.

AVM	Samuel Richardson, *The Apprentice's Vade Mecum* (1734; reprint, New York: Garland, 1974).
BP	Elaine Scarry, *The Body in Pain* (New York: Oxford University Press, 1985).
BN	J. Paul Hunter, *Before Novels* (New York: Norton, 1990).
CC	Terry Castle, *Clarissa's Ciphers* (Ithaca, N.Y.: Cornell University Press, 1982).
DP	Michel Foucault, *Discipline and Punish*, trans. Alan Sheridan (New York: Vintage, 1979).
EDF	Laura Brown, *English Dramatic Form, 1660–1760* (New Haven, Conn.: Yale University Press, 1981).
HFL	Martin Battestin, *Henry Fielding: A Life* (London: Routledge, 1990).
HFT	Robert Hume, *Henry Fielding and the London Theatre, 1728–1737* (Oxford: Clarendon Press, 1988).
"Int*TJ*"	Martin Battestin, Introduction to the Wesleyan Edition of *Tom Jones* (Middletown, Conn.: Wesleyan University Press, 1975).
LB	Elaine Scarry, ed. *Literature and the Body* (Baltimore, Md.: Johns Hopkins University Press, 1990).
LT	Robert Hume, ed., *The London Theatre World, 1660–1800*, (Carbondale: Southern Illinois University Press, 1983).
"MNF"	Terry Castle, "Matters Not Fit to be Mentioned: Fielding's *The Female Husband*," *English Literary History* 49 (1982): 602–22.
OF	J. Paul Hunter, *Occasional Form* (Baltimore, Md.: Johns Hopkins University Press, 1975).
PK	Michel Foucault, *Power/Knowledge*, ed. Colin Gordon (New York: Harvester Press, 1980).

PW   Martin Battestin, *The Providence of Wit* (New York: Oxford University Press, 1974).

RS   Robert Hume, *The Rakish Stage* (Carbondale: Southern Illinois University Press, 1983).

"SI"   Martin Battestin, "Henry Fielding, Sarah Fielding, and 'the dreadful Sin of Incest,' " *Novel: A Forum on Fiction* 13 (1979): 6–18.

SVP   William Empson, *Some Versions of Pastoral* (New York: New Directions, 1974).

TCI   Martin Battestin, ed., *Twentieth-Century Interpretations of Tom Jones* (Englewood Cliffs, N.J.: Prentice-Hall, 1968).

"TJ"   William Empson, "*Tom Jones*," in *Twentieth-Century Interpretations of Tom Jones*, ed. Martin Battestin, (Englewood Cliffs, N.J.: Prentice-Hall, 1968), 33–55.

Introduction

This study examines the London stage of the 1730s and the English novel of the 1740s. More specifically, it explores the representations of the human body and the attempts to enact or narrate certain physical experiences both on stage and in print during this period. It also attempts to establish that the performance conventions and print narratives of this era shared a preoccupation with the relationship between certain kinds of physical experience and the processes by which individual human identities—or the fictional approximations thereof—are constructed and transformed.

The critical approach used here might best be described as a version of cultural materialism. In their recent anthology of essays sharing this perspective, Jonathan Dollimore and Alan Sinfield have characterized the critical project of cultural materialism as a broadly based challenge to traditional forms of literary interpretation and valuation, carried on through a type of inquiry that combines "historical context, theoretical method, political commitment, and textual analysis" (vii). Although this introduction is concerned primarily with providing the historical and theoretical contexts for my argument, I want to pause briefly here to justify both my choice of texts and the relatively narrow scope of this project.

In their foreword to *Political Shakespeare*, Dollimore and Sinfield suggest that their emphasis on textual analysis is designed to "[locate] the critique of traditional approaches where it cannot be ignored" (vii). Much the same impulse is behind my choice of subjects for this study. With the exception of Charlotte Charke's autobiographical *Narrative* (1755), all of the works that receive detailed consideration in my discussion are canonical texts that have been regularly included in undergraduate literature courses over the past half-century. Some of the best recent works in cultural studies have been organized around interpretations of social practices rather than literary texts, and many of the critics who currently embrace this perspective have also sought to abolish or at least to expand the literary canon. The fact that this study is primarily concerned with texts rather than practices, and with canonical texts at that, should by no means be construed as a tacit endorsement of those critical practices that emphasize New Critical readings, old historicist contexts, and great traditions. In fact, one goal of this study is to appeal not only to those who already recognize the value of examining social practices and noncanonical texts, but also to those casually traditional readers and scholars who may be pleased to find that this new perspective has the potential to complicate their readings of well-known texts in interesting and valuable ways.

This study also offers another sort of challenge to traditional models of generic change for this period. Most literary histories of the early eighteenth century agree that the drama "declined" during this period while the novel "rose." It seems to me that the theoretical assumptions underlying these claims ought to be examined more carefully before we accept them (do these terms represent aesthetic judgments or a set of facts pertaining to the production and relative popularity of these works?), but that is beyond the range of this project. By limiting myself to the period bounded by the premiere of *The Beggar's Opera* in 1728 and the publication of the final volumes of *Clarissa* twenty-one years later, I have effectively refused to generalize about either Restoration and eighteenth-century drama or seventeenth- and eighteenth-century English fiction. Instead, I wish to pursue a more synchronic analysis, with the goal of demonstrating that certain literary and extraliterary developments involving or pertaining to the English theater of the 1730s helped to determine both the contents and the social status of the English novel of the 1740s and thereby allowed the new genre to supplant irregular dramatic satire as the preeminent source of literary narratives during the middle eighteenth century. The remainder of this introduction will seek, first, to present certain ideological concerns that permeated English society at this point in history; second, to provide a more detailed overview of the London stage and the English literary public of this era; and finally, to examine two crucial theoretical issues associated with the general question of whether and how these particular stage plays can or should be connected to these particular novels.

*   *   *

Throughout the first half of the eighteenth century, England was in the process of evolving from a post-feudal, predominantly agrarian society into a consumer society that would be increasingly dominated by the largely preindustrial capitalism of London. One general characteristic of

this evolution was a gradual redistribution of wealth and educational opportunities across what appeared to be a much broader spectrum of social
classes and individuals. As is typical of this sort of change, it served as the
catalyst for rivalries that pitted old money against new, tradition against
innovation, and literary ancients against literary moderns. This evolution
also produced an ongoing competition between landed wealth and merchant capital which set the Tory landowners against the Whig merchants
and the growing middle class, with various court factions and elements of
the increasingly restless urban masses contributing to the larger struggle
on certain occasions.

From a purely numerical standpoint, the courtiers represented a
rapidly shrinking minority of the country's population, and in all of
eighteenth-century Britain, only London was large enough to contain
"urban masses"; however, both the court and the mob played major roles
in the life of the city, and London dominated the economic and ideological life of the country to such an extent that its own political landscape
seems to have been generally mistaken for that of the nation as a whole.
According to historian E. A. Wrigley, by 1750 London contained more
than 11 percent of the population of England, and more than eight thousand people entered the city each year. As a result, nearly one of every six
adults living in Britain at this time had direct experience of the capital
(64). Furthermore, since the literacy rate was higher in London than it
was anywhere else in Great Britain, and since London contained far more
printers and booksellers than the rest of Britain combined, we can safely
assume that the reading public was even more likely than the general
population to confuse the political contours of the metropolis with those
of the country as a whole. Eighteenth-century London was an enormous
modern city, by far the largest in Europe, and it dominated the political
and social life of the country that surrounded it to a degree unequaled by
any other European city in the modern era.

Recent studies of British social history have suggested that the shift
from a post-feudal to a precapitalist social and economic system was accompanied by an equally disruptive shift in the way individuals conceived
of themselves. In his pathbreaking study of the effects of the Industrial
Revolution on English society, Peter Laslett has argued that the socioeconomic changes of this era undermined the traditional role of the family as
an arbiter of individual economic destinies; ultimately, he declares, "the
removal of the economic function of the patriarchal family at the point of
industrialization created a mass society." Laslett also argues that this new

society "turned the people who worked into a mass of undifferentiated
equals, . . . bereft for ever of the feeling that work was a family affair, done
within the family" (19). Although by no means industrialized, London
during the first half of the eighteenth century was certainly, as he puts it,
"a city on an industrial scale" (55), and it was thus in London that the new
pressures of mass urban living first exposed the weaknesses of traditional
roles and relationships and prompted the literati to explore at least a limited range of alternatives to those time-honored models.

In *The Family, Sex, and Marriage in England, 1500–1800,* Lawrence
Stone takes a different path to reach roughly the same conclusion. Stone
notes that much of the political, philosophical, and theological discourse
of the seventeenth century sought to reinforce the institution of patriarchy
in the context of the nuclear family, but he argues, first, that this preoccupation was spurred by an anxious awareness of certain social changes that
threatened the traditional system, and second, that by the early eighteenth
century, a variety of factors had begun to undermine parental authority in
significant ways.[1] Stone contends that throughout the late seventeenth and
early eighteenth centuries, English parents were becoming noticeably
more indulgent toward their offspring, while at the same time English
masters and mistresses were becoming more arbitrary and more authoritarian toward their apprentices and servants (170).[2]

In retrospect, the disparity between the treatment accorded to children and that accorded to adolescent workers helps to confirm the tension
between two competing conceptions of the family: essentially, the sons
and daughters of this era were increasingly likely to experience the family
as a source of protection and emotional sustenance, while apprentices and
maidservants were more likely to be disciplined than nurtured by the families for whom they toiled. Eighteenth-century social commentators continued to defend the status quo with conventional but forced analogies
that described every conceivable kind of institutional authority as a parent
deserving of both love and respect (Thompson 397ff.), but the interest in
this subject on the part of the literati suggests at the very least that this
equation could no longer be taken for granted. Anxiety about this issue is
reflected most prominently for our purposes in George Lillo's *The London
Merchant* (1731), where the title character is presented as both a loving father
figure and an economic mentor. This characterization attempts to gloss
over two increasingly unavoidable facts: (1) that many parents could not
or did not help their children find a place in the adult world, and (2) that
many masters could not or did not provide the quasi-parental nurtur-
ing that was generally assumed to be implicit in the indenture agreement.

The well-known emphasis on adolescent workers in eighteenth-century English literature can also be connected to these sweeping social and economic changes. What is interesting about the arrival of apprentices and servants on the English literary scene is that they appeared almost simultaneously as both readers of and subjects for narrative literature. There was no obvious economic justification for this coincidence. Although contemporary critics often attacked individual texts on the grounds that they appealed *only* to lower-class readers like apprentices and servants,[3] it seems unlikely that any of these groups had enough purchasing power to establish or disestablish a writer's reputation. Even if apprentices or maidservants had wanted to see only those plays or read only those novels that dealt exclusively with their own experiences—an assumption that is dubious on any number of grounds—they could not have produced enough economic pressure to get what they wanted. Thus it seems likely that the emphasis on apprentices, servingmaids, milliners, and footmen reflected not only the workers' interest in themselves, but also an interest in them and in what they represented on the part of the writers and the broader reading public.

Both apprentices and servants could be characterized as increasingly literate but economically marginalized aspirants to middle-class status; interestingly enough, both groups also seem to have been cohesive enough that their apparent unity alarmed those who wrote about social issues during this era.[4] To the literate public of the time, the mobs of apprentices and footmen who figured prominently in the social tracts and in various reports of disturbances in the London theaters represented the advance guard of Laslett's "mass society." The conventional view seems to have been that if the London crowds were any indication, under the new system one's individual identity would be derived not so much from one's position within a narrowly defined household, but rather from a much larger matrix of relationships that included but was not limited to purely familial connections. Because this matrix of relationships generally included the individual's connection to a large group of Londoners who shared roughly the same set of economic and social concerns—that is, to a group that was at least potentially a mob—the new model of identity apparently made some elements of the literary public profoundly uneasy. Conventional morality dictated that each apprentice should learn how to behave properly from his respective master; he was not supposed to join a crowd of his peers in order to run wild in the streets or create disturbances in the theaters. Social commentators looked on associations among working women with a similarly jaundiced eye. In 1725, the first page of Daniel Defoe's

"Everybody's Business is Nobody's Business" denounced "the inconveniences daily arising from the insolence and intrigues of our servant-wenches, who, by their caballing together, have made their party so considerable, that everybody cries out against them."

This fear of collective activity by certain segments of the lower classes was justified to some degree by the often unruly behavior of city mobs and by the widespread awareness that London's criminal underworld contained a large number of formerly respectable members of the urban underclass. The thief and the prostitute were closely connected in the popular imagination to the runaway apprentice and the young women who had been seduced or forced away from service and into prostitution. The anxiety generated by the operation of these various sociohistorical forces was reflected both on stage and in print throughout this period.

As we shall see in the first two chapters, both *The Beggar's Opera* and *The London Merchant* deal not merely with the phenomenon of urban crime, but also with the means by which casually virtuous young people were led into vice. Both explicitly invoke a conceptual polarity which sets up two competing versions of an individual identity: one defined by familial or quasi-familial relationships and the other by some stylized representation of London's urban masses. Nor is this trope located only in stage plays. Charke's *Narrative* is organized around a competition between the identity she hoped to recover—that of "Mr. Cibber's youngest daughter"—and the one she hoped to put to rest—that of "the well-known troublemaker"[5] who was associated with Henry Fielding's alternative theater troupe, with the denizens of London's sexual underground, and with the strolling players of the 1740s. Similarly, each of Richardson's exemplary female protagonists is confronted by a male villain who hopes to mistreat her as he has mistreated other women with roughly the same social backgrounds. Moreover, both Pamela and Clarissa seek at crucial moments to escape their tormentors by returning to the houses of their respective fathers. And in *Tom Jones* (1749), this thematic opposition connects the mystery of Tom's origins—his apparent lack of family connections—to the narrator's frequently repeated suggestion that he was (like the marginalized criminals of *The Beggar's Opera*) "born to be hanged."

It should also come as no surprise that all of these texts and performances are concerned to one degree or another with the issue of individual sexual misconduct. Michel Foucault once told an interviewer that "the political significance of the problem of sex is due to the fact that sex is located at the point of intersection of the discipline of the body and the control of the population" (*PK* 125).[6] This assertion does more than simply identify the regulation of sexual conduct as both a personal and a political issue. It also defines the political side of this question in explicitly demographic terms, and thereby implies a broadly based interest in perpetuating and reinforcing the institution of the nuclear family, partly as a means of strengthening a society by increasing its numbers, and partly as an alternative to the mobs that were more difficult to govern and less productive, in both the material and the biological senses of the word.

*   *   *

Even if they accept the argument that the London stage of the 1730s and the realistic novels of the 1740s reflected some of the same political concerns in some of the same ways, skeptics may wonder whether there is anything to be gained by focusing on these connections. In order to defend the proposition that these common tropes and concerns reflect more than a superficial link between the stage and the print media during this era, I will need to begin by glancing briefly at the economic history of English literary production between 1728 and 1749.

Before the Stage Licensing Act was passed in 1737, the London theaters dominated in the English literary marketplace. Certain poetic forms—the epic, for instance—might have been more prestigious, but a successful stage play tended to be more lucrative and to reach a wider audience than any other kind of literary production. The theater enjoyed a fashionable reputation among the general population and the reading public, and it provided the subject matter for a small but significant community of literary critics whose essays appeared in newspapers, periodicals, and pamphlets.[7] After the Licensing Act was passed, interest in the drama seems to have plummeted sharply, at first because playgoers angrily refused to accept new plays that had been cleared by the censor, and later because the lack of new works forced essayists and audiences alike to find new focuses for their critical interests and new sources for their entertainment.

The Licensing Act did not simply grant the Lord Chamberlain's office the power to censor plays; it also limited the number of state-sanctioned theaters to two. There had been five playhouses operating before the legislation was passed, and many of the period's most interesting experiments—including the early works of Fielding and Lillo—had been produced first by the smaller companies competing with the relatively wealthy and somewhat complacent groups headed by Colley Cibber, Charles Fleetwood, and John Rich. The smaller companies had sprung up and flourished partly because the number of playgoers had increased steadily throughout the first third of the century, and partly because Cibber, Fleetwood, and Rich were temperamentally averse to risking their money on new plays. By the mid-1730s, the managers of the two patent theaters had moderated their policies in response to the increased competition, but once the Licensing Act was passed they returned to their tight-fisted ways almost immediately. According to Robert Hume, Rich's Covent Garden Theatre produced exactly three new full-length plays between 1740 and 1747 (*RS* 307).

The effects of these new restrictions reached far beyond the London theatrical community. Throughout the 1720s and 1730s, large segments of the English reading public had been accustomed to reading plays; in fact, a number of plays from this era apparently had more readers than auditors. New plays were almost invariably published, regardless of their reception on stage, usually within two weeks of their first performance (Kenny 314–15), and anecdotes about reading dramatic texts recur frequently in a variety of contexts.[8] In June of 1732, Thomas Cooke began his satirical essay in *The Comedian* with an account of a visit to

> a Yorkshire gentleman . . . who told me that several in the Country entertain a Suspicion of the Booksellers presuming to publish bad Plays which were never performed on any Stage . . . and this Art, say'd he, they are supposed to use as an Imposition on their Customers who live at a great Distance from *London*; some of which buy every play that is acted.

Sales figures for the period are difficult to locate, but those that are available corroborate the claim that printed plays were widely read. The number of piracies and squabbles among printers and booksellers about the rights to popular pieces attests to the financial success of such ventures, and that in turn indicates a sizable reading public for dramatic works. Some 10,500 copies of Gay's *Polly* were printed for the author in 1729, and, given the number of pirates who were attempting to cash in on his success, the actual number of copies in circulation must have been even larger (Kenny 325). Even though *Polly* was clearly an exceptional case—Walpole had obligingly banished it from the stage, thereby turning it into a cause célèbre and boosting sales—the number of copies in print was remarkable. By way of comparison, *Tom Jones*, which was offered to the larger reading public of 1749, sold 6,500 copies (out of a printing of 10,000) during its first year (Battestin, "Int *TJ*," xxi).

Polly was also exceptional in that it sold well without being staged. After the Stage Licensing Act was passed, a few dramatists tried publishing their works before submitting them to the censor, apparently in the hope of using popular support to pressure the authorities into allowing their plays to be staged. Since very few publications of this sort appear after 1738, it can be inferred that the booksellers had no notable success with such efforts. Cooke's joke assumed that provincial readers would refuse to read plays that had not been acted. Had the Licensing Act not been passed, no modern critic would dare to make or defend such a claim, but the historical record of the period is actually quite clear on this point: both urban and rural English readers stopped reading new plays when new plays stopped being performed.

Thus the advent of institutionalized censorship on the London stage altered the English literary marketplace in at least two important ways. First, as a purely practical matter, the upheaval in the theater world and the extremely negative public reaction to it deprived the printing industry and the reading public of a profitable and fashionable source of entertainment. The noisy reception of *Pamela* in 1741 demonstrated to authors and audiences alike that prose fiction might be able to fill that void, and there is anecdotal evidence to suggest that a number of writers were spurred by Richardson's success to begin writing novels themselves.[9] Second, the reduction in the number of theaters and the resulting complacency of the two remaining managers stifled the further development of certain generic experiments and indirectly cleared the way for a kind of theater that would place more emphasis on acting technique and less emphasis on what was being enacted.

The irregular satires that were so popular during the 1736–37 theatrical season might have fallen out of favor after only another season or two, but there is no convincing evidence to support this claim. Nevertheless, the acclaim that greeted the debut of David Garrick and his new style of acting in October 1740 signaled a relatively sudden shift away from an overtly political theater that emphasized new dramatic works to a theater that emphasized individual virtuosity and made a fetish out of decency. The groundwork for this change was laid in a kind of critical vacuum; despite Garrick's growing fame, there was much less theatrical criticism published in the newspapers and periodicals during this decade than there had been during the 1730s (Gray 97). The issues taken up by critics toward the end of the decade included Garrick's style of acting and his projects of establishing a national repertory and cleansing the stage of immorality. Thus the irregular satires of the 1730s could have been excluded from Garrick's theater because they provided few showcase opportunities for actors, or because they were not timeless, or because they were immoral.

The Lord Chamberlain had banished plays like these because they offended powerful individuals connected with the government. By the mid-1740s, the theater community had developed a set of aesthetic standards that tended to obscure the extremity of the interventions ordained by the Stage Licensing Act by promoting and defending the kind of drama that would be unlikely to arouse the censor's ire. This is not to suggest that this set of standards can or should be traced to the machinations of sinister forces within or outside that community. Unlike, say, Colley Cibber, the later generation of reformers seems to have taken its own rhetoric seriously, and in any case, the question of agency with regard to this particular institutional change is vexed and probably unanswerable. For the purposes of this study, however, we only need to recognize that in the decades immediately following the passage of the Stage Licensing Act, the London theater community declared its allegiance to an assortment of virtues that effectively masked the necessity of acceding to the censor's demands.

In 1736, Great Britain's popular culture was dominated by the London stage. The theaters were not the only form of entertainment available, nor were they universally respected, but they were exceedingly profitable, and they did provide a variety of opportunities for individuals who sought to break into the literary world of their day. In 1740, the stage was moribund. Because the number of theaters had been drastically reduced, very few new works were being produced, and critics, writers, and readers had turned their attention elsewhere. Domestic tragedy, a genre which had arisen partly in response to experimental satires like those of Gay and Fielding, resurfaced during Garrick's reign, but by that time the ideological debate underlying the original competition between the two dramatic forms had changed venues.

Given this array of circumstances, it seems reasonable to conclude that the audience for the novels of the 1740s overlapped to a considerable degree with the audience for the plays of the 1730s. And yet this connection, like that which pertains to the sociohistorical forces detailed in the previous section, continues to go largely unremarked. With very few exceptions, historians of the eighteenth-century English novel have focused exclusively on the relations of the new form to other kinds of prose narratives. Over the past thirty-five years, novels have been connected in one way or another to prose romances, newspaper stories, sermons, conduct books, travel narratives, personal letters, periodical essays, legal documents, biographies, autobiographies, and histories.[10] The difficulties created by turning a blind eye to the stage are perhaps best illustrated with a brief mention of J. Paul Hunter's most recent book about the early English novel. Although Hunter acknowledges that "[o]nly readers of plays seem to have moved easily and naturally to the new narrative fiction from motives that suggest continuity of desire, need, and pleasure" (*BN* 87), he does not explain why this should be so or how this assertion should change the way we think about the rise of the novel. In fact, in a study that is three hundred and fifty pages long, he refers to eighteenth-century readers of plays fewer than five times.

I do not intend this as an attack on Hunter's book, which has a great deal to recommend it on other grounds; it is only the combination of his isolated comment with the absence of other studies exploring the connection between reading plays and reading novels that makes this particular silence so suggestive. It is unclear whether this collective silence has been prompted by conscious judgments about the value of discussing this connection, or whether it is simply an accident caused by the relatively recent tendency of academic critics to specialize not only in a particular historical period, but also in a particular medium or genre. In either case, this silence has affected the current debate about the origins of the English novel in a manner analogous to the way that David Garrick's professional demeanor and management practices affected the critics and playgoers of the mid-eighteenth century. The Stage Licensing Act cleared the way for the legitimation of the new form by depriving the literary public of a fashionable source of reading matter, by all but eliminating the possibility that an unknown or otherwise marginalized writer could get his or her work performed, and by forcing the critics and the coffeehouses to turn their attention away from a moribund stage. To the extent that critics ignore these material interventions in the literary marketplace, they perpetuate the myth that literary forms develop according to a purely internal logic that is somehow protected from the vicissitudes of everyday life. If we are to understand why the English novel established itself when it did, and why and how it shared certain ideological concerns with the drama of the 1730s, we must be willing to test these myths against more sophisticated models of the relationships between literary forms, between literary media, and between literature and history.

*   *   *

Although historians of the early novel have been loath to connect the eighteenth-century London stage to the rise of the novel, a few modern critics have been willing to explore the manner in which specific novelists were influenced by the drama of this era. Surprisingly enough, Henry Fielding, who wrote plays and managed a theater, does not get much of this sort of attention; rather, it is Samuel Richardson, who professed a deep distrust of the London stage and all it touched, who is often credited with creating something called the "dramatic novel."[11] Critics who have pursued this line of reasoning have often combined several strategies—the tracing of specific allusions, the identification of plot conventions and character types that were evidently borrowed from the London stage, the assertion that the author's way of presenting specific incidents is somehow "dramatic" or "theatrical"—in order to establish that the novelist has consciously or unconsciously tried to create the impression that the unfolding of a narrative plot is a species of performance. Even before the poststructuralist revolution in literary criticism, this approach might have seemed excessively positivistic. Despite this weakness, however, such a model can provide a point of departure for a brief discussion of exactly which of the many differences between performance and printed narrative most need to be theorized.

Before any critic can make claims about the relationship between printed texts and theater, or about the imagining of physical experience in either medium, certain theoretical problems must be addressed. For the relatively restricted purposes of my own analysis, these problems can be presented in the form of two basic questions. First, how do the fundamental differences between theatrical performances and printed texts facilitate or obstruct the effort to compare specific performances to specific texts? Second, since neither reading a narrative of a physical experience nor seeing that experience enacted on stage is the same as actually having that experience, on what basis can we claim a connection between either of these literary processes and the physical experiences they claim to represent?

Insofar as this discussion is concerned, the most important distinction between theatrical performance and print narratives is that the basic elements of theatrical performance are both multifarious and predominantly material (in the broadest sense of the word). These elements appeal primarily to our eyes and ears in a straightforward, sensory mode; they include spoken words and sound effects, gestures and costumes, activity and scenery, all of which depend upon a series of more or less productive interactions between animate beings and inanimate objects. By way of contrast, although the component elements of printed texts are also material (one needs at least ink and paper), they are by no means sensual. No print narrative actually contains a spoken word, a gesture, a sound, an image, a being, or an object; texts can only use language to describe such things and attempt to arrange them into a coherent pattern. This is not to suggest that printed texts are incapable of producing physical responses in readers. I do, however, wish to assert that even when print narratives succeed in producing such responses, they do not produce them by the same means that performances produce them, for the simple reason that in the former case the means of presentation is almost exclusively verbal, while in the latter case the means of presentation is predominantly material. On the face of it, the two literary systems would seem to be generally incommensurable, and yet there are occasions when the connections between specific stage pieces and specific printed texts seem both obvious and significant. What is needed, then, is a way of defining and evaluating such local connections within the larger context of general incommensurability.

In his discussion and reenvisioning of the letters and manifestos authored by Antonin Artaud, Jacques Derrida posits the existence of a kind of theatrical experience that antedates writing and thereby liberates the audience from the binarism of both critical and clinical discourses. For both Derrida and Artaud, this liberating effect seems to be derived largely from what might be termed the unscriptable elements of performance (185 ff.). Over the past half-century, these ideas have provided the basis for many sophisticated explorations of theater history and performance in general—so many, in fact, that at this point we may need to be reminded of the limited nature of the claims made initially by Artaud and elaborated later by Derrida. Artaud's goal was to purge the mid-twentieth-century theater of the discursive elements that Derrida identifies as critical and/or clinical, but his utopian vision was rooted in a conviction that the theater that immediately preceded his own experiments was decidedly *not* exempted from the conceptual limitations of the bourgeois audience that supported it. The traditional conception of theater claims a relatively straightforward correspondence between the onstage and offstage worlds. Plays are presumed to hold up a mirror to the world of the audience, and the range of possibilities available for the development of both plots and characters is defined and limited by (often unarticulated) local beliefs about human nature and social or material reality. In a sense, any playwright or theatrical company working from this sort of conceptual foundation has already placed significant limits on the possibility of liberating either the theater or its audience from the discursive structures they share with the world of printed texts.

Claims about the incommensurability of works drawn from different media are rooted in the assumption that different potentialities translate in every case to substantially different results. However, what a particular performance does with the matrix of potentialities available to playwrights, performers, and theater people in general is profoundly influenced by local historical and individual factors. Virtually any historical study of any stage will contain innumerable instances where local pressures led to greater or lesser emphasis on either the discursive or the nondiscursive elements of particular productions. My claims about the relationship between certain plays of the 1730s and certain novels of the 1740s are based in part on my belief that, whatever the potentialities that were available to either the London stage or the printing industry of that era, the shared actualities of these specific works provide opportunities for a limited sort of quasi-intertextual analysis. As we shall see in Chapter 4, both Charles Johnson's *Caelia* (1732) and Richardson's *Clarissa* presented their respective audiences with a linear narrative involving substantially similar characters in substantially similar circumstances. Clearly, it would be absurd to argue that Richardson's novel is only or essentially a retelling of Johnson's tragedy. It seems to me, however, that it would be equally wrong to dismiss the connections between these two works simply because each medium engenders such a vastly different array of potentialities; the different ranges of these two sets do not preclude the possibility of extensive overlaps in particular cases.

The second question—that regarding the relationship between lived experience and experience as represented either in performance or on the printed page—presents us with yet another version of the problem of incommensurability. Obviously, characters are not people, and the events recounted in a narrative or enacted on stage are therefore not equatable with the events they claim to represent. Given these undeniable truths, is there any justification either for talking about imaginary characters as if they were people, or for talking about fictional episodes as if they had actually occurred? [12]

Once again, it seems to me that we need to distinguish between an absolute claim that the word represents the thing and the more limited claim that words frequently attempt to represent things, with varying degrees of success. The word "rose" cannot be equated with the flower that goes by that name among English-speaking people; the question, however, is whether the term needs to do more than invoke the flower before we can talk coherently about a connection between the word and that which it claims to signify. Similarly, when we refer to Caelia, or to Clarissa

Harlowe, we understand on some level that we are referring only to a specific collection of words created by Charles Johnson, or, perhaps, to the enactment of that collection of words by Jane Cibber in December 1732, or to another completely distinct verbal construct written into and out of existence by Samuel Richardson. At the same time, we also understand and accept the writer's or the performer's implicit claim that the thoughts, experiences, and actions of these characters will invoke thoughts, experiences, and actions that are conceivable within our own horizon of expectations.

The connections between these imaginative constructs and our own realities may well be approximate and provisional, but we need not assume on that account that they are utterly inaccessible. A great deal may be lost or changed by attempting to represent the flesh in words (or, in the case of traditionally discursive theater, by attempting to represent the word in flesh), but we need not assume that those losses and changes place either the process of representation or the material reality being represented entirely beyond our grasp. Obscuring a connection is not the same as severing it.

I am not convinced that the general question of what it means to be a body in a play or in a print narrative can or should be answered transhistorically, and I will certainly not attempt to arrive at that sort of answer in this study. I do, however, wish to argue that certain specific connections between the theatrical performances and print narratives of this era can be played off against the general incommensurability of plays and novels to arrive at a new vision of literary change. It is my hope that this vision will allow for more extensive consideration of the relationship between specific generic changes and the extrageneric and even extraliterary forces that help to shape and define those changes.

* * *

During the second quarter of the eighteenth century, both the London stage and the matrix of prose works that Lennard Davis has christened "the news/novels discourse" were more or less exclusively narrative media. Both texts and playtexts contained plots that were easily recognizable as such, and characters interacted with each other in ways that were supposed to change either them or their situations. As Peter Brooks has pointed out, one of the defining characteristics of narrative is its transferability (4); plots retain their basic shape even when they are shifted from one medium to the next. The same is true, though to a somewhat lesser extent, of the characters and settings that figure in those narratives. At least in a limited sense, Sam Spade remains Sam Spade, with or without the effects created by Dashiell Hammett's prose or John Huston's direction or Humphrey Bogart's performance. At the same time, the experience of attending a play is profoundly different from the experience of reading a novel. Theater is a public event; it does not exist in any abstract form, and each concrete instance of it can be viewed as an almost infinitely mediated negotiation. If I attend a play, the distance between the playtext and myself is defined, enacted, and acted upon to a greater or lesser degree by the theater managers, by the director, by the actors, and by any fellow spectator who chooses to make his or her response to the play part of my experience on that particular evening. Reading a novel is a private experience that provides at least the illusion of an essentially unmediated relationship between the writer and the reader; it is also unavoidably abstract.

Although these characteristics do not in themselves determine the meaning of particular texts or performances, they do tend to push audiences in certain directions. The materiality of stage performance all but eliminates the possibility of writing drama that entirely devalues the realm of physical experience, if only because any attempt at communication inevitably valorizes the means by which it is attempted. For analogous reasons, print narratives have an inherent tendency to valorize abstract verbal structures. And in the middle decades of the eighteenth century, this process of valuation often seemed to require the devaluation of certain kinds of experience and modes of perception that had been associated with the social and literary practices of the London stage.

To carry this point a bit further, we might return briefly to the mysterious refusal of the eighteenth-century English reading public to read plays that had not been acted. Cooke's vignette suggests that the audience for printed plays was seeking some sort of connection to the London theaters of this era. When the provisions of the Stage Licensing Act effectively severed that connection, they suddenly focused a great deal of attention on the epistemological barrier between the material medium of performance and the symbolic medium of print. In a sense, of course, the barrier was always already there—presumably, even Cooke's Yorkshire gentleman would have acknowledged that reading a play was not the same as seeing it performed—but the English reading public prior to this moment seems to have supposed that a printed edition of a play could and did establish some sort of link between the world of print and the material world of performance. Even the editorial treatment of printed plays seems calculated to establish the priority and greater authenticity of the stage production. Title pages of the printed scripts from the seventeenth and eighteenth centuries invariably indicated where the play was being performed at the time of the printing, and all but the cheapest editions included cast lists as well. The orthographic conventions of printed scripts continuously disrupt the narrative flow of the text; both the insistent repetition of the characters' names and the printing of stage directions in a different, harder-to-read typeface continuously remind readers that they are dealing not just with a script, but rather with a transcript—that is, an account of something that happened somewhere else, at a different time and in a different place.

Speculating about the presuppositions of a particular literary public is always a risky business, but I feel reasonably safe in concluding first, that for eighteenth-century English readers, the activity of reading plays tended to emphasize an apparent but illusory connection between the page and the stage; and second, that the shift away from that activity involved the loss of that sense of connection. Thus the movement away from printed plays and toward other kinds of printed texts can be viewed as reproducing and reinforcing the shift away from the material world of performance that was engineered by the Stage Licensing Act. This is not to suggest either that the stage of the 1730s tended as a whole to promote the material at the expense of the spiritual or sentimental, or that the English novel of the 1740s sought to reverse that process. My point is simply that in each case, the individual writer could be conceived as swimming either with or against the current of potentialities defined by the medium of presentation. With respect to the works involved in this discussion, I hope to show, for example, that *The London Merchant* resists the materialist tendencies of performance by a certain aggressive economy of scale, while both *Tom Jones* and *The Beggar's Opera* are saved in a sense by the continual resurgence of the material in the role of the necessary opposition to the idealizing and hence dehumanizing tendencies of their respective moral visions.

The discussion that follows has a tripartite structure. The first section, which deals with the London stage in the decade before the passage of the Stage Licensing Act, is divided into two chapters, one focusing on *The Beggar's Opera*, and one focusing on *The London Merchant*. The middle section consists of my chapter on Charlotte Charke, the transvestite actor and memoirist who was also the youngest daughter of Colley Cibber.

Since Charke was not only a successful stage actor, but a celebrity and a writer as well, my exploration of her life and career will, I hope, provide a smooth transition between the first section and the third, which concentrates on the two most important novels of the 1740s. Like the opening section, the last section is split into two chapters, the first of which focuses on *Clarissa*, and the second of which focuses on *Tom Jones*.

My discussion of *The Beggar's Opera* begins by exploring the play's rendition of two peculiar eighteenth-century social practices: that of allowing female convicts to escape execution if they were pregnant, and that of selling the bodies of executed criminals to medical doctors and their students. I believe that the play sets up a thematic struggle between the world of disembodied words that is invoked and defined by Macheath and Polly and the world of collective physical experience that is constituted in the form of a demographic portrait of the London underworld. Although the celebration of Macheath and Polly at the end of the play seems on one level to suggest that the world of words can triumph over the world of the body, the structure of the ending produces a subtext that complicates and compromises that claim.

George Lillo's *The London Merchant* seeks to undermine what the playwright perceived as the romanticization of the urban criminal in *The Beggar's Opera*. In *Discipline and Punish*, Foucault alludes briefly to the "juridical theology of the Middle Ages" in order to cite the notion of the king's "double body" (28). According to this view, the individual ruler's body was only the material representation of the sacred abstraction of the king; that abstraction was invested with the metaphorical equivalent of some physical characteristics, but it was not situated in any one individual. In a sense, *The London Merchant* substitutes this sort of symbolic body for the literal bodies that demanded our attention in *The Beggar's Opera*. Lillo's tragedy postulates a fundamental link between individual sexual transgressions and parricidal violence by focusing repeatedly on the blood of the patriarch. Although Lillo, like Gay, seems to be interested in the demography of the urban underworld, the conception of the underworld as a kind of mass society is condemned in *The London Merchant* as immoral and socially irresponsible. In place of this model, the play presents a vision that demonizes women in order to use them as scapegoats for the Oedipal struggle between his title character and his protagonist.

Although Lillo makes a point of rejecting misogyny as such, both the logic of his plot and his symbolic use of blood and money imply that neither good women nor bad women can be trusted. The boundless and dispassionate greed of the evil Sarah Millwood represents a direct threat to Thorowgood's patriarchal order, but even a good women like his chaste heroine Maria is capable of betraying that order when she is blinded by desire. This essentialist view of the female character was current both on and off the London stage during the second quarter of the eighteenth century, but it was one of the cultural clichés that was being vigorously contested by the experimental dramas written and performed in the decade before the passage of the Stage Licensing Act.

The pivotal chapter of my study focuses on the life and career of Charlotte Charke as a startling instance of the myriad ways in which a single individual could be affected by the historical and ideological currents I have laid out in the earlier chapters. Charke became famous during the 1730s for playing breeches roles on stage; then she became notorious during the 1740s for her offstage transvestism. When she wrote her autobiographical *Narrative* in 1755, she was trying (at least at first) to supplant the disreputable public image of her earlier years with a more acceptable persona. My discussion begins by using three of her onstage roles (Mother Lupine in Charles Johnson's *Caelia*, Mrs. Otter in Ben Jonson's *Epicoene* [1609], and Mr. Hen in Henry Fielding's *Historical Register* [1737]) to examine the different ways that gender could be constituted on the London stage of this period. Her successful portrayals of male characters in Fielding's plays tended to subvert conventional conceptions of gender as being rooted in biological essences, but those successes were stifled by the provisions of the Licensing Act, and the printed accounts of her stage career and its aftermath oversimplified her attitudes and distorted her accomplishments. The *Narrative* initially attempts both to mend fences with her wealthy father and to defend her extraordinary activities. My reading of certain episodes from this text casts this split purpose as a kind of a debate between the performative and the essentialist models of individual identity. At the end of the chapter, I return to the subject of literature per se (and turn from the London stage to the pages of the early English novel) by using Elaine Scarry's analysis of the representation of the human body in narrative to connect Charke's fate to that of Richardson's Mrs. Sinclair.

Scarry contends that the degree to which an individual human being is materially represented in a particular narrative is inversely proportional to the degree of power accruing to that individual; those without power are deeply embodied, while those with power can appear, if they wish, as disembodied (and hence invulnerable) voices (*BP* 207). In this third section of my argument, I use Scarry's discussion and an awareness of the historical connections between the London stage of the 1730s and the novels of the 1740s to structure my treatments of both *Clarissa* and *Tom Jones*.

My primary goal in this part of the study is to explore how the relationship between performance and embodiment came to be represented on the pages of the early English novel. Richardson's well-known opposition to theater in general is reflected in his presentation of the evil characters in *Clarissa* as actors, stage managers, and co-conspirators. All of these characters are eventually punished for their theatrical misbehavior with illness, injury, or worse; the recurring motif here suggests that deep embodiment eliminates the possibility of false performances. At the same time, the trajectory followed by Clarissa herself over the course of the novel seems to reproduce this pattern: she is accused of performing by her family and by Lovelace, then deeply embodied as both a rape victim and a dying martyr, and only the latter version of her deep embodiment is enough to put to rest the doubts about her behavior up to that point. Virtue may triumph at the end of the novel, but that victory depends on the transformation of Clarissa the character into *Clarissa* the text, and that rhetorical maneuver tends to trivialize both the political content of the story and the physical suffering of the heroine. It is Lovelace who suggests that he cannot know that Clarissa is truly virtuous without testing her, but it is the novel itself that reconstitutes this remark as an ironic truth.

Several recent critical and historical discussions of the eighteenth-century English novel have praised Richardson for his sympathetic treatment of women's issues and condemned Fielding as both less subtle and less sympathetic. In swimming against this particular tide, I have not sought to deny or defend Fielding's occasional tendency (especially in his early prose works) to present his readers with misogynistic comments or characterizations. By focusing on the roles played and the purposes served by the female characters in *Tom Jones*, I hope to demonstrate that the treatment of gender issues in this novel is both more complicated and more sympathetic to women than has been generally conceded. Like *Clarissa*, *Tom Jones* is explicitly concerned with the matrix of issues linking performance, embodiment, and individual identity; however, where Richardson's plot suggests that performance is invariably misleading and embodiment is invariably tragic, the plot of *Tom Jones* suggests that material existence and physical experience have a certain redemptive potential that compensates for the inevitable effects of decay and mortality.

Both Fielding and Richardson apparently thought of women primarily as physical rather than spiritual or intellectual beings, but this shared assumption was manifested very differently in their respective works. On the one hand, although Richardson's female heroes are clearly more concerned with matters of the spirit than with those of the flesh, the novelist's insistence on their exemplary status indirectly confirms his opinion of those women who in his view did not measure up to the exalted standard of a Pamela or a Clarissa.[13] On the other hand, Fielding's attitude toward physical experience leads him to avoid and even to subvert many of the stereotypes and conventional moral judgments that other writers of this era derived from that original assumption.

At various points in this study, I hope to identify and explore certain formal devices in *Clarissa*, *Tom Jones*, and the *Narrative* of Charlotte Charke that help to illuminate the relationship between the London stage of the 1730s and the novels of the following decade. Perhaps the most important consequence of the shift from the stage to the page during this era was the fact that in the new medium the human body could no longer be represented by a real human body. This change made it easier to assert, suggest, or imply that physical experience was less important than any of the abstract values that were set up in opposition to it in fictional plots.

In general, this drive to write the body out of existence seems to me to be an inherently regressive impulse. One signal of this regressive tendency is the recurring plot device whereby illicit sexual activity is punished by what are construed as salutary assaults on the bodies of individual transgressors. In a sense, the heroes of my study are those who refuse to accept or sanction such punishments. I am thinking here of Charlotte Charke, whose career and autobiography demonstrate the individual's ability to transcend the modes of thinking that cast her (as one anonymous commentator put it) as "a mere Female in the Dark,"[14] and Henry Fielding, who resisted even his own moral judgments when they seemed to require that he abandon his healthy regard for the exigencies of physical existence.

1. Life Among the "Otamys": Gender and Demography in *The Beggar's Opera*

Act II of John Gay's *The Beggar's Opera* begins with a conversation between two members of Macheath's gang which contains the following exchange:

> BEN. But pr'ythee, *Matt*, what is become of thy Brother *Tom*? I have not seen him since my Return from Transportation.
> MATT. Poor brother *Tom* had an Accident this time Twelve-month, and so clever a made Fellow he was, that I could not save him from those fleaing Rascals the Surgeons; and now, poor Man, he is among the Otamys at *Surgeon's Hall*.
> (II.i.1–6)[1]

Becoming an "Otamy"—that is, one of the corpses sold to and subsequently dissected (an "anatomy") by surgeons and medical students—was a real and much-feared possibility for any criminal who was hanged in eighteenth-century London. In fact, it was primarily on this account that riots sometimes broke out after hangings, when the friends and partisans of the deceased fought with various officers of the court to gain custody of bodies they hoped either to revive or, at the very least, to bury decently.[2] Gay's allusion to this phenomenon serves locally to authenticate the underworld atmosphere of his satire, but—as I hope to show in the following pages—it also contributes to the larger project of establishing both figurative and literal connections between the material world of performance, the symbolic realm of language, and the social world that both literary media claim to reflect and represent.

In its bare outlines, the plot of *The Beggar's Opera* is very conventional. The hoped-for union of two charismatic lovers is threatened by various blocking figures—at first by parents with other plans, and later by rivals with other hopes—who manipulate legal and social conventions to promote their own ends, but the lovers manage somehow to overcome every obstacle and to meet at center stage in time for a happy finale. Obviously, there is a great deal more to the play than this outline might suggest. Despite its veneer of tradition, the plot provides Gay with a series of opportunities for mounting timely satirical attacks against Italian opera and the Walpole Ministry, and against the self-serving codes of the eighteenth-century aristocracy and the pretentious moralizing of the eighteenth-century bourgeoisie. The middle term in this equation—the means by which a traditional plot is enlisted in the service of a fairly specific topical satire—is the fictionalized and stylized version of the London underworld that provides the framework for the interaction between plot and theme. Gay's vision of the underworld is what distinguishes his plot from a thousand other comic plots, and what gives his satire its bite; the pieties and pretentions of his characters are funny chiefly because their highflown sentiments seem absurdly incongruous in relation to their low-down context.

The Beggar's Opera supposedly began as a response to Swift's suggestion that Gay should write a "Newgate pastoral." During the playwright's lifetime, stories of his research expeditions into prisons and thief-taker's offices were widely circulated, and his interest in *The Newgate Calendar* and the sort of criminal biographies being churned out by Daniel Defoe and others during the 1720s is reflected in a series of references and obvious quotations in the play itself. Gay's fascination with urban crime and urban criminals was as much journalistic as it was literary; whatever his satiric aims may have been, he was also genuinely interested in how the underworld worked. However, one need not resort to an old-fashioned biographical reading in order to demonstrate that *The Beggar's Opera* is especially concerned with the question of how and under what circumstances the members of London's criminal underclass succeeded in reproducing themselves. I do not mean to suggest that *The Beggar's Opera* can or should be taken seriously as a demographic profile of even this small, rather narrowly defined segment of the population of eighteenth-century London. I do, however, wish to suggest that the coherence of both Gay's plot and his characters depends to a great extent on the quasi-scientific portrait of the urban underworld that is embedded in the script of the play.

The theoretical foundation for this discussion is derived from a 1977 interview in which Michel Foucault was asked to explain and elaborate on the eighteenth-century "discovery of population as an object of scientific investigation." In his reply, Foucault argued that

> In the seventeenth and eighteenth centuries a form of power comes into being that begins to exercise itself through social production and social service. . . . And in consequence, a real and effective "incorporation" of power was necessary, in the sense that power had to be able to gain access to the bodies of individuals, to their acts, attitudes and modes of everyday behaviour. . . . But at the same time, these new techniques of power needed to grapple with the phenomena of population, in short to undertake the administration, control and direction of the accumulation of men . . . I believe that the political significance of the problem of sex is due to the fact that sex is located at the point of intersection of the discipline of the body and the control of the population. (*PK* 125)

Like the public executions themselves, the practice of selling the bodies of convicted felons to the surgeons serves as a particularly graphic demonstration of "incorporated power." Given the rather draconian nature of the English criminal justice system during this era, it is perhaps not surprising that this practice was not only tolerated but celebrated by some of those charged with the tasks of enforcing the laws and meting out punishments. According to a recent study, the criminals themselves were terrified by the prospect of becoming an "Otamy," and many authorities believed that their terror made the threat of death and dissection a more effective deterrent than that of death alone (McLynn 272). Of course, people do not need to be hanged and dissected in order to be deprived of their individual autonomy and identities. Even in the absence of overt violence against individual citizens, the longterm political interests of those in power can create a tendency to conceive of human beings not as individuals, but rather as biological or demographic functionaries whose desires and capacities are tolerated or condemned according to how much and how well they contribute to some larger demographic goal.

We need not accept Foucault's model as universally valid in order to recognize that *The Beggar's Opera* seems to be very much in tune with the pattern described by the twentieth-century theorist. From the very beginning, the script plays on the connection between individual immorality and the demography of the criminal underclass, so that this broadly based anxiety about losing one's identity and becoming little more than a demographic functionary mingles with the more specific fear of becoming an "Otamy." This connection is registered on a number of occasions, but one of the most striking occurs in the thief's original description of his brother's fate. When Matt places Tom among a group of bodies which were sold to the surgeons, the grammatical shift from singular to plural envisions the process of death and anatomization as a dissolution of the individual identity in the collective anonymity of the merely material.[3] Like the riots at Tyburn, which pitted those who were attached to the deceased individual against those who claimed dominion over a no-longer-individuated body, Gay's plot sets up a series of oppositions between individual identity and collective anonymity. Ultimately, this series resolves itself into a rather equivocal settlement which acknowledges the permanence of both the anonymous world of "Otamys" and the urge to find a purely imaginative means of transcending that world.

In *The Beggar's Opera*, the opposition between identity and anonymity is figured along two parallel trajectories. The first, which is reflected primarily in Macheath's relationship to Peachum and Lockit, presents this dichotomy as a struggle between words and things. The second, which follows Macheath's attempts to evade the competing claims of Polly and Lucy, is more explicitly concerned with demographic questions. In the latter case, the material world is represented not by inanimate objects, but rather by the human body in all its gendered frailty. Taken as a whole, the play makes two implicit claims about the relationship between language and the material world. First, Gay's plot suggests in various ways that the most effective way for individuals to distinguish themselves from the mass of humanity is through the creation and deployment of verbal structures. Second, it also suggests that when the material world obtrudes on human affairs, individuals tend to lose part of their individuality in the common struggle against the thousand natural shocks that flesh is heir to.

The Beggar's Opera has a double ending, and both halves of that ending exploit the conflicting impulses generated by these two thematic matrices. The first, false ending of the play—where Macheath, who has just declared that he would rather be hanged than confront the six women who claim to be his wife, starts off stage with the Sheriff's officers, only to be interrupted and rescued by the reappearance of the Beggar and the Player—asks the audience to resist the world of "Otamys" by celebrating the imaginative vision that distinguished Macheath and Polly not only from their material surroundings, but even from their material selves. However, the structural disruptions involved in the second part of the ending suggest that choosing between words and things, or between words and bodies, may be neither as simple nor as advisable as it seems at other times in the play. The major part of this chapter attempts to explore these parallel developments in some detail. It begins with a discussion of Macheath's relationship with Peachum and Lockit, which is succeeded in turn by a discussion of Polly and Lucy. Once that foundation is laid, my analysis turns again to the play's double ending.

✳   ✳   ✳

Critics have tended to view Peachum and Lockit as more or less interchangeable,[4] and indeed, it would be foolish to deny that Lockit is in some respects a less fully developed version of his better-known compatriot. Certainly the two villains appear to be equally and analogously corrupt. Moreover, Lockit's scenes frequently run parallel to those of Peachum, and the language and manners of both men seem to be modeled on what the playwright perceives as the language and manners of middle-class shopkeepers. Finally, their rather ceremonial quarrel in Act II, scene x seems calculated to emphasize their interdependence rather than their differences. Nevertheless, I wish to begin this section of my discussion by identifying and elaborating those differences, primarily because I hope to demonstrate that the notion of interdependence should lead us to recognize not only that Peachum and Lockit share certain interests and attitudes, but also that each man provides a particular service that the other somehow cannot duplicate.

We can begin to explore the distinctions between Peachum and Lockit by looking closely at their names. In each case, the name clearly describes what the character does, but the two labels are by no means synonyms. Peachum impeaches a "him" or a "them," while Lockit is connected to an inanimate "it" (presumably either Newgate or some part of Newgate); in other words, while "Peachum" refers to a species of verbal performance, "Lockit" refers to a simple physical act. Essentially, Peachum is identified with the predominantly verbal and textual processes by which criminals were apprehended, tried, convicted, and punished, while Lockit is identified with the material trappings of that system. When Lockit first appears (II.vii), he takes the part of a tailor, talking about the fetters Macheath must wear in jail as though they were fine clothes. In his first scenes (I.ii, iii), Peachum demonstrates that his chief commodity is information concerning the people he exploits. The point becomes even more explicit when Macheath escapes from Newgate at the end of Act II. When he offers Lucy twenty guineas with which to bribe her father, she tells him that she will simply steal her father's keys. There is no need to suborn a witness here; there is simply a lock that needs a key.[5]

In the jargon of their day, Lockit was a (jail)-"keeper" and Peachum was a (thief-)"taker"; Lockit is a member of the old guard, someone who wants to keep the old conventions in place, while Peachum rides the crest of the new wave. This is perhaps most evident in their fight scene, where the new professional criminal takes the old-fashioned cheat to task for shortcomings which threaten the smooth operation of Peachum's criminal organization:

> PEACHUM.   Here's poor *Ned Clincher*'s Name, I see. Sure, Brother Lockit, there was a little unfair proceeding in *Ned*'s case: for he told me in the Condemn'd Hold, that for Value receiv'd, you had promis'd him a Session or two longer without Molestation.
> LOCKIT.   Mr. *Peachum*,—This is the first time my Honour was ever call'd in Question.
> PEACHUM.   Business is at an end—if once we act dishonourably.
> LOCKIT.   Who accuses me?
> PEACHUM.   You are warm, Brother.
> LOCKIT.   He that attacks my Honour, attacks my Livelyhood.—And this Usage—Sir—is not to be born.
> PEACHUM.   Since you provoke me to speak—I must tell you too, that Mrs. *Coaxer* charges you with defrauding her of her Information-Money, for the apprehending of curl-pated *Hugh*. Indeed, indeed, Brother, we must punctually pay our Spies, or we shall have no Information.   (II.x.27–44)

In part, this exchange reflects the shifting class dynamic of early eighteenth-century London: Lockit claims the right to emulate aristocratic capriciousness by repeatedly invoking the concept of his honor and by referring to his accuser (with more than a hint of condescension) as "Sir," and Peachum makes his case for sound business practices and reveals his bourgeois political sympathies by addressing his colleague as "Brother." Lockit and Peachum are not simply partners in crime; rather, they are natural enemies joined in a rather tenuous alliance to serve distinct and sometimes conflicting self-interests. On the one hand, Lockit represents the old, the liminal, the material; his currency is that of bricks and mortar, keys and fetters, of material things. On the other hand, Peachum represents the new, the orderly, the verbal and textual; his currency is chiefly that of information, contracts, and testimony—of words.

The probability that this pattern would have been recognized by an eighteenth-century audience seems to me to be very high, not only because of the various signals described in the last few pages, but also because of the playwright's obvious allusions to well-known historical sources and analogues for these three characters. In other words, the editorial decisions that translated Jonathan Wild into Peachum and Jack Sheppard into Macheath—and, to a somewhat lesser extent, those that recreated City Marshall Charles Hitchen as Lockit—help to configure the obstacles arrayed before Macheath and Polly as deriving from either the world of words or the world of things.

Like Jonathan Wild, Gay's Peachum keeps an account book detailing his inventory and explaining where and how his stolen goods were procured, and maintains a network of informers and seducers. Peachum's pretense to bourgeois respectability also recalls Wild, who at one point applied (in the guise of a legitimate businessman) to become a freeman of London (Howson 273–76). Connoisseurs of rogue literature might also have recognized the quarrel between Peachum and Lockit as Gay's dramatization of a brief but relatively well-known pamphlet war between Wild and Hitchen which took place in 1718.[6] Hitchen's link to the world of things is often reflected in footnotes to Jonathan Swift's "Description of the Morning" (1709), which mentions a Newgate jail-keeper who lets the prisoners out at night "to steal for fees"—that is, for the "garnishes" Macheath pays to Lockit in Act II, Scene vii in order to obtain a lighter pair of fetters. On the other hand, Wild's connection to the world of language figures prominently in Defoe's biography, which spends a great deal of time explaining, for example, the pains taken by Wild to make certain that nothing he said to those who were trying to recover their stolen property could be used against him in court.[7] One suspects that this cautious rationality contributed a great deal to the sinister image of Wild which figured so prominently in the crime literature of the 1720s. Unlike Lockit, Wild could not reasonably be expected to fall asleep and allow his own pocket to be picked, and consequently he would have been much more difficult to resist or ignore.

Macheath's connections to Jack Sheppard are less exact, and hence slightly more complicated, than those involving Peachum, Wild, Lockit, and Hitchen. There were more than a dozen pamphlet biographies of Sheppard printed between 1724 and 1729. Most of these works presented Sheppard as a bold and charismatic housebreaker and highwayman with strong appetites for drink, women, fine clothes, and games of chance. One of the most popular, *The History Of the remarkable Life of John Sheppard* (1724), reported that Sheppard "declar'd himself frequently against the practice of *Whidling* or *Impeaching*, which he said, had made dreadful Havock among the *Thieves*, and much lamented the depravity of the *Brethren* in that respect" (61). Several biographies of Sheppard also noted that after his second escape from Newgate, the legal authorities concluded that no jail could hold him, and they made special arrangements to have him hanged almost immediately after he was recaptured. The similarity to Macheath's habits, opinions, and circumstances—including the detail about the early execution (III.xiv.1–2)—should be evident.

Sheppard's example provided a true case of a near-mythical figure whose fondness for female company led to his capture by the authorities, but his three escapes from prison bore very little resemblance to those accomplished by Macheath. Sheppard was wiry and agile and, perhaps more importantly, a former locksmith's apprentice. He used these various skills and attributes so effectively that he once broke jail despite having been chained to the floor in a locked room in the tower at Newgate. Though apparently something of a slave to his desires, Sheppard was also in some sense a master of the material world. Macheath, on the other hand, is a master of the word; he is obviously more proficient with a promise than he is with a picklock.

As Michael Denning has observed (43), each act of *The Beggar's Opera* ends with an escape; the first two are engineered by Polly and Lucy, respectively, while the last one is credited to what the Player calls "the Taste of the Town" (III.xvi.16–17). The rhythm of Gay's plot shows Macheath repeatedly traversing the boundary between Peachum's world and Lockit's world. He gets into trouble by immersing himself in the material—that is, by drinking and womanizing—and gets out of trouble by making promises that appear to have no connection with that reality. When he falls out of Peachum's world and into Lockit's, it is only through a kind of free-floating, purely verbal creation—a promise of fidelity to Polly, a promise of marriage to Lucy, an unexpected reprieve credited to the town—that he can rise out of that world again.

*   *   *

The opposition between Peachum and Lockit carries over to their respective daughters, where it is complicated in some interesting ways both by Gay's treatment of gender issues and by the repeated allusions to the demographic issues mentioned earlier. Peachum introduces us to both of these themes in Act I, Scene ii, when he informs his companion Filch that a woman named Black Moll would not need his assistance to escape hanging, because "she may plead her Belly at worst; to my Knowledge she has taken care of that Security" (I.ii.4–5). Soon afterward, Peachum reassures the young thief that he will suppress the evidence against a prostitute and pickpocket named Betty Sly because of her abilities in "train[ing] up young Fellows to the Business [of stealing]" (I.ii.27). He also adds that he "love[s] to let Women scape. A good Sportsman always lets the Hen Partridges fly, because the breed of the Game depends upon them" (I.ii.19–22). Given Peachum's metaphor and the earlier reference to Black Moll, we cannot be sure at this point whether "the breed of the Game" depends in this case on seducing young fellows or pleading one's belly, but Gay's plot suggests eventually that the recruitment model is less appropriate in this context than the model based on reproduction.

Eighteenth-century social commentators seem to have assumed that the population of the London underworld was sustained chiefly by recruitment. According to this view, innocent men and women did not turn to crime of their own accord; instead, they were seduced or tricked into criminal behavior by people who had already committed themselves to lives on the wrong side of the law. The description of Betty Sly obviously alludes to this narrative paradigm, and Filch himself acknowledges that "'twas to her I was obliged for my Education" (I.ii.25–26). However, when Macheath boasts of his skills as a recruiter of "free-hearted Ladies" (II.iii.5), and when one such free-hearted lady prides herself on her ability to persuade apprentices to steal from their masters (II.iv.110–12), the playwright adds a new twist to what was, even in the eighteenth century, a time-worn cliché. Essentially, Gay's demographic emphasis—his series of allusions to the *numbers* of thieves and prostitutes created by these activities—repackages seduction as a socially productive gesture.

The more conventional social commentators of this era presumably had something to gain by propagating the idea that urban crime was no more than an unfortunate result of the combustible association of the weak with the vicious. If nothing else, such a fiction helped to obscure the degree to which poverty and certain kinds of worker alienation were involved in the process of spawning urban criminals. To the extent that Gay's use of the recruitment paradigm helps to recast a widespread social phenomenon as a collection of ritualized seductions, it contributes to this larger project of converting the political to the merely personal. At the same time, his treatment of the practice of impregnating female prisoners to help them escape the gallows inverts this process by transforming sex itself into a dispassionate and defensive political gesture. In thematic terms, this shift from the personal to the political recapitulates the loss of individuality accomplished in the physical sphere through the interventions of the hangman and the surgeon's messengers.

By the middle of *The Beggar's Opera*, the early emphasis on traditional (parental) blocking figures has been supplanted by an intragenerational conflict between Macheath and Polly on the one hand, and the various representatives of the anonymous world of "Otamys" on the other. Particularly in the latter half of the play, the obstacles facing Macheath and Polly are configured in a way that emphasizes this opposition between being a person and being no more than a body, a component element of a population. This opposition is exploited for comic purposes in Gay's portrayals of Filch and Lucy Lockit—two secondary characters who function as materialist doubles for Macheath and Polly, respectively. Like Macheath, Filch has had sexual relations with a number of women; like Polly, Lucy has lost her heart and her virginity to Macheath. By the end of the play, however, both Filch and Lucy seem to be at risk of losing both their physical integrity and their personal identities. Their shared role in the reproductive economy of Gay's underworld threatens to reduce both to the status of "Otamys."

Filch's destiny is foreshadowed in the second scene of the play, where, as I mentioned earlier, Peachum alludes to the phenomenon of women pleading their bellies to escape execution. However, it is not until Act III that the young thief's role in this process is revealed:

> LOCK.   Why, Boy, thou lookest as if thou wert half starv'd; like a shotten Herring.
> FILCH.   One had need have the Constitution of a Horse to go thorough the Business.—Since the favorite Child-getter was disabled by a Mis-Hap, I have pick'd up a little Money by helping the Ladies to a Pregnancy against their being call'd down to Sentence.—But if a Man cannot get an honest Livelyhood any easier way, I am sure, 'tis what I can't undertake for another Session.   (III.iii.1–9)

Filch's plight reenacts Matt's shift from singular to plural with comic rather than tragic consequences. Although it is clearly preferable to death followed by dissection, "helping the Ladies" has reduced Filch to the level of a biological functionary, and his duties seem to be wearing him down. The connection between Filch's joyless husbandry and Macheath's manic pursuit of any and every woman may seem tenuous at first, but it is reinforced by Lockit's celebration of the child-getter Filch is replacing, whose fertility was such that "the Vigor and Prowess of a Knight-Errant never saved half the Ladies in distress that he hath done" (III.iii.11–13). By presenting the practice of child-getting in terms of chivalric romance, Lockit reminds us of the considerable gap between Macheath's courtly rhetoric and his behavior. Regardless of whether the latter term is construed as referring to his criminal occupation or his series of onstage seductions and abandonments, the gap itself seems calculated to produce the same confusion that is generated by Lockit's comparison. To strengthen the connection even further, we need only suggest that the first half of the play's ending reveals Macheath, somewhat to his chagrin, as another sort of "favorite Child-getter."

The joke about Macheath's surfeit of wives and children suggests that in Gay's view the feminine complement to the shotten herring is simply the mother. We are prepared for this conclusion by Lucy's first appearance, where she rails at Macheath for deserting her:

> You base Man you,—how can you look me in the Face after what hath passed between us?—See here, perfidious Wretch, how I am forc'd to bear about the load of Infamy you have laid upon me—O *Macheath*! thou hast robbed me of my Quiet—to see thee tortur'd would give me pleasure.   (II.ix.1–6)

Lucy's "see here" demands not only Macheath's attention, but our own as well; it is tantamount to a stage direction that the actor should appear to be largely pregnant. That circumstance places her in the same relation to Polly that Filch bears to Macheath; they are post-coital shadows of the two leads, as close to the world of "Otamys" as they are to the stylized world of sentimental devotion that is evoked by the two protagonists. In Act III of *The Beggar's Opera*, Lucy is threatened with a metamorphosis that seems reminiscent of the one experienced by Filch. It begins when her father announces his plan to make her "fast and mortify yourself into Reason, with now and then a little handsome Discipline to bring you to your Senses" (III.i.71–73). The intensity of Lockit's threat presents an odd contrast to the locker-room humor of the shotten herring discussion that follows close on its heels, but the two scenes share an odd emphasis on the grotesque as it is manifested in the physical phenomenon of wasting away.

What separates Macheath and Polly from Filch and Lucy is their intense interest in and attachment to language. I mentioned earlier that the rhythm of Macheath's career shows him getting into trouble because of his physical appetites and getting out of trouble by making promises. Polly Peachum is of course well suited to such a silver-tongued lover. She claims to get many of her ideas from reading plays (I.x.66) and prose romances (I.xiii.16–17), and no reader or auditor of the play can fail to notice the verbal extravagance of the exotic similes and feverish pledges of love between the two leads.

This opposition between the word and the body shapes much of the dialogue between Polly and Lucy. When the two women first confront Macheath and each other in Newgate, Lucy notes, characteristically, that "Flesh and Blood can't bear my Usage" (II.xiii.39), while Polly stakes her claim on etymological grounds ("there ought to be some Preference shown to a Wife! At least she may claim the Appearance of it" [46–47]). In Act III, shortly before Macheath's reprieve, the two women share a duet which emphasizes this division:

AIR LII.	*The last time I went o'er the Moor.*	
POLLY.	Hither, dear Husband, turn your Eyes.	
LUCY.	Bestow one Glance to cheer me.	
POLLY.	Think with that Look, thy *Polly* dyes.	
LUCY.	Oh, shun me not—but hear me.	
POLLY.	'Tis *Polly* sues.	
LUCY.		'Tis *Lucy* speaks.
POLLY.	Is thus true Love requited?	
LUCY.	My Heart is bursting.	
POLLY.		Mine too breaks.
LUCY.	Must I	
POLLY.		Must I be slighted? (III.xi.12–22)

In the first five lines, Polly's flowery language is contrasted to Lucy's bluntness. The inverted syntax and the appeal to the imagination in the first and third lines is deflated by the directness of the second and fourth; while Polly sues and dies, Lucy speaks and asks to be heard.

A somewhat subtler effect is achieved by juxtaposing Polly's question about true love with Lucy's bursting heart. The difference between "Love" and "Heart" uses a common metaphor to register the distinction between sentimental abstraction and physical substance once again, and Polly's claim that her heart "breaks" essentially corrects Lucy's usage by shifting away from the anatomical accuracy of "bursting" toward the more conventional language of lovers.[8] Shortly afterward, when the two women try to intercede on Macheath's behalf with their respective fathers, these modes of thought and speech are reflected in how each of them perceives the risks involved in the upcoming trial. Thus it is Polly, not Lucy, who begs her father to "sink the material Evidence" (III.xi.36) and thereby reveals her fear of the unfamiliar world of things. Meanwhile, Lucy tells *her* father that "Cannons, or Bombs, or clashing of Swords" are less deadly than "Witnesses' Words," and then returns to form by urging him to "nail up their Lips" (III.xi.56–58).

The double ending of *The Beggar's Opera* reproduces the dichotomy that contrasts the entrapment of bodies to the escape through words. When Macheath announces that he would rather be hanged than confronted with his six wives and four children (III.xv.25–26), he presents death by strangulation as the only appropriate way to avoid monogamy and at least the semblance of contrition—two kinds of physical limitation that represent the long-deferred consequences of his past promises. However, when the Beggar provides Macheath with a reprieve and allows him to recover his relationship with Polly simply by reasserting his love for her, the primacy of the word is quickly reaffirmed.

Since this reaffirmation involves what appears to be a final rejection of the pregnant Lucy and four mothers with children, it is tempting to see this ending as yet another version of the kind of misogyny described by Susan Gubar in her controversial essay "The Female Monster in Augustan Satire." Gubar contends that the Scriblerians' jealousy of the reproductive capacities of women led them to demonize women by associating them with what they conceived as a filthy materiality. She traces this pattern through Swift's scatological poems into Pope's *Dunciad*, as well as into other, more obscure works. If we pursued this line of argument into *The Beggar's Opera*, we might argue that Gay, like Swift, is finding a way to exclude women based on biological characteristics that are presented as exclusively female. Of course, in the case of this play, the characteristic that Gay seizes on *is* exclusively female: Lucy is disqualified from goddess-hood not because (like Swift's Caelia) she shits, but because she—like every one of Macheath's paramours except, apparently, Polly—is fertile.

In any case, I think it would be unfair to Gay to frame the discussion only in these terms, for two reasons. First, although it would be absurd to deny Gay's interest in the trope of filthy materiality, it would be equally wrong to imply that he uses that trope only or even predominantly with respect to women. The plot of *The Beggar's Opera* may indeed suggest that motherhood is a condition which is roughly analogous to that of a shotten herring, but it also suggests that the filthy materiality of men is less productive in the demographic sense, and therefore closer to death and the world of "Otamys," than the materiality of women. Second, there is a sense in which the experience of pregnancy is more closely connected to the experiences of Filch and Tom that we might care to admit. Not only do all three situations threaten the physical integrity of the individuals involved; they also involve turning one's own body over to another person: to the surgeons in the first case, to the ladies in the second, to the child in the third. From this perspective, Gay's association of pregnancy with mortality can be viewed not as an effort to blame women for the materiality of the human condition, but rather as a reasonably sympathetic invocation of the hazards of being female in eighteenth-century England.

*　*　*

For the first two and a half acts of *The Beggar's Opera*, Macheath is hunted and imprisoned by Peachum and Lockit, only to be loved and released by Polly and Lucy. Nevertheless, when Macheath is forced to choose between the world of the fathers and the world of the daughters, his first impulse is to choose the former—even when that means choosing death. In this section of my discussion, I will examine Macheath's choice in terms that reflect both the highly gendered structure of Gay's plot and the tension between identity and anonymity that is endemic to both the male and female characters in the play.

The first ending of *The Beggar's Opera* (III.xv) shows Macheath responding to the presence of six wives and four children by asserting that he would rather be hanged than forced to untangle his past promises. I suggested earlier that this surfeit of wives and children defines the marriage half of this analogy (at least for the moment) in demographic rather than individual terms. By doing so, the playwright significantly complicates the conventional eighteenth-century joke equating marriage with hanging. Given the misogynistic baggage that accompanied this joke in many other cases, we should perhaps be grateful that he presents a hanging as only a little better than a wedding. By the time that Macheath announces his choice, both sides of the dilemma have been defined as fundamentally similar descents into the collective anonymity of the material world. In any case, it is this rather bleak stereograph that provides the serious undertone to the Player's claim that such an ending would have to be construed as "a downright deep Tragedy" (III.xvi.8–9).

Although there are allusions to the highly ritualized public executions at Tyburn sprinkled throughout *The Beggar's Opera*, it is not until the latter half of Act III that Gay confronts both his audience and his hero with the imminent prospect of Macheath's own death sentence. Remarkably enough, when this prospect finally appears, it is not presented as the kind of eroticized, celebratory rite evoked by the comments of Polly (I.xii.1–10) and Mrs. Peachum (I.iv; Air III). Instead, death by hanging is treated as the rough equivalent of being a husband to six women—that is, as a fall into a different (but equally anonymous) kind of oblivion. Shortly after the recaptured Macheath is escorted offstage by Peachum and Lockit, Polly and Lucy are left alone in Newgate, only to be quickly driven from their places by "a dance of prisoners in chains" (III.xii). This dance seems designed partly to signal the passage of time involved in getting Macheath tried and sentenced, but it also connects the group to Gay's hero, who was wearing chains when he was escorted from the stage shortly before (III.xi). In effect, Macheath the gang leader has become Macheath the gang member; he seems to have lost his ability to make use of his verbal skills to define or discover a new means of escape.

This loss is registered quite powerfully by the interlude that immediately follows the prisoners' dance. The only scene in the play where Macheath appears alone, it presents us with an odd and very dark portrait of drunken despair.[9] In what is likely to be no more than fifteen minutes' stage time, he starts ten different songs and finishes only the last of them. Six of the first seven concern his efforts to get drunk enough to face his death with the right degree of insouciance, and their cumulative effect is to create a disquieting image of a man fighting a losing battle against a breakdown.[10] The last three, however, set the stage for the fall from heroic individualism to collective anonymity which is reflected in Gay's idiosyncratic version of the hanging/marriage joke:

> Air LXV.   *Did you ever hear of a gallant sailor.*
>   But can I leave my pretty Hussies,
>   Without one Tear, or tender Sigh?
> Air LXVI.   *Why are mine eyes still flowing.*
>   Their Eyes, their Lips, their Busses,
>   Recall my Love.—Ah, must I die?
> Air LXVII.   *Green Sleeves.*
>   Since Laws were made for ev'ry Degree
>   To curb Vice in others, as well as me,
>   I wonder we han't better Company,
>   Upon *Tyburn* Tree!
>   But Gold from Law can take out the Sting;
>   And if rich Men like us were to swing,
>   'Twould thin the Land, such Numbers to string
>   Upon *Tyburn* Tree!   (III.xiii.18–29)

The coherence of the quatrain about Macheath's love of women is clearly at risk; what the words put together, the music pulls apart. Even so, this part of Macheath's soliloquy holds together better than the six song frag-ments which precede it. (In the earlier part of the sequence, each shift disrupts not only the melody but the meter and rhyme scheme as well.) In general, the scene moves from disintegration toward a limited sort of syn-thesis: the fragments about drinking are followed by a more cohesive ver-bal unit which attempts to bridge the gap created by yet another melodic shift, and that in turn is succeeded by the most elaborate and sustained song in the group.

Perhaps more importantly, the passage quoted above helps to connect and contrast Gay's treatment of gender to his treatment of demography, and to clarify the relation of both to the larger conflict between the body and the word. The vaguely romantic tone of Macheath's generalized love song is answered and undermined by the sardonic commentary of the song about Tyburn. The singer of the love song is an "I," while the singer of the Tyburn song refers to "we" and "us." Even more explicit is the contrast between the stark individualism of "must I die?" and the sarcastic quasi-demographic analysis of "'Twould thin the Land, such Numbers to string." Macheath associates the loss of female companionship with his own death, but that death is quickly subsumed in a contemplation of the body politic; pre-romantic individualism is supplanted by census-taking, and Gay's hero is in the process of becoming a statistic.

The ending of Macheath's song-soliloquy implies that being involved with women and becoming an "Otamy" are somehow mutually exclusive, but the two scenes that follow this one quickly correct this impression. Act III, Scene xiv shows Macheath saying good-bye to two trusted mem-bers of his gang, while Scene xv shows him taking his leave of Polly and Lucy; the reversal of the gender order established at the end of Macheath's Gethsemane scene coincides with the repetition of the shift from the hero to the functionary, so that in this case it is his connection with women which carries with it the bitter taste of mortality. Ultimately, this theme-and-variation pattern suggests that it is not the involvement with women but the nature of that involvement that determines whether an individual's identity will remain intact or dissolve into the sea of collective anonymity.

The first of Macheath's formal good-byes shows him lamenting the fact that one of his gang members has been suborned against him, and urging his two subordinates to see that Peachum and Lockit are them-selves hanged. His suggestion would have been recognized by Gay's au-dience as a more genteel version of the sentiment attributed to the thief who assaulted and nearly killed Jonathan Wild when the latter came to visit him in Newgate. According to Defoe, the criminal, a sometime partner of Jack Sheppard named Joseph "Blueskin" Blake, swore that "if he had murdered [Wild] he should have died with satisfaction" (195). If the previous scene had called Macheath's courage and character into question, a reference of this sort might help to reestablish his credibility as a hero. Like any hero worth his salt, Macheath is not about to allow his death to pass unnoticed by the world, but the extremity of his last intervention should not go unnoticed. Combined with his own execution, the death sentence he passes against Peachum and Lockit means the virtual end of the underworld as it has been constituted in the play. The equation of one's self with the world—an equation implicit in the belief that the destruction of the former can or should entail the destruction of the latter—obviates the whole notion of demography, since no collective entity could possibly compete with the self for the attention of the egocentric individual.

The beginning of Macheath's farewell to Polly and Lucy is gentler and more self-effacing than anything in the previous scene, but he lapses quickly into an almost sullen self-absorption until the arrival of four more wives and their children is announced. When Macheath responds to this visitation by expressing his desire to be hanged forthwith, the whole plot is suddenly collapsed into the double-edged demographic joke I described at the beginning of this section. Under these circumstances, Peachum and Lockit are rendered irrelevant, and indeed, their fates go unremarked for the remainder of the play. And although both Polly and Lucy are momentarily eclipsed by the crowd of new wives and the prospect of a hanging, they both figure prominently in the second ending of *The Beggar's Opera*. If the first ending suggested a willingness to choose the world of the fathers over the world of the daughters, the second ending makes a case for choosing the latter rather than the former.

In an essay written in 1987, Robert Markley argues that the sentimental identification of the eighteenth-century spectator with a suffering victim required two closely related rhetorical moves. The first and more obvious of these was the decision to focus one's attention on a particular object of contemplation and sympathy, while the second, less benign element of this process called for the exclusion of any rival claims by other individuals in the same situation. Focusing on Sterne's *Sentimental Journey* (1768), Markley demonstrates that the novel dramatizes the "necessary suppression of political consciousness" involved in Yorick's charitable acts.

Later in the same paragraph, he contends that Sterne was troubled by Yorick's "inability to imagine the suffering of the poor as anything but an individual misfortune" (225). If we apply this model to the competition between the female leads in *The Beggar's Opera*, we can see that our sympathy for Polly and our emotional assent to Macheath's reunion with her depends at least in part upon a judgment that her claim on Macheath is more valid than those of Lucy and the other wives. And as we have already observed, the playwright deprives Lucy of our sympathy partly by making her predicament a collective one.

Although Macheath does not confirm his love for Polly until just before the final dance in the play, the competition between Polly and Lucy is resolved in Polly's favor just before Gay's hero is led off in the direction of the gallows, when the hitherto somewhat tentative connection between Lucy and the anonymous world of the demographic functionaries is suddenly confirmed and reconstituted as a literal reality. The final dance—the latter half of the play's double ending—finishes what is begun in this earlier scene by placing Macheath and Polly at center stage, while Lucy must settle for an unnamed partner and a place in the chorus line with the other wives. On its surface, this conclusion suggests that the survival of Macheath and Polly is contingent at least in part upon the playwright's ability to consign their post-coital shadows to anonymity and oblivion: Polly dispatches Filch to observe and report on Macheath's trial, but he never reappears, and Lucy becomes merely one more dancing "Wife," matched up with a partner assigned to her by Macheath. The Beggar's reprieve allows Macheath to escape hanging, and Macheath's confession that he and Polly are really married separates her from her predecessors. In a gesture reminiscent of the end of Alexander Pope's *The Rape of the Lock* (1714), Gay uses an obtrusive authorial fiat to make certain that the material world and its various representatives are pushed into the background, so that the names of Macheath and Polly, like that of Pope's Belinda, can be inscribed mid'st the stars.

In fact, however, the second ending of *The Beggar's Opera* does not succeed in banishing the body in favor of the word; instead, it seems to establish a precarious balance between the two. This balance is accomplished in two ways, the first of which is an odd sort of structural joke. Properly speaking, *The Beggar's Opera* does not have an epilogue. However, the two characters who spoke the Induction—the Beggar and the Player—do resurface just before the end of the play to redirect the action. Macheath is reprieved, and he and his wives celebrate his liberation with a dance. The structural conventions of theatrical mainpieces during this era dictated that the piece itself should be framed by a prologue and an epilogue, each of which was usually spoken by a single individual. Gay uses two characters to introduce his play, and he uses the same two characters to comment on what is offered as the play's original ending. This is very much in keeping with what happens in most of the epilogues written during the Restoration and early eighteenth century. Then, however, he brings a crowd of characters back on stage and ends the play with a dance that is *not* followed by an epilogue of any sort. The impression created here is that of a world which cannot be contained within the conventional dramatic structure, a world whose physical vitality can break through the dictates of literary form. The ambivalence of this gesture is emphasized by the opera's final song, where Macheath describes himself as the master of a harem ("though willing to all[,] with but one he retires"). Since Macheath is standing center stage with Polly at this point, the words and the gesture are once again at odds with each other, and we are left with a verbal suggestion that desire in general may outlast any specific relationship.

The second way in which the ending insists on the ineradicable presence of the material is by including Lucy Lockit in the final dance. Although the happy reunion of Macheath and Polly suggests that they belong together because they are truly married and because they love one another, the attempted erasure of Lucy in the final scene also implies that Polly is to be preferred because she is the only one of his wives who has not (yet) threatened to burden him with a child. But if that is indeed the case, why should Lucy (or, for that matter, the other wives) be on stage at all? The conventions of Restoration and eighteenth-century comedy dictated that female antagonists should be banished from the stage before the happy ending occurs. The list of plays that makes use of this convention would include well-known works like *The Man of Mode* (1676), *The Way of the World* (1700), *The Careless Husband* (1704), and *The School for Scandal* (1777), just to name a few. Obviously, there are good reasons for these exclusions. In most cases, happy endings seek to discredit the perspectives and behaviors enacted by those characters, and when such an antagonist is allowed to reappear at the end of a play—as, for example, in the case of Angellica Bianca in Aphra Behn's *The Rover* (1677)—that allowance can and should be viewed as an acknowledgment that the problems raised by that character ought to be considered less tractable, less susceptible to easy dismissal, than those which might be connected with other, less problematic blocking figures.

If we use this context to examine Lucy's presence in the closing dance, we can see how Gay's playtext—meaning, in this case, the historically informed, hypothetical construct of the play-as-it-might-have-been-performed—undermines the purely textual message that asserts the primacy of the verbal construct over its material surroundings. Regardless of what the script says about or what the choreographer does with the ending of *The Beggar's Opera*, the woman who plays Lucy will inevitably attract our attention; we recognize her and we know her story, and (depending on how obviously pregnant she is made to appear) her figure would remind us once again of who she was and how she differed from her fellow dancers. The script may seek to reduce the character to anonymity, but the playtext undermines that project, and it does so in a manner that, for the first time in the play, pits anatomy *against* anonymity.

* * *

If the play stopped before the Beggar's second appearance, we would be faced, if not with "a downright deep Tragedy," at least with the sort of satire which insists on the animal nature (and thus on what is often construed as the ultimate depravity) of human beings. The real ending of the play takes a more complicated and somewhat equivocal stance on this question; it valorizes and defines certain conventional institutional abstractions (in this case, love and marriage) at the same time that it suggests that the pursuit of those abstractions will invariably be hindered by the resurgence of the material. This equivocation is underscored and further complicated by the shift in setting which occurs at the end of the play. When the Beggar and the Player reappear, the prison setting effectively disappears. The painted flats and props remain on stage, but they no longer signify "Newgate"; instead, they signify something like "scenery." Moreover, since the Beggar and the Player apparently remain on stage throughout the last scene and final dance, the backdrop for the condemned hold remains defamiliarized and insignificant even after Macheath returns. In the absence of Peachum and Lockit—in the absence, even, of Newgate itself—we are left with Polly and Macheath on the one hand, and a group of mostly anonymous dancers on the other, all inhabiting what might be characterized as a generic theatrical space.

Like most physical spaces, the space in which theater occurs is filled with material objects: painted scenery, props, human bodies, the stage itself. The technical skills involved in any performance provide the means by which these material objects are made to represent the collective imaginative vision of the human beings involved in the production, and when any of the technical elements of a performance are taken out of commission, greater pressure is placed on and greater attention is paid to the other elements of that performance. At the end of *The Beggar's Opera*, the pseudomanagerial presence of the Beggar and the Player challenges not only the imaginary version of the London underworld conjured up in the play, but also the equally imaginary characters who inhabit that world. However, since the Beggar and Player are themselves imaginary characters, and since they are usually played by performers who are considerably less prominent than those who are playing the lead roles in the play, their ability to challenge the existence of Macheath and Polly will be limited at best. Thus the hierarchy established by the second ending places the two lovers at the top of the ladder, Lucy and (by implication) humanity in general on the second rung, the Beggar and the Player on the third, and every other character and technical element of the production below those figures.

The primacy of Macheath and Polly in this arrangement is confirmed by the familiar historical responses to Gay's masterpiece—by the sermons and pamphlets that insisted that too many poor Londoners thought Macheath worthy of emulation, and by the vogue for Polly Peachum merchandise that accompanied the first run of the play. But what is perhaps even more striking is the manner in which an awareness of these characters sometimes transformed the lives of real people who fell under their spell and, to one degree or another, internalized the conflicts and processes that Gay and the theater company at Lincoln's Inn Fields had created on stage. Two particularly remarkable instances of this phenomenon are those of James Boswell and Lavinia Fenton.

In an article published in *The Age of Johnson* in 1991, Michael Friedman examines Boswell's obsessive interest in the figure of Macheath. Drawing on the *London Journal* and some later essays, Friedman argues that Boswell habitually describes both his encounters with prostitutes and his pursuit of a wife in terms that refer explicitly or implicitly to Macheath, and that Boswell's ambivalent fascination with public hangings (he attended many, and he was usually thrown into deep depression by what he saw) should likewise be traced to his understanding of Gay's highwayman-hero (101).

Remarkably enough, both Boswell's behavior and his choice of citations suggest that he was also fascinated by the play's equivocal response to the competition between bodies and words. Friedman notes that when the young Scotsman discusses his plans to marry, he often quotes Macheath's second song (which claims that "ev'ry Flower is united" in Polly [I.xiii; Air XV]), but that when he indulges in "concubinage," he often refers to Macheath's last air, which describes him as "a Turk, with his Doxies around" and acknowledges that "for black, brown, and fair his Inconstancy burns, / And the different Beauties subdue him by Turns" (III.xvii; Air LXIX).

Boswell apparently made a habit of seeking out prostitutes after he had witnessed an execution, and Friedman argues that in at least two cases, this impulse was in a sense scripted by *The Beggar's Opera*. In the earlier case, the young Boswell finally shakes off a depression contracted at the hanging of one Paul Lewis by singing "Youth's the Season" (II.iv; Air XXII) to two teen-aged prostitutes before having intercourse with each of them in turn. Friedman contends that the self-conscious theatricality of this situation allows Boswell to regain the control of his emotions, which had been threatened by the spectacle of the execution he had witnessed more than two weeks earlier (103). We might also argue that the therapeutic effect of this particular adventure is derived from the relationship between what Foucault has labeled "incorporated power" and the connection Gay makes between Filch and the "Otamys." Seen in these terms, Boswell's boasting—not one young girl, but two, bedded "one after the other, according to their seniority" (Boswell 264)—carries with it a suggestion that he is trying to prove that he could be Macheath by proving that he is not a shotten herring.

Friedman also notes that Boswell spent the early part of his adult life searching for a woman who would play Polly to his Macheath (106); if so, his ambition was by no means unique. Eighteenth-century London audiences could and did purchase thousands of Polly Peachum fans and Polly Peachum jest-books, and they were also treated to a number of new ballads that pretended to be written either to or by Polly Peachum. By the mid-1730s a pamphlet war between the partisans of Susannah Cibber and Katherine Clive demonstrated that the actors of this period believed the role was worth fighting about. But perhaps the most telling consequence of the vogue for this character was the elevation of Lavinia Fenton, the first Polly, who was wooed away from the stage as soon as the initial run was completed to become the mistress of the Duke of Bolton.

In a sense, Fenton's subsequent life gave the lie to Mrs. Peachum's claim that in marrying a highwayman, her daughter would "be as ill used, and as much neglected, as if thou hadst married a Lord!" (I.viii.26–28). The duke kept Fenton as his mistress for twenty-three years and then married her after the death of his wife, and she was cited by William Cooke, a theater historian writing at the beginning of the next century, as having "conduct[ed] herself with that propriety and conduct, as to attain the first rank in the country, with the esteem and approbation of the public" (qtd. in Straub 155). In its general outlines, this version of Fenton's story reproduces the path laid out for Polly in the play; Polly's father is only a shopkeeper, she seems to have been at least technically illegitimate, and Macheath is a nobleman of sorts. However, other contemporary accounts charged her with infidelity to and financial exploitation of the duke.[11] Lavinia Fenton was an illegitimate child of poverty who had spent time as a barmaid—a detail which connects her not to Polly, but rather to Lucy, who blames her "education" in an alehouse for her inability to resist the advances of Macheath (III.i.25–35). She also had at least three children out of wedlock before the duke finally married her—another fact that connected her to Lucy and the wives who preceded her. Fenton's detractors characterized her as a whore and accused her of trying to have her bastard children legitimated after the fact, but nothing has ever been produced to corroborate either claim. In any case, there seems to be too little information available to settle the dispute as to which of these various portraits is closer to the truth. And it is perhaps this lack of evidence that constitutes the most significant link to the theatrical role that gave Fenton her first big break.

Neither Polly nor Lucy is given anything to say after the Beggar's reprieve. In Lucy's case, that is hardly surprising, but the playwright's treatment of Polly's silence is remarkable both for the emphasis it receives and for the manner in which it is announced. "Ladies," says Macheath,

> I hope you will give me leave to present a Partner to each of you. And (if I may without Offence) for this Time, I take *Polly* for mine.—And for Life, you Slut,—for we were really marry'd.—As for the Rest.—But at present keep your own Secret. [*To Polly.*   (III.xvii.7–11)

Given the nature of the relationship between Macheath and Polly, asking her to keep her own secret, even if it is only "at present," seems like an unnecessarily severe restriction; after all, if he can speak to her without being heard by the others, why can't she speak privately to him in the same situation? There is also the matter of how this injunction is connected to the cryptic threat contained in "As for the Rest." The bargain being struck here is old-fashioned even by eighteenth-century standards. Macheath offers to give her what she wants and to protect her from the jealousy of other women; in return, he wants the right to have the last word, and the right to organize the dance. The nature of the agreement dictates that the private rewards or penalties of this arrangement must remain obscure, but the public consequences of a woman's assent to it are reflected in history's ambivalent treatment of Lavinia Fenton.

*   *   *

In a 1986 study entitled *The Politics and Poetics of Transgression*, Peter Stallybrass and Allon White explore the relations between what Mikhail Bakhtin has termed "the classical body" of "high official culture" and "the grotesque body" of the carnival and its analogues (19–23). Stallybrass and White suggest that even in the literary productions of high culture, the project of expelling the grotesque body never fully succeeds; instead, that body lurks just below the surface as "an unpalatable and interiorized *phobic* set of representations associated with avoidance and with others" (108, their italics). In *The Beggar's Opera*, the grotesque body is represented by the corpse hanging from the gallows, soon to be dissected; by the knight-errant who will soon resemble a shotten herring; and by the pregnant woman who becomes the one individuated dancer in Gay's closing number. With respect to the institutional aims of high culture—at least insofar as they are elaborated by Foucault, and by Stallybrass and White—Lucy's presence has to be considered an oversight. At the same time, her presence serves as an indication of how difficult it is to eradicate the material elements of theatrical performance. Actors' bodies, like our own bodies, are ephemeral, and any and every body runs the daily risk of ending up among the "Otamys." At the same time, actors also outlast the characters they play, and an ending like that of *The Beggar's Opera* can and should serve to remind us that the abstractions which are frequently exalted above the mundane concerns of everyday life—love, honor, language, art—mean little or nothing unless and until they are attached to specific human and material contexts.

2. "The storm that lust began must end in blood": The Physical Economy of *The London Merchant*

In 1734, Samuel Richardson wrote and published *The Apprentice's Vade Mecum*, a conduct book in which he strongly admonished his young readers against spending their time and money in London theaters. In a section subtitled "the shameful Depravity of the *British* Stage," Richardson complains that

> all our late Heroes and Heroines of the Drama, have been fetch'd from *Newgate* and *Bridewell*. . . . [T]he wretched Group of Rogues, form'd from the Characters of *Shepherd, Jonathan Wild, Blueskin*, and, in fine, from every Rogue that has made a Noise in the World by his superlative Wickedness, has yielded the principal Characters exhibited, and that not for the Sake of Poetical Justice, in their *Execution*, but to divert the Audience by their *Tricks* and *Escapes*; and if they have been brought to Justice at last, it has been in such a Manner, as to move the Pity of the Audience for them. (*AVM* 12–13)

Perhaps to demonstrate that he could be somewhat open-minded on these issues, Richardson then went on to exempt "One Play only" from his general condemnation of the London stage:

> I know but of one Instance, and that a very late one, where the Stage has condescended to make itself useful to the City-Youth, by a dreadful Example of the Artifices of a lewd Woman, and the Seduction of an unwary young Man; and it would savour too much of Partiality, not to mention it. I mean, the Play of *George Barnwell* which has met with the Success that I think it well deserves; and I could be content to compound with the young City Gentry, that they should go to this Play once a Year, if they would condition, not to desire to go oftner, till another Play of an equally good Moral and Design were acted on the Stage. (*AVM* 16)

"The Play of *George Barnwell*," now generally known as *The London Merchant* (1731), is a sentimental tragedy set in the London underworld and aimed directly at city apprentices. Written by a goldsmith and jeweler named George Lillo, it was staged ninety-six times between its premiere in 1731 and the publication of *Pamela* nearly ten years later. Although *The Beggar's Opera* was performed more than twice as many times during this same period, Lillo's play is by far the most popular and most discussed tragedy of its era. Its supporters included not only Richardson but Fielding as well; in fact, Fielding later staged Lillo's *Fatal Curiosity* (1736) at the Little Haymarket Theatre.[1]

The London Merchant seems to have been written at least in part to attract the attention of the audiences who had flocked to see *The Beggar's Opera*. Like Gay's satire, Lillo's tragedy focuses on life among the urban lower classes, and it draws on the same sources for its particular subject matter. In fact, Lillo seems to have modified his mid-seventeenth-century source specifically in order to strengthen the connection between his story and more contemporary treatments of crime in an urban setting. In the ballad called *George Barnwell*, the murders take place in Shropshire and the murderer escapes to sea following his betrayal by Millwood; with the exception of the murder scene, the play is set in London, and it ends in Newgate. To a certain extent, the configuration of Lillo's plot also recalls that of Gay's satire. Like Macheath, Barnwell finds himself suspended between two women, one a sentimental heroine and the other a homicidal monster. In each case, the hero finds himself more or less unexpectedly in conflict with the heroine's father, who in each case exercises a great deal of political power in the world created on stage. Finally, of course, in each case the threat of hanging looms as an imperfect resolution of that central conflict.

However, if we turn our attention from plot and setting to characters, these parallels seem merely to provide occasions for a series of antitheses. In some respects, Lillo's merchant—an upstanding and wealthy patriarch named Thorowgood—can be viewed as an amalgam of Peachum and the Beggar: like Peachum, he is the patriarch of his little urban world, and like the Beggar, he issues pronouncements about certain themes and changes the direction of the plot at crucial moments. At the same time, Thorowgood's sententious didacticism has little in common with either Peachum's chilling but generally good-humored cynicism or the Beggar's willingness to follow the shifting currents of fashion. Similarly, where Macheath happily acts on whatever impulses possess him, Barnwell cannot stop ruminating about the morality and consequences of his past, present, and future actions. Lillo's Maria has none of Polly's vivacity, and his Sarah

Millwood displays a gothic extravagance that would be entirely inappropriate in Lucy Lockit.

Even more important—at least for the purposes of this study—are the differences between these plays which have to do with the matrix of issues that Elaine Scarry has encapsulated in the phrase "persons and populations."[2] In certain respects, the plot of Lillo's tragedy suggests that he shared Gay's interest in the demographics of the London underworld. Like *The Beggar's Opera*, *The London Merchant* contains several references to the macabre carnivals that erupted spontaneously around every public execution at Tyburn, and Millwood's repeated efforts to excuse her exploitation of Barnwell on the grounds that she herself is a victim (I.iii.31–41; IV.xviii.11 ff.)[3] are cast in terms that echo Gay's descriptions of the social conditions that produced prostitutes and pickpockets. In the previous chapter, I suggested that Gay explored certain demographic issues by providing post-coital materialist shadows for his two protagonists, and that the ending of *The Beggar's Opera* exhibits a deep ambivalence about the role of physical experience in human affairs. Although *The London Merchant* uses some of the same doubling effects, the terms of the implied comparison are quite different, and in general Lillo's play is not the least bit ambivalent about what it presents as the inevitable consequences of illicit sexual activity.

The difference between these approaches is reflected in the scale of each production. By eighteenth-century standards, the cast of *The Beggar's Opera* is huge; it has more than twenty speaking roles, and the presence of the orchestra and the inclusion of three dance scenes could easily have doubled the number of performers involved in the production. By way of contrast, *The London Merchant* could be performed with as few as nine actors. In *The Beggar's Opera*, Gay uses Filch and Lucy to establish connections between the individual protagonists and the populations they were assumed in some sense to represent. In *The London Merchant*, there are no "Otamys," no shotten herring, no thieves other than Barnwell, no seducers other than Millwood. The occasional references to Tyburn notwithstanding, Lillo's tragedy reduces the whole phenomenon of eighteenth-century urban crime to what amounts to a purely internecine struggle.

The ballad that provided the source for *The London Merchant*[4] has only two speaking characters: Millwood, and the apprentice himself. Contrary to the impression created in Richardson's conduct book, Lillo transforms this story by recasting the central conflict not as a struggle between a young man and a "lewd woman," but rather as a battle between two very different families. The play pits Thorowgood, his dutiful daughter Maria, and a good apprentice named Trueman against Millwood and her two servants. Although the plot of *The London Merchant* clearly revolves around Barnwell, he does not appear on stage until the first act is more than half over. The four scenes that precede his appearance present us first, with a tribute to the noble city merchants who have used their financial influence to hinder the building of the Spanish Armada; second, with a conversation between Thorowgood and his daughter Maria, designed to demonstrate the virtuous consideration they show for each other's feelings; third, with an introduction to the predatory Sarah Millwood and her maidservant Lucy; and finally, with a brief soliloquy in which Millwood plans how she will receive Barnwell when he visits for the first time.

The structure of this beginning defines the ideology of domestic tragedy as a genre. On the one hand, Thorowgood presents the ethical context of the play, first by asserting the virtue and political power of the group he represents and then by demonstrating his role as an exemplary parent. On the other hand, Millwood's first two scenes present the challenge to that ethical stance—the Hobbesian principles, learned in the urban underworld, that account for her opposition to Thorowgood's well-regulated household. Lillo's particular version of this opposition is rooted in his sense of what he considers to be essential differences between men and women. The first explicit allusion to these differences occurs in Millwood's soliloquy, when she explains where she has learned the skills necessary to deceive and manipulate Barnwell:

> I'll trust to nature, who does wonders in these matters. If to seem what one is not in order to be the better liked for what one really is, if to speak one thing and mean the direct contrary, be art in a woman, I know nothing of nature.   (I.iv.9–13)

Millwood's plan is to appear to be a modest woman ("to seem what one is not") so that Barnwell will like her better when she turns out to be a woman who will take him to bed ("what one really is"). This statement damns her twice—once because she is dissimulating, and once because she acknowledges the need to dissimulate. It also completes the orientation process begun with Thorowgood's opening scene, where he advises the worshipful Trueman to "take heed not to purchase the character of complaisant at the expense of your sincerity" (I.i.29–30).

If Millwood is drawing upon the resources of her female nature, what force is animating Thorowgood? William Empson has suggested that *The Beggar's Opera* contains some verbal and physical signals that cast Macheath as a fertility god whose body is destined to be killed and divided up among his worshippers (*SVP* 225–26, 230–31). Cultural anthropologists and social theorists of various stripes often read this ritual of dismemberment and dispersion as a means of erasing the boundary between the abstract notion of the god or king and the physical substance of the particular individual who represents the abstract principle or divinity. In the particular cases of *The Beggar's Opera* and *The London Merchant*, this narrative paradigm can be read in the context of Foucault's description of the early modern body politic as bounded on the one end by the body of the king and on the other by the body of the condemned (*DP*, 28–29).

The exaltation of the state and its quasi-divine representative depended on the abjection of the individuals who threatened the social fabric in concrete ways. Consequently, any perceived threat to the structural integrity of the abstract authority had to be answered with public gestures that simultaneously emphasized the vulnerable materiality of the violator and reaffirmed the invulnerable abstraction of the judge. One way to achieve such a reaffirmation was through the production of texts about the convict and the execution. Regardless of whether the fragmented body was associated with a divine spirit, an extraordinary villain, or a misunderstood victim of circumstances, the purely verbal construction of that character invariably outlasted the body itself. In my discussion of *The Beggar's Opera*, I argued that performance conventions could be manipulated to suggest that bodies can indeed outlast the verbal structures attached to them. In *The London Merchant*, however, the body at the center of the text is singular, not plural, and it is thus primarily a symbolic rather than a physical presence. Lillo sets up a network of verbal figures that are presented as concrete realities on stage only intermittently; in this play, both the abstract authority over and the concrete reality of human existence are located in the idea and person of the patriarch.

In the pages that follow, I hope to demonstrate that Lillo's tragedy seeks to establish Thorowgood as the authoritarian abstraction whose structural integrity is placed at risk by the activites of his erstwhile subjects, and that the playwright employs the symbolic equivalents of dismemberment, dispersion, and reconstitution to shape his plot. This narrative paradigm determines the ethical framework for the tragedy: if most of the characters in *The Beggar's Opera* were judged according to how much they contributed to the underworld community, the cast of *The London Merchant* are judged according to whether and how they contribute to the symbolic health not only of their local merchant-deity, but also of the socioeconomic regime he represents. As in Gay's satire, Lillo's highly gendered treatment of physical experience occurs within a social context that emphasizes the conflicting demands placed on the individual by private desires on the one hand and by implied demographic responsibilities on the other. In *The London Merchant*, however, this dilemma is not left unresolved at the end of the play. Instead, Lillo's tragedy asserts the ethical priority of demographic and economic responsibilities over individual desires, because that choice allows both the body of the merchant-king and the body of the state to remain intact.

*   *   *

Like the vast majority of plays written during the eighteenth century, Lillo's tragedy had a sort of double name: the first page of the original edition called the play "The London Merchant; or, The History of George Barnwell." In cases like this one, the conventional twentieth-century critical practice has been to ignore and often even to delete one of the two titles. Generally speaking, this sort of omission is relatively harmless, but in the case of *The London Merchant*, the use of the first title alone is somewhat misleading. During the eighteenth century, Lillo's play was known as the history or tragedy of George Barnwell. Using the second title rather than the first is atypical, and it helps to suggest what eighteenth-century audiences thought was important about this play. George Barnwell is identified in the Prologue as a "London 'prentice ruin'd" (Prologue 21); the combination of this particular occupational label and a prophecy of doom provides a very particular social context for what follows.

The eighteenth-century apprentice was uniquely susceptible to the pressures created by the shift away from the family-oriented socioeconomic structures of the sixteenth and seventeenth centuries, toward the mass society that would become characteristic of the modern world. On the one hand, apprentices were supposed to be treated as members of their masters' families. For most of the century they were required to live in their masters' houses, and they were expected to accept their masters' right to control their behavior and their social activities. On the other hand, their masters were legally bound to teach them a trade, and it seems to have been assumed that apprentices who did in fact learn trades could reasonably expect to achieve independent livings when their indentures were finished. In other words, although apprentices were expected to submit themselves to their masters as to surrogate parents, that submission was balanced by an explicit promise of a particular economic benefit; thus the indentures artificially replicated a preindustrial socioeconomic system. In such a system, the family and the family business were still essentially indistinguishable, and any threat to the latter could and was easily construed as an attack on the former.

In theory at least, the success of the apprentice/master relationship depended only on the technical and pedagogical skills of the master and the industriousness of the apprentice. However, the problems that surfaced in connection with this arrangement during the first half of the eighteenth century suggest that the potential for serious abuses was embedded in the structure of the institution as a whole.[5] Even under the best of circumstances, the last three years of any indenture obviously exploited the apprentice. By that time he[6] was worth as much as any journeyman, but his earnings still belonged entirely to his master. In theory at least, this inequity was balanced by the early years of the apprenticeship, when the boys involved—those, at least, who were decently cared for, and who were not forced to work beyond their physical capacities—must invariably have cost their masters more than they contributed to the business. Still, even where the economic obligation was understood, nearly every young man in this situation must have chafed under the infantilizing restrictions of the indentures, which forced him to subsist on an allowance set by his master and which forbade him to get married, to drink, or to frequent taverns or playhouses without his master's permission.

Any effort to exert such total control over the lives of young adults is probably doomed to failure, and in early modern London this particular effort produced failure on a grand scale. By the early 1700s, apprentices had been banding together in the streets of the capital for more than two centuries, often for the purposes of disturbing the peace in one way or another. Lawrence Stone has noted that the London apprentices were "by far the largest adolescent peer-group in the country" throughout the eighteenth century, and that as such they "were inevitably a constant threat to social order" (376). Because the enforced bachelorhood of the group helped to create an extraordinary demand for prostitutes in the city, Lillo's pairing of a prostitute and a city apprentice must have seemed not merely plausible but unmistakably familiar; it metonymically reproduced one of the fundamental demographic facts of life in eighteenth-century London.

Neither the apprentices nor the authorities were happy with this situation, but there was no solution available at this time, largely because the two groups were so obviously working at cross-purposes. While eighteenth-century apprentices wanted and would eventually obtain more freedom to do as they pleased, the authorities sought to keep the old restrictions in place throughout this period. In fact, they even tried to strengthen those controls by prohibiting apprentices from attending a variety of popular entertainments, including dances, cock-fights, and bowling (Stone 376). Even Richardson's suggestion that apprentices should see only one play per year echoes this broader social policy. Such restrictions were defended on the grounds that they encouraged the apprentices to spend more time on their work, but they seemed also to reflect an unspoken belief that the "City-Youth" should not be allowed to associate with one another under even the most innocent of circumstances. They were expected to remain home, where each household business establishment could keep its own apprentices in line.

The apprentices' intense dislike of these programmatic attempts to control their private lives was reflected not only in their often unruly behavior, but in their literary tastes as well. One of the very few holidays alloted to the "young City Gentry" fell every year on the Lord Mayor's Day (October 29), and the proprietors of the London theaters traditionally helped them to celebrate by staging productions that were calculated to please apprentices in particular. During the second quarter of the eighteenth century, the play offered most frequently on these occasions was a ribald Restoration farce by Edward Ravenscroft called *The London Cuckolds* (1681). In fact, it was presented at Covent Garden on every Lord Mayor's Day between 1733 and 1749, and it drew such large crowds that theater managers often recorded their receipts for posterity. The plot of this rather poorly crafted play concerns three wealthy old citizens whose young wives are coveted by three young men of modest means. One of the wives is foolish, one aspires (unsuccessfully) to wit, and one makes a great show of her piety; the play consists primarily of slapstick routines that revolve around the seductions of these women.

Given the degree and number of physical restrictions placed on London apprentices during the first half of the eighteenth century, we should perhaps not be surprised to find them applauding a play that offered them forbidden sex, forbidden revenge against the city's upper crust, and forbidden community, all at the same time. The competition thrown against the Covent Garden productions of *The London Cuckolds* during this era tends to confirm this interpretation of Lord Mayor's Day tradition. At various times between 1728 and 1749, the apprentices were offered productions of *The Beggar's Opera*, of Christopher Bullock's *A Match in Newgate* (1715), and of George Farquhar's *The Beaux' Stratagem* (1707)—all plays that celebrated these forbidden possibilities in one way or another. Nor should we be surprised to discover that *The London Merchant* ran on Lord Mayor's Day only twice during this period (in 1731 and in 1740), or that neither performance was successful enough to warrant a repetition of the experiment on the following year. Where Ravenscroft's farce celebrated the energy and resourcefulness of youth, Lillo's tragedy urged the necessity of subordination, isolation, and, above all, abstinence. In his dedication, Lillo defends his effort to reform the apprentices of London in terms which hint at this emphasis on physical restraint:

> If princes, &c., were alone liable to misfortunes arising from vice or weakness in themselves or others, there would be good reason for confining the characters in tragedy to those of superior rank; but, since the contrary is evident, nothing can be more reasonable than to proportion the remedy to the disease. (Dedication 26–31)

The diseased body in the last line is presumably that of the city, or perhaps the state as a whole, and "proportion the remedy" in this sense means to direct one's clinical attention to the group of individuals who composed the diseased part of the body politic.[7] In a fairly conventional conceptual inversion, people who actually have bodies become mere cells in a larger body, and the quasi-medical needs of that larger organism provide an occasional justification for certain kinds of social microsurgery. That goal is also reflected in the way that the passage seeks to establish limits at every conceivable syntactical juncture. This barely submerged text bobs to the surface in Lillo's use of "confining" (or even "good reason for confining"!), and in the circumlocution that establishes "nothing" as a kind of boundary in the last clause.

The terms of the eighteenth-century debate about apprentices echoed the opposition between individual identity and collective anonymity that helped to shape the plot of *The Beggar's Opera*. Good apprentices stayed home, avoided contact with external temptations, and remained loyal to their business families; bad apprentices joined other bad apprentices to form the unruly crowds of unsupervised adolescents in the bear gardens, brothels, and theaters. In other contexts, the impulses that drove them to such places might have been construed as natural, but in *The London*

Merchant, Lillo uses the standard familial construction of the apprentice's obligations to emphasize what he believes to be their perversity. According to this view, the business of the apprentice's master is not limited to making money or educating his inferiors; like any good patriarch, he must also regulate the desires of those inferiors, partly so that the pursuit of those desires will not interfere with the efficient conduct of business, and partly so that the political and social power of one generation can be handed on to the next in an orderly fashion.

∗   ∗   ∗

The plot of *The London Merchant* establishes Thorowgood's household as natural and normative, while Millwood's household is cast as a dark parody of that model. The impulse that drives Barnwell to Millwood's doorstep is that of unregulated sexual desire, but what is most remarkable about Lillo's plot is not the young protagonist's inability to govern his own lust, but rather the way in which that lust is translated by Millwood into crimes against property that are also violations of sexual taboos. Nearly every critic who has written on the play has noted Lillo's effort to absolve Barnwell of blame for his crimes,[8] but such comments have tended to focus on larger thematic issues rather than on the particular mechanism which leads, at least in the playwright's view, to that absolution. In the soliloquy that follows her opening conversation with Lucy, Millwood tells the audience that "if I have any skill in physiognomy, [Barnwell] is amorous and, with a little assistance, will soon get the better of his modesty" (I. iv.7–9). Whether Millwood does in fact have any skill in physiognomy is open to question—this is the first and only time that that pseudoscience is mentioned, so there is no way to evaluate her claim—but in any case this description presents "amorousness" as the kind of personality trait that is tantamount to a medical condition. It implies a susceptibility to sexual desire that is quite beyond the individual's ability to resist. Barnwell himself describes it as "the fever of the soul and madness of desire," and adds that "[i]n vain does nature, reason, conscience, all oppose it" (III.v.24–26).

Although Thorowgood describes "the bitter fruits of passion's detested reign and sensual appetites indulged" as "severe reflections, penitence and tears" (V.ii.1–3), his plot suggests that the more immediate consequences of Barnwell's lust are theft and murder of a peculiarly sacrilegious nature. Furthermore, since the plot of *The London Merchant* is arranged in a manner calculated to make Barnwell as innocent as possible (given the circumstances), it might ultimately be more accurate to say that Millwood deliberately perverts Barnwell's sexual appetite in order to suit her own purposes. The blueprint for this transformation appears in her opening scene, when she tells Lucy that "I would have my conquests complete, like those of the Spaniards in the New World, who first plundered the natives of all the wealth they had and then condemned the wretches to the mines for life to work for more" (I.iii.24–27). The playwright presumably equated Millwood's treatment of Barnwell with the barbarities of Spanish colonialism because too many London merchants depended for their livelihoods on the English variety. However, by the end of the first act, Lillo has discovered another way to take advantage of this implicit comparison. Barnwell closes Act I with a somewhat cryptic vision of colonial conquest which both explains his decision to do as Millwood asks him and passes judgment on the earlier figure of speech:

> I would not—yet I must on.
> Reluctant thus, the merchant quits his ease
> And trusts to rocks and sands and stormy seas;
> In hopes some unknown golden coast to find,
> Commits himself, though doubtful, to the wind;
> Longs much for joys to come, yet mourns those left behind.
>
> (I.viii.24–29)

This passage is clearly intended to contrast Barnwell's male innocence with Millwood's female experience, but it also serves indirectly to reinforce the tendency of eighteenth-century male writers to blame women for what troubled them about the national economy. If Millwood presents herself as a conquistadora, Barnwell locates himself in the context of a considerably more benign expansionism. The "unknown golden coast" of his vision, like the highly sanitized version of the colonial enterprise that Thorowgood and Trueman dream up in the opening moments of Act III, is presumably free of both slaves and mines.

Millwood's comment is criticized not only by the three male characters, but by Lucy as well. In fact, Millwood claims the role of the colonial conqueror for herself only after Lucy has joked that men are women's slaves, "for we lay them under contribution" (I.iii.19–20). A military conqueror would place a subject population under contribution in the sense of demanding that they pay tribute (this sense of the phrase is reinforced by Millwood's reference to Spanish colonists soon afterward), but of course Lucy is also punning on another sense of the verb "to lay," and the "contribution" she has in mind in that case may be either the customary fee demanded by prostitutes or semen. In either case, Lucy's cheerful lust is expressed in a manner that implies that women can take from men whatever they want. The playwright uses her to establish a connection between power and desire which does not appear to be threatening at this point, but which quickly becomes threatening when the dispassionate Millwood demonstrates how it can be exploited.

Millwood's relationship with Barnwell recapitulates the difference in their respective economic visions. Essentially, it is Barnwell who is laid under contribution by Millwood, who succeeds in conquering him chiefly because he thinks of Millwood herself (at least at first) as that "golden coast." Moreover, since it is this relationship that drives Barnwell both to steal and to kill his uncle, we can conclude that Lillo's script is seeking to establish a connection between mercenary females and the perversion of mercantile capitalism into theft and murder for financial gain. At first, the text implies that Barnwell, had he not been subject to Millwood's demands, would have made a good capitalist; later on, after he has become involved with her, it suggests that those demands will transform Barnwell into either a great capitalist (in the tradition of Gay's Peachum) or a slave toiling in the mines.

In relation to the other Augustan works which connect women and economic change in this way,[9] *The London Merchant* stands out, chiefly because it explicitly and idiosyncratically links the economic consequences of an exaggerated version of female consumerism to what is presented as the irresistable imperative of male heterosexual desire. In the next section of my discussion, I will attempt to explain how Barnwell's institutional identity and Millwood's economic role are reflected in the symbolic dismemberment that ultimately directs the audience's attention back to Lillo's merchant-god.

*   *   *

Lillo's understanding of the psychopathology of Barnwell's enslavement is laid bare in the climactic scene of the play, where the distraught apprentice returns to Millwood with blood on his hands (the expression must in this case be taken quite literally) only to be repudiated and betrayed. Although we have been told by various characters that Barnwell has brought Millwood money several times before this episode, this is the first and only time in the play that we see her waiting with that specific expectation. Waiting for money, she receives blood instead; the substitution of the latter for the former suggests that everything she has done to Thorowgood through Barnwell has suddenly been shifted from the realm of the abstract to that of the concrete. The connection between blood and money is reinforced when Millwood upbraids the distraught Barnwell for failing to rob his uncle after he has murdered him. After pointing out that his uncle no longer had any use for his wealth, she accuses Barnwell of bringing her only "penury and guilt" (IV.x.42)—two abstract terms that reflect a lack of money and an abundance of blood, respectively.

Millwood would obviously prefer to have an abundance of money and no blood at all, but the substitution is appropriate in light of the way in which the swift or slow circulation of money has been treated as a symptom of strength or weakness for each of the patriarchs in the play. The first reference to this model occurs in the opening scene, where Thorowgood exults in his judgment that the king of Spain, who needs funds to build his Armada, "must now attend the slow return of wealth from his New World to supply his empty coffers" (I.i.6–7); soon afterward, we discover that Thorowgood himself pays his bills promptly (I.i.55–59), and that he is a generous host (I.ii.1–2). The latter detail is important because Millwood is equally generous (I.vii.1–3), but her hospitality is funded by illegitimate means. This point of comparison is registered in a series of inconspicuous references to the dinner parties held in both Thorowgood's and Millwood's houses. Thorowgood's first speech to Maria asks whether she has made arrangements for that evening's "entertainment" (I.ii.1); before Act I has ended, Millwood has used the same term to refer to the elaborate supper she has prepared for Barnwell's first visit (I.vi.3), and she claims later that although she is confident of her ability to attract Barnwell to her house against his better judgment, she is "afraid that he [might] come without money," for "a house of entertainment, like mine, is not kept with nothing" (II.xii.4–6). In the opening scene of Act III, Thorowgood tells Trueman in effect that "getting wealth" is less important than "open[ing] and . . . keep[ing] up an intercourse between nations far remote from one another . . . [and] by mutual benefits diffusing mutual love from pole to pole" (III.i.5–9). But this is a far cry from Millwood's conspicuous consumption.

With the connection between blood and money as background, we can see how the repudiation scene situates Thorowgood's circulatory metaphor within the larger context of the body politic. After a brief aside from Millwood, the scene itself begins rather strangely, with her extraordinary and totally unexpected offer of a safe refuge:

> BARNWELL.   Where shall I hide me? Whither shall I fly to avoid the swift, unerring hand of justice?
> MILLWOOD.   Dismiss those fears! Though thousands had pursued you to the door, yet being entered here you are safe as innocence. I have such a cavern, by art so cunningly contrived, that the piercing eyes of jealousy and revenge may search in vain, nor find the entrance to the safe retreat. There will I hide you if any danger's near.   (IV.x.4–11)

This is wholly uncharacteristic of Millwood, partly because she seems to sympathize with his fear and remorse, and partly because she seems at least temporarily willing to assume openly the dominant position in the relationship. It is, however, the specific content of her reassurances—in particular, her reference to the cavern, cunningly contrived and hidden—that gives such a surreal quality to the moment. William McBurney annotates this passage with the comment that "Millwood's cavern may be a property common to enchantresses (no specific source has been found), or simply an oblique reference to a grave" (56n). Since (as Laura Brown points out) the play occasionally encourages a perception of Millwood as some sort of supernatural being (*EDF* 159), there is little reason to quarrel with McBurney's use of the term "enchantress." However, his use of the term "property" is less clear and more problematic. Does he mean to designate a piece of real estate or a personal attribute? And if the latter, exactly what sort of attribute are we discussing here?

Like the Cave of Spleen in Pope's *Rape of the Lock*, Millwood's cavern constitutes a less than oblique reference to the conventional male conception of the womb as an empty space;[10] read in these terms, her offer becomes the opening gambit in a highly compressed and stylized enactment of what the playwright perceives as the connections between theft, parricide, and unregulated desire. Like the staging of the murder (III.v–vii), this scene attempts to render crimes against property horrifying by connecting them to the primal nightmares of male psychosexual development. Barnwell himself describes the murder as a parricide (III.vii.34–35), and the phallic imagery employed in the struggle with his uncle/father is embarrassingly obvious: the younger man tries to use his pistol but cannot, and then finds himself forced to defend himself with a dagger against his uncle, whose sword is drawn. In the repudiation scene, Millwood's first words to Barnwell offer him a return to the womb, a place where he will be "safe as innocence" from the twin Oedipal demons of "jealousy and revenge." It is thus an entirely appropriate beginning to a scene which quickly evolves into a heated argument about the morality of rifling the corpse of the uncle/master/father. The passage may also hint at an explanation for why the guilty Barnwell keeps returning to Millwood, or it may represent simply her attempt to regain control of a situation that is rapidly disintegrating. In either case, the details of her description help to infantilize Barnwell (whose blood-spattered appearance may also remind us of a newborn), and that appearance in turn contributes to the equally important exposure of Millwood in the guise of the bad mother who rejects her own child.

Although Millwood's relationship to Barnwell over the first three acts of the play might be aptly described as parasitic, it is not until the repudiation scene that this metaphor is used to recast her as a vampire. Obviously, this is not to suggest that Millwood conceives of herself in these terms. When she thinks that Barnwell has money, she is willing to play the receptive mother—the one who, given the opportunity, would prefer the child to the father—in his Oedipal drama. When she believes that Barnwell no longer has money—as she does when she learns that he has deserted Thorowgood's household (III.iv.34–66)—she reveals herself as a monster in the shape of a bad mother. In either case, the logic of Lillo's plot places the responsibility for that conflict with the mother, not the son; the role that Millwood chooses to play is determined not by Barnwell's behavior, but by what she gets from him. In the terms established by Lucy's joke, Millwood is ultimately not interested in contributions which take the form of what Stanley Kubrick's General Jack D. Ripper called precious bodily fluids; what Millwood wants is money. In the repudiation scene, the literalization of these various metaphors reveals her as the bad mother who rejects her children, who exposes them instead of protecting them, who takes life instead of giving it.

Given the rather monstrous nature of his chief villain, we may be somewhat surprised to discover that Lillo tries very hard to arrange his plot and his dialogue so that Millwood's sins are not construed as those of the female sex as a whole. In fact, he seems to have invented the character of Thorowgood's daughter solely for the purpose of using her as a counterexample to Millwood's female monster. This is only implicit in Maria's first scene, where she provides a contrast to Millwood's misandry and rebelliousness by expressing her love for her father and her willingness to defer to his wishes in all things (I.ii.51–54), but it becomes much more explicit the next time that she appears on stage, when Trueman tells her of Barnwell's embezzlement and she decides to use her own money to conceal the fact from her father. The scene ends with her request that her assistance be kept secret, because "[a] virgin's fame is sullied by suspicion's slightest breath; and, therefore, as this must be a secret from my father and the world for Barnwell's sake, for mine let it be so to him" (III.iii.65–68). Both the request for anonymity and the gesture itself reverse the pattern set by Millwood's parasitic relationship to Barnwell, a point that is empha- sized—some might say overemphasized—by Lillo's use of the theatrical equivalent of a cinematic match cut. Maria's conversation with Trueman ends with the speech just cited, and the next words spoken on stage are Lucy saying to Blunt "Well, what do you think of Millwood's conduct now?" This pattern is carried to a further extreme in the final scenes of the play, where Lillo at last allows Maria to confess her love for Barnwell (V.vii–ix). The episode clearly implies that if the virtuous apprentice had succeeded in resisting Millwood's advances, he would in time have married his master's daughter and inherited Thorowgood's business.

Maria's final appearance inverts the pattern of Millwood's vampirism in much the same fashion that her second appearance did, and by doing so it also provides Lillo with an opportunity to get in one last dig at the demographic perspective on crime which Millwood had championed ear- lier in the play. The playwright drives the point home in this case by hav- ing the distraught Maria compare a private death in the arms of a lover to the spectacle at Tyburn:

> MARIA.   What is her misery and distress who sees the first, last object of her love, for whom alone she'd live—for whom she'd die a thousand, thousand deaths if it were possible—expiring in her arms? Yet she is happy when com- pared to me. Were millions of worlds mine, I'd gladly give them in exchange for her condition. . . .
> TRUEMAN.   Time and reflection cure all ills.
> MARIA.   All but this; this dreadful catastrophe virtue herself abhors. To give a holiday to suburb slaves and, passing, entertain the savage herd who, elbow- ing each other for a sight, pursue and press upon him like his fate. A mind with piety and resolution armed may smile on death. But public ignominy, everlasting shame (shame, the death of souls, to die a thousand times and yet survive even death itself in never-dying infamy), is this to be endured?
>
> (V.ix.54–70)

Although these two kinds of death are very different, in both cases her descriptions are heavily laced with numbers. In the first instance, the many deaths of the heroine and the many worlds she possesses recall the money Maria supplied to cover up the fact of Barnwell's embezzlement; they also, of course, invoke the long-term prospects of sexual satisfaction and economic advancement which have been sacrificed to Barnwell's ill-considered lust and Millwood's all-too-considered greed. The second description envisions the chaos at Tyburn as a peculiarly voyeuristic version of a bacchanal; the mob pursues and presses on the condemned criminal not because it wishes to tear him to pieces, but because it wants to see him, and this in itself is somehow shameful.

Kristina Straub has recently argued that the eighteenth-century London stage provides an important site for "the ongoing process of naturalization by which the powerful, gendered tropes of the male spectator and the female spectacle become encoded in modern ideology" (19). *The London Merchant* helps this process along by suggesting that good women shy away from spectacles of all kinds, while bad women search out opportunities to display themselves. The first time Millwood suspects that Barnwell has lost interest in her, she visits Thorowgood's shop, ostensibly to tell her lover that she is leaving London. On this occasion, she arranges for Lucy to tell Barnwell that she, Millwood, has been ruined by a corrupt guardian who wanted to make her his mistress. By the time this narrative actually comes out, Lucy's asides (II.ix.28–30; xi.11–12) have already established that none of this is true, but it is the story's circumstantial plausibility rather than its falseness that calls Millwood's prior self-analysis into question. Millwood claims that she became wicked herself because she was abused by wicked men. However, when the only wicked man in Lillo's plot turns out to be imaginary, the general proposition that wicked men exist becomes—at least within the context of this play—questionable. Lucy's use of stage jargon to indicate that she is deceiving Barnwell (she speaks of playing her part and getting her cue) is in fact somewhat misleading, because the crucial opposition here pits the story she tells against the plot being enacted for the audience. Millwood-the-victim is the subject of a discredited narrative, while Millwood-the-seducer is the character performed for us.

If Straub's hypothesis is correct, the specular economy of the eighteenth century evolved out of a relatively fluid and open situation at the turn of the seventeenth century to the point where a rigid, male-dominated paradigm came to be conceived as normative and natural. At first glance, Lillo seems to be swimming against this tide, because he repeatedly shows Millwood placing herself on display as a means of using

Barnwell's desire to control him. The most explicit example of this tendency occurs when Millwood finds that Lucy's story about the abusive
guardian has failed to persuade the apprentice to come back to her:

> Look on me, Barnwell! Am I deformed or old, that satiety so soon succeeds
> enjoyment? Nay, look again! Am I not she whom yesterday you thought the
> fairest and the kindest of her sex? Whose hand, trembling with ecstacy, you
> pressed and molded thus, while on my eyes you gazed with such delight as if
> desire increased by being fed?   (II.ix.40−45)

Barnwell's initial response to her ploy is a peremptory "No more," but his
resistance soon fades altogether. And although this appears to be a case of
power residing with the spectacle rather than with the spectator—that is,
of a specular economy which inverts the power structure that will be established by later in the century—we need to recognize that this is part of
a rhetorical effort by a male playwright to hold this particular woman
responsible for the sexual transgressions of a particular man. In other
words, this power is granted to Millwood solely for the purpose of demonstrating that she should not have it; thus the episode provides a negative
example that helps to legitimize the model of the active male spectator and
the passive female spectacle.

   This model is also promoted by the playwright's treatment of his female protagonist. For example, Maria's description of Barnwell's death
reveals that the public nature of that death is more of a problem for her
than it will be for him; she is the one who will sense his shame and igno-
miny "each hour of [her] devoted life." Since Barnwell has already accepted his role as (in Richardson's words) a "dreadful example," Maria's
fear may seem a bit incongruous, but in fact this is by no means a new
concern for her. In her first scene, she asks her father to be excused from
an entertainment that she herself had planned; though she claims to be
indisposed, Thorowgood reminds her that "you are not insensible that it
is chiefly on your account these noble lords do me the honor so frequently
to grace my board" (I.ii.16−18). Within the logic of the plot, it is Maria's
love for Barnwell that makes her unwilling to display herself in this fashion, but the recurring contrast between the virtuous woman who hides
herself and the vicious woman who manipulates men by playing on their
lusts and sympathies is difficult to ignore.

✳   ✳   ✳

Lillo's plot contrasts the promise of both sensual and material rewards within a socially sanctioned relationship to the triple threat of incest, Oedipal violence, and the ignominious death reserved for those who violate such deep-rooted taboos. Given the symbolic content of the relationship between Barnwell and Millwood, it is somewhat surprising to discover that the relationship the playwright offers as an alternative to it is in certain respects even closer to literal incest than the path Barnwell has chosen. Since Maria is wholly Lillo's invention, he could easily have given her a different background, or even a different guardian. The fact that he did not do so helps to define the difference between Maria and Millwood in terms of what anthropologists call endogamous and exogamous relationships. Structuralists like Claude Lévi-Strauss have long argued that the nearly universal taboo against incest serves to establish the normalcy and propriety of exogamy as a way of knitting disparate family groups into a community.[11] Thus it is remarkable that *The London Merchant* seeks to valorize a virtually endogamous relationship as safer and more productive than any exogamous alternative.

Of course, Maria is not actually Barnwell's sister; what brings the two young people together in a sibling-like relationship is the apprenticeship system. I suggested earlier that this system evolved partly as a means of reintegrating certain potentially unattached individuals—the second sons of some aristocrats and gentry, the children of the middle class, the wards of the parishes—into a socioeconomic system which still wanted to equate families and family businesses. In a recent essay entitled "Bawds and Merchants: Engendering Capitalist Desires," Laura Mandell argues that the social criticism of Bernard Mandeville uses gender distinctions "to quarantine the vicious part of capitalism in order to idealize the capitalist enterprise of trading" (109). Over the past few pages, I have tried to suggest that *The London Merchant* is structured around the same sort of dynamic: where Thorowgood's economy produces, protects, and nurtures, Millwood's economy consumes, betrays, and destroys. However, Lillo's play is distinguished from Mandeville's tracts because he does not demonize Millwood as a representative of the "grotesque body" defined by Stallybrass and White. Indeed, in Lillo's tragedy, both the grotesque body and the classical body are defined in exclusively male terms. On the one hand, it is ultimately the body of the male apprentice that is bought and sold, wracked with and controlled by desire, and finally reduced to mere matter by acts of individual or institutionalized violence. On the other hand, although Mandeville's prostitutes are presented as evil-because-filthy and although Macheath is shadowed by "Otamys" and shotten herring,

Millwood is judged to be evil not because she is too deeply immersed in the material world, but rather because she seeks certain illicit appropriations of the precious bodily fluids of the patriarch—that is, of Thorowgood's money and the uncle's blood.

Given this last detail, the distinction between Maria and Millwood becomes slightly blurred. Though Lillo does not emphasize the point, when Maria gives some of her own money to Trueman in order to cover Barnwell's losses, she becomes an accessory to embezzlement and a perpetrator of fraud. Early in the play, we learn that Maria is "melancholy" (I.ii.13), and that she is uninterested in the parade of wealthy and well-born suitors who have asked her father for permission to court her. Eventually, of course, the reason for her sadness is discovered to be her love for Barnwell. Though it is never made explicit in the script, Maria apparently believes that her interest in Barnwell must be kept secret from her father; moreover, her reticence continues despite both Thorowgood's avowedly open mind and his direct questions on this point. Later on, when Lucy reveals Millwood's plot to him, he expresses doubts about her account because he has seen no evidence of Barnwell's thefts (IV.iii), but it is Trueman's agitation, not Maria's sudden exit, that convinces him that Lucy may be telling the truth. Even after Barnwell and Millwood have been apprehended, Thorowgood seems not to have bothered to find out what had happened in his own household; instead, in a somewhat elliptical final speech to and about his former apprentice (V.ii.52–58), he follows the pattern he had already established of focusing on Trueman's love for Barnwell while remaining oblivious to Maria's. In other words, both the merchant and his creator seem deliberately to avoid the question of how Maria's actions might affect her relationship with her father.

The silence about Maria's concealment of Barnwell's theft signals the collapse of a distinction that seems crucial to Lillo's moral vision. Even if, as Trueman suggests, both earth and heaven must approve her actions (III.iii.63–64), we cannot be certain that her father would or does approve them. And if he does not, Maria loses not only her money but a degree of her security and integrity as well. One tentative explanation for Thorowgood's silence on this subject might be that the playwright simply hoped Maria's transgressions would be equally unnoticed by his audience. We might also argue, however, that her father cannot comment on her behavior because to do so would implicate her further by connecting her passion and her crime in a way that echoed the earlier connection between the blood and the money of the patriarch.

As Thorowgood's sole heir, Maria controls the future of both the merchant's bloodline and his fortune. At the beginning of the play, we can hypothesize either that Maria's unwillingness to confess her interest in Barnwell to her father has something to do with the financial expectations connected with marriage in the upper middle classes, or that she herself is troubled by the endogamous nature of her passion. The incest taboo looms large in either case. Her father's aspirations for her marriage emphasize the manner in which that institution commodifies daughters as items in a social exchange; when Thorowgood expressed his belief that "intercourse between nations" produces both economic and social benefits (III.i.6), he recasts the structuralist explanation of the incest taboo as a kind of political economy. Maria may be bothered by the propriety of falling in love with someone who is like a brother to her, or she may believe that she has a responsibility to enlarge her father's fortune by marrying. In either case, when she uses her own money to cover for Barnwell, she has in effect threatened both Thorowgood's health and his line of succession by reversing the process by which merchants enrich themselves; her gesture guarantees that what her father counts as profit will, in the context of the family fortune as a whole, ultimately have to be considered a loss.

Since marriage to Barnwell is obviously out of the question (she is allowed only "a chaste embrace" with him before he is hanged [V.x.7]), the end of the play is doubly disastrous for her and for Thorowgood, whose patrimony is apparently consigned to sterility and loss. Maria appears at last as a kind of secondary scapegoat, because her love for Barnwell has led her to impede the circulation of wealth and blood that register the health and well-being of her father. Shortly before Barnwell is taken away to be hanged, Maria asserts that when "women like Millwood . . . smile in prosperity and in adversity forsake," it should be "the pride of virtue to repair or partake the ruin such have made" (V.ix.26–29). In material terms, however, there is little difference between Millwood's appropriations of Thorowgood's money and Maria's concealment of those crimes. The logic of Lillo's plot ultimately marginalizes both good women and bad women, because both honorable desire and dishonorable greed are revealed as obstacles to a more extensive intercourse of nations.

＊   ＊   ＊

At the outset of this chapter, I suggested that the plot of *The London Merchant* enacts the symbolic dismemberment, dispersion, and reconstitution of its resident fertility god. I have tried to demonstrate that the

processes of dismemberment and dispersion are rendered in both positive
and negative forms: Thorowgood's model economy, with its rapid circulation of wealth—and, perhaps, with its circulation of daughters as
well—is opposed to Millwood's parasitism. The final phase of this narrative paradigm—the reconstitution and reaffirmation of the authoritarian
abstraction represented by the patriarch—is embedded in both the structure and language of Lillo's ending. At the end of his reunion scene with
Maria, Barnwell is led off stage by the officers of the court. As he leaves
the stage, he speaks directly to the audience:

> If any youth, like you, in future times
> Shall mourn my fate, though he abhors my crimes,
> Or tender maid, like you, my tale shall hear
> And to my sorrows give a pitying tear,
> To each such melting eye and throbbing heart,
> Would gracious Heaven this benefit impart:
> Never to know my guilt, nor feel my pain.
> Then must you own you ought not to complain,
> Since you nor weep, nor shall I die in vain.   (V.x.23–31)

The speech is quite literally self-effacing. Instead of talking about himself
directly, Barnwell offers us a series of abstract possessions ("my fate," "my
crimes," "my tale," "my sorrows," "my guilt," "my pain"); the only use of
"I" in the paragraph is a direct reference to his impending death. Each of
the first four epithets implies an extended narrative of some sort; since the
only "I" here is used to emphasize the mortality of each individual human
being, the passage rather aggressively asserts both that the story will last
and that the human being will not. The point is also registered both visu-
ally and aurally when Barnwell exits immediately after this speech, only to
be replaced on stage by Lucy, Trueman, and Blunt—the lower-class audience for whom the play was supposed to have been intended—who briefly
discuss what they have learned from witnessing the deaths of Millwood
(who has not been seen since the end of the fourth act) and Barnwell.[12]

I suggested earlier that the cast of *The London Merchant* was very
small, and that the more narrow scope of this production helped to undermine the kind of analyses that were based on various conceptions of
broader social phenomena. That narrowness of scope also indirectly provides the means of defining the reconstitution of Thorowgood in the closing moments of the play. Since Blunt and Lucy had been allied with
Millwood at the beginning of the play, their appearance at this point directs our attention to a limited sort of demographic success: Thorowgood

may have lost an apprentice (and, of course, the silence about his daughter's fate continues to be problematic), but he has gained two new converts. Essentially, the erasure of the individuals who played Barnwell and Millwood eliminates most of the opposition to Thorowgood's regime, and the association of Lucy and Blunt with Trueman gets rid of the rest. The void at the center of the action—the space once occupied by Millwood and Barnwell—signals the victory of abstract authority over the concrete individuals, and the final conversation between the three servants expresses their sense that only by learning the lessons of this tale will they be able to forestall their own mortality.

My analysis of *The London Merchant* has suggested that the play is in some respects both socially regressive and misogynist. Before I finish my discussion, I would like to take a moment to distinguish between the ideological project defined and promoted by this playtext and the personality and behavior of George Lillo. Very little is known about the man who wrote *The London Merchant*, but he seems to have been loved and respected by a remarkable range of eighteenth-century writers and performers (see McBurney xiv–xv). Furthermore, his religious convictions were remarkably compassionate, especially given the kind of views that were more conventional during this age. As I mentioned earlier, he does seek to mitigate some of the misogynistic elements in the play, and in the scene he appended to the fifth edition of his play in 1735, he even held out the possibility that Millwood herself might find mercy after death (Appendix B, 26 ff.). My argument here is simply that the play, as produced on the eighteenth-century stage, became a means of promoting the virtues of the middle-class merchant at the expense of women and apprentices, and that the good intentions of the playwright could not—or at least in this case, did not—produce a means of softening the effects of a rigid paternalism whose primary goal seemed to be to save those marginalized individuals from themselves.

At the end of the previous chapter, I spent some time discussing James Boswell and Lavinia Fenton as historical figures whose private lives were shaped to varying degrees by *The Beggar's Opera*. Despite Lillo's hopes of reforming apprentices, *The London Merchant* apparently never attained that degree of influence over any player or any member of its audience. There is, however, one detail concerning the original cast for the play which will become increasingly important as my study continues. The first actor to play the role of Lucy in this play was Charlotte Charke—the daughter of poet laureate and Drury Lane manager Colley

Cibber, and the sister and sister-in-law of Theophilus and Jane Cibber, who first played Barnwell and Maria. The role of Lucy is relatively uncomplicated; she serves as Millwood's confidante until she becomes frightened by the latter's excesses, at which point she shifts her allegiance to Thorowgood's household, where she is welcomed with open arms. Although it would have been very difficult to predict this in 1731, Charlotte Charke would spend the last decade of her life attempting to live down a series of institutional and individual judgments that had repeatedly labeled her guilty by association—the fate that Lucy narrowly avoids in the play by going over to Thorowgood's side of the conflict very shortly before Millwood is finally arrested. In Lillo's generally benevolent universe, Lucy was presumably forgiven for her transgressions, and perhaps even welcomed into her new home. In the more rough-and-tumble world of the London stage establishment, redemption was harder to come by.

3. "Not the Person she conceived me": The Public Identities of Charlotte Charke

Charlotte Charke, the youngest daughter of the actor and playwright Colley Cibber, was born in 1713. By the time she began her stage career in 1730, her father was one of the patent holders of Drury Lane Theatre, and he was named poet laureate later that year. After a disastrous marriage and five years spent mostly with acting companies controlled to a great extent either by her father or by her brother Theophilus, Charke joined Henry Fielding's company at the New Haymarket Theatre. Soon afterward, she broke off relations with her family, and shortly after that the Stage Licensing Act cast her abruptly into unemployment and poverty. From 1737 to 1745, she eked out a precarious hand-to-mouth existence in London. She became notorious during this period for wearing men's clothes on the streets of the city, and in various masculine disguises she held several jobs, including those of a street peddler, a gentleman's valet, and a tavern bouncer. Somewhere near the end of this period, she married a second time, but nothing is known about her second husband except his name and the fact that he died or disappeared very soon after the ceremony, with the result that Charke soon found herself dunned for his debts as well as her own. Perhaps to evade these new legal and financial pressures, she went into the English countryside around 1745 and spent nearly a decade alternately performing with strolling companies and trying to establish a place for herself in the small towns between London and Bristol. Her autobiographical *Narrative* suggests that for much of this period she wore men's clothes and presented herself in public as "Mr. Charles Brown." By the time she returned to London in 1754, she had apparently given up cross-dressing; she set herself up as a novelist and memoirist, but neither pursuit made her rich, and she died alone and destitute in 1760.

Most of the critical attention that has been paid to Charke over the past decade has emphasized the schizophrenic nature of the *Narrative*, which presents its author as both a resourceful female rogue and a penitent prodigal daughter.[1] The proximate cause of this shift can be found in the circumstances surrounding the composition of the autobiography. When she began the *Narrative*, Charke hoped to use her public forum to plead for her father's forgiveness, but when she was approximately halfway through her project, it became apparent even to the unreasonably optimistic author that her father had no intention of forgiving her. Faced with the prospect of his continued neglect, she essentially abandoned her submissive pose and struck out in another vein entirely.[2] Critics who focus exclusively on the *Narrative* have argued that this split focus reflects Charke's inability to reconcile the conflicting impulses governing her own life; according to this view, the structural incoherence of the *Narrative* reflects the author's equally incoherent sense of her self. The chief difficulty with this analysis, it seems to me, is its circularity. With the exception of Fidelis Morgan's recent biography, every scholar who has stumbled across Charke in his or her studies has accepted the *Narrative* more or less without question, as a statement of facts.[3] And if the *Narrative* is accepted as the primary—and with respect to many details, the only—source of information about Charlotte Charke, we should not be surprised to discover that the version of her self which is constructed by these readers replicates both the form and the content of that text. Partly in an effort to avoid this difficulty, and partly to take full advantage of the very few other sources of information about Charke's life and career, my own attempt to understand her character begins by focusing not on the structural flaws of the *Narrative*, but rather on the writer's extraordinary willingness to dissolve and reconstitute her identity while her readers looked on. Essentially, I wish to contend that the sudden shift at the center of the autobiography can best be understood in terms of the author's experiences on stage, where the issue of self-definition invariably becomes entangled with the reception of individual plays and the phenomenology of theatrical performance.

Actors are neither free agents nor puppets; the control they exercise over themselves is compromised and contested by the controls imposed on them by other people—playwrights, directors, fellow performers, spectators—and by a variety of circumstances representing the material effects of social, literary, and historical contexts. Although both Charke's relatively brief career on the London stage and the public record of her intermittent celebrity status in later years provide a number of interesting opportunities for investigating the dynamics of this struggle, my study deals with only three of the characters played by Charlotte Charke on the

London stage between 1731 and 1737, and with an equally small number of printed accounts concerning these and other performances both on and off stage. In the pages that follow, Charke will appear as a number of dramatic characters, and as the individual performer who enacted those characters. She will also appear as a character in her own narrative and in Samuel Richardson's *Clarissa* (1748), and as the real individual who was masked at first by the autobiographical "I" and later by the novelist's usual welter of conscious and unconscious designs, memories, and intentions. The "real individual" is of course inaccessible to any modern investigator. In my discussion, she exists only as the sum of a series of triangulations involving first-, second-, and third-hand accounts of her activities, filtered through my own welter of precepts and concepts. I have conjured up this being because it seems to me that the fascinating juxtapositions invoked by the cryptic narratives of her life provide me with certain opportunities to explore both the degrees of embodiment associated with these various disguises and the consequences of her gradual loss of control over that process.

The theoretical underpinnings for my analysis are derived in part from an essay by Elin Diamond in which she defines what she calls "gestic feminist criticism," and from a book by Bruce Wilshire titled *Role Playing and Identity*. Diamond's analysis provides a way of focusing on crucial moments in performance, where the issue of the actor's self-creation becomes entangled with those of social and literary production. Her model combines feminist theories of spectacle and spectatorship with the Brechtian concept of the "gestus" (a word, gesture, action, or image through which "the social attitudes encoded in the playtext become visible to the spectator" [89]) in order to "highlight sex-gender configurations as they conceal or disrupt a coercive or patriarchal ideology" (91). Wilshire combines phenomenological insights with more literary kinds of performance theory to argue that role-playing on stage is analogous to role-playing in real life—that the ways in which actors and spectators construct and construe the meaning of their shared experiences correspond to similar processes that figure in human relations in the world at large (44).

Two of Wilshire's terms—"authorization" and "engulfment"—will be of particular value in this discussion. According to Wilshire, theater audiences always begin by assuming that there is a fundamental connection between the onstage and offstage worlds; the presence of an audience authorizes specific actors to "stand in" for specific characters, and each individual spectator also authorizes each character to stand in on some level for him- or herself (40, 43). This does not mean that the spectators must adopt every character's feelings and motives as their own, but it does mean that they have to find a place for each character within their collective horizon of expectations.[4] Like the audience, the actors must also authorize the characters to stand in for themselves; consequently, every emotional connection between an actor and a character is (like the character itself) always at risk. If the character is rejected, some part of the actor's identity has also been condemned. This condemnation can take at least two different shapes: the spectators can either simply refuse to authorize the performance, in which case they might choose either to leave or to seek some way to disrupt it; or they can pursue the course Wilshire describes as engulfment, where a character is more or less deliberately misinterpreted and made to serve an agenda set not by those who are staging the production, but rather by their audience (44). Each of the four sections of my argument show Charlotte Charke searching for authorization and finding only refusal or engulfment.

Perhaps more importantly, each of these episodes raises questions about the social and institutional functions of eighteenth-century gender categories, particularly insofar as they are related to the evolution of the London stage. Kristina Straub has recently argued that between 1660 and 1800, the London theater community was increasingly concerned with the perceived need to establish clear and effective boundaries between the spectacle and the spectator. Drawing on the work of Nancy Armstrong and Michel Foucault, Straub suggests that as the eighteenth century wore on, the role of the spectator came to be seen as more exclusively and essentially masculine, while the spectacle became more passive, more submissive, and therefore, according to the social conventions of the early modern period, more essentially feminine (4–5). Such a change represented a considerable departure from the plasticity of Renaissance performance conventions, and it was not accomplished in a quick or orderly fashion. At least in retrospect, the lifelong struggle of Charlotte Charke to stake out and claim her own discursive space in an increasingly rigid specular economy provides a striking example of how agonizing and disorderly—not to mention unjust and destructive—this process could be.

Since the latter part of my argument focuses on narrative accounts of performances rather than performances per se, some readers may be disturbed by what they perceive as an inappropriate use of performance-oriented critical theory. Without going into too much detail, I would like to defend this strategy on three related grounds. First, each of the narrative paradigms considered in this section of my discussion speaks directly to the question of what happens between the actor, the character, and the spectator in situations that are explicitly and unmistakably theatrical. Second, if Wilshire's primary assertion is correct, there is a sense in which the identity of any individual can only be constituted through processes that are best understood in terms of their similarities to the processes that define the shape and significance of theatrical performances. Finally, since the differences between a particular performance and a narrative account of that performance are both undeniable and ineradicable, I would argue that every student of performance is faced with this same problem to one degree or another, and that nearly every one of them solves it the same way—by recognizing that before any performance can be studied, it must be in some sense narrativized, and by keeping that fact before themselves and their readers as part of the hermeneutic puzzle.

*   *   *

Early in her *Narrative*, Charlotte Charke suggests that she had been cross-dressing on an irregular basis ever since she was four. As I indicated earlier, a number of scholars have taken this claim at face value, but there is no evidence to corroborate it in the Cibber family papers (Morgan 27), and it is certainly possible that she invented or at least revised certain episodes in her autobiography to suit her rhetorical purposes. If she could recast her adult transvestism as a childish prank, that behavior might seem less threatening and more forgivable, especially since the male she was impersonating on this early occasion happened to be her father (Charke 18).[5] In any case, her first three seasons at Drury Lane provided her with no opportunities to display this talent; before the summer of 1733, her only breeches role on stage was a rather anemic female adventurer named Clarinda in Colley Cibber's comedy *The Double Gallant* (1707).[6] Given both the kind of character she became and the extraordinarily large number of breeches roles available in the eighteenth-century repertory, she seems almost exceptionally reserved in this respect.[7] Still, the London theater audiences of this period were notoriously fractious, and the surface calm of Charke's relative anonymity was interrupted on at least one occasion by an incident that foreshadowed some of the conflicts that burst into the open later in her career.

Charles Johnson's *Caelia* was performed only once, on the night of 11 December 1732; the play apparently upset its audience to such an extent that the actors refused to stage it a second time. From the perspective of the modern critic, Johnson's domestic tragedy is remarkable chiefly because an odd chain of circumstances involved not only Charlotte Charke but also both Henry Fielding and Samuel Richardson in the production and subsequent reception of this otherwise obscure work. First, nearly four months after the first-night disaster, the play was summarized and reviewed in an influential theater periodical called the *Grub-Street Journal*; it was also featured prominently in a bookseller's advertisement in the same issue. It is difficult to say whether this sort of attention indicated that Johnson's tragedy had had some success as a so-called reading play, or whether it was the result of some backroom deal designed to engineer a success that the play had not yet achieved on its own. In either case, it is at least conceivable that there was something about Johnson's plot that the literary public of this period found more palatable on the page than on the stage. Presumably, one of Johnson's readers was Samuel Richardson, who disliked theater in general, but who obviously constructed a large part of the plot of *Clarissa* on the model established in *Caelia*. Johnson's play begins shortly after an innocent young woman has been seduced away from her familial estate by a rake named Wronglove. Soon afterward, the rake sells the virtuous heroine to a bawd named Mother Lupine who presides over a notorious London brothel. The house is raided by the authorities, and Caelia dies in prison before her newly sympathetic family members can find and rescue her. Like Richardson's Clarissa, Johnson's heroine is presented as an exemplary figure, a paragon of wronged innocence; and like Lovelace and Mrs. Sinclair, Wronglove and Mother Lupine seem to grow more sinister as the heroine moves closer to martyrdom. Later in this chapter, I will use these details to explore the relationship between the stage and print versions of the brothel madam's character.

The epilogue for *Caelia* was written by Henry Fielding, whose acquaintance with Charke may date from this production. In his own irregular dramas, Fielding frequently called attention to the generic expectations of his audience, and he returned to this habit when he had his speaker ask Johnson's audience "what are all our comic Heroes famed for / But such exploits as Wronglove has been blamed for?" But while the audiences of this period were willing to contemplate the possibility that the comic heroes of a previous age could be villains by their more enlightened standards, they were apparently much less willing to tolerate Johnson's innovative treatment of prostitution. More than any extant play of its generation, *Caelia* dramatizes the mechanics of entrapping and selling

young women. During the first act, the playwright shows his rake arranging to abandon the heroine at Mother Lupine's brothel, and he shows
Mother Lupine sizing her up "as a Horse-Courser does a Filly." Soon
afterward, he shows the more experienced prostitutes teasing the new victim, followed by Mother Lupine again, who on this second occasion
shows Caelia a letter from her seducer which makes it unmistakably clear
that she has in effect been sold to the brothel. The audience response to
these scenes was so violent that Johnson in his preface to the printed text
of *Caelia* apologized for putting characters like Mother Lupine and her
prostitutes on stage. In retrospect, he wrote, "I should not have made 'em
necessary to my design."

When she stepped on stage that night to play Mother Lupine, Charlotte Charke was a nineteen-year-old single mother.[8] She apparently already knew what brothel madams looked like and how they behaved; in
the *Narrative*, she claims that even during the first year of her marriage she
had found herself "tracing [my] Spouse [Richard Charke] from Morn to
Even through the Hundreds of Drury" (53). She also had firsthand experience of economic exploitation as it was practiced by her estranged husband, who in 1732 continued to exercise his legal right to claim his wife's
earnings—this despite the fact that he had abandoned her and their infant
daughter more than a year earlier. Finally, as a woman who later succeeded
in presenting herself in public as another woman's husband, Charke might
also have been able to infuse Mother Lupine's predatory gaze with a
threatening and "unnatural" erotic interest in Johnson's virtuous heroine.

It is difficult even to speculate about what Charke might have been
willing or able to do with her personal experiences in the context of early
eighteenth-century acting styles,[9] but the stage direction referring to
horse-coursers does seem to suggest that Johnson might have been happy
to have those elements brought into Charke's portrayal of Mother Lupine.
A horse-courser at an auction was both an entrepreneur and a voyeur; his
financial success depended on his ability to produce and manage a particular public spectacle, and on his ability to look carefully at what he was
about to buy. By analogy, Mother Lupine's commentary—and perhaps
more importantly, her gaze—implicated the spectator in the exploitation
of women in general and female actors in particular; it demonstrated that
the economic value of both Caelia and the woman who played her (Jane
Cibber, the much-abused first wife of Theophilus) depended entirely on
their shared status as objects of desire. As Straub's analysis suggests, by
the fourth decade of the eighteenth century such a gaze would also have

been seen as a transgression of conventional gender boundaries, if only because it attempted to appropriate to itself a prerogative which by that time was generally presumed to belong exclusively to men. To the extent that Charke's personal background led her to enact this stage direction effectively, the spectators' reaction meant that they would authorize neither her erotic interest, nor her awareness that the desires of others could be exploited for financial gain—neither her appropriation of masculine assurance and worldliness, nor the implication of complicity which was derived from Mother Lupine's dispassionate inspection.

*   *   *

Eight months after the *Caelia* debacle, Theophilus Cibber and a group of veteran actors revolted against Drury Lane manager John Highmore and set up shop at the New Haymarket Theatre. Charlotte Charke walked out along with her brother, and played a number of important parts with the rebel company, including many breeches roles.[10] Her new characters included Fainlove in Richard Steele's *The Tender Husband* (1705), Charlotte Weldon in Thomas Southerne's *Oroonoko* (1695), and Silvia in George Farquhar's *The Recruiting Officer* (1706).[11] Unlike Clarinda, each of these characters spends a significant amount of stage time in breeches, and none of them relies on a male rescuer to preserve and protect her double identity. In addition to the breeches roles, Charke also played a few ambiguously gendered monsters. For example, Theophilus had begun his season at the New Haymarket with Nicholas Rowe's *Tamerlane* (1701), a patriotic tragedy that pitted solid English heroism against baroque Oriental villainy. In this production, Charke played Haly, a eunuch whose chief purpose seems to have been to procure innocent female victims for his evil master. She also played Mrs. Otter—a termagant wife who shared Haly's exotic ethnic background—in the company's revival of Ben Jonson's *Epicoene, or the Silent Woman* (1609). Of the eighteen roles credited to Charke in *The London Stage* summary of this season, ten required either cross-dressing or behaving in what was presumed at the time to be an inappropriately masculine fashion, or both.

Given this collection of roles, we might expect Charke to have encountered more reactions like the one that greeted Mother Lupine. In general, however, the rebels were kindly received, and Charke seems to have shared in their good fortune. This treatment may have been due largely to the advertising strategy of Theophilus Cibber, who presented the company as being engaged in the glorious task of defining a national repertory. In practice, this amounted to little more than deciding to produce the well-known plays mentioned above, but Theophilus was a good publicist. Unfortunately, this public image did not make it any easier for Charke to control the responses to the characters she played. The appeal to conventional tastes might have reduced the chances that the spectators would refuse to authorize a particular performance, but it seems on occasion to have predisposed those spectators toward the kinds of engulfment that reflected a conventional, essentialist approach to matters of gender—even when the play itself tended in another direction. Perhaps the best illustration of this process can be found in the rebel company's revival of Ben Jonson's *The Silent Woman*.

First, however, a bit of background. Jacobean audiences believed that otters were hermaphroditic (see Knoll 110–11), and on that basis they would have assumed that Mrs. Otter's name alluded directly to her jarring combination of masculine aggressiveness and feminine costume. Indeed, for Jonson's audience, Mrs. Otter's dress defined her transgression; since the character would have to have been played by a male actor during this era, it could be said that Mrs. Otter's costume provided the single most important means of defining "her" monstrosity. It might be objected that because such transvestism was one of the defining characteristics of Jacobean public theater, audiences of this period would have been slow to make anything of a particular instance of that fact. This claim cannot, however, be applied to *The Silent Woman*, because the end of the play focuses the spectator's attention directly on this issue. The climax of the comedy occurs when Epicoene (the title character) is revealed to be "a gentleman's son" (V.iv.182ff). The effect must have been especially unnerving to Jonson's audience, because no one besides Dauphine (one of the play's protagonists) and his accomplice knows Epicoene's secret before he is unmasked; nothing is said to anyone about the possibility that she is a he until Dauphine removes "her" wig. Dauphine's trick confronts Jonson's audience with the fact that none of the ostensibly female figures on stage were actually women; rather, they were all male enactments of female characters. Although Jonson's script ridicules every one of his female characters, the animosity directed toward those characters is undermined to some degree by a gestus which forces the audience to recognize its own complicity in a performance style that effectively reduced all women to silence.[12]

Shortly after Charles II reopened the public theaters in 1660, he decreed that female roles should be played only by women. When the king issued the patents which licensed two new theatrical companies, the proclamation accompanying the patents expressed the hope that if women's roles were indeed enacted by women, the plays themselves would soon be "esteemed not only harmless delights but useful and instructive representations of human life" (qtd. in Maus 598). Lesley Ferris has recently argued that Charles believed this new policy would help to differentiate the theater of his era from the all-male Renaissance stage, which he saw as promoting homosexuality (70). Since the court of his grandfather James I had been publicly attacked on the grounds that it tolerated openly homosexual relationships, Charles II also stood to benefit politically from what amounted to an ostentatious display of his and his court's heterosexuality. Since women were first allowed on the London stage partly in order to involve them in an effort to stage a return to gender normalcy, it is ironic that Restoration playwrights and performers turned so quickly to the transvestite tricks of yesteryear.

Of course, the female-to-male cross-dressing of the Restoration and eighteenth-century stage was qualitatively different from the male-to-female cross-dressing of the Renaissance era. After the Restoration, theatrical cross-dressing by men seems to have been limited to cases of obvious parody, while women on the Restoration and eighteenth-century stage wore breeches for a variety of reasons. Although the "breeches part" on the Restoration stage seems to have come into vogue largely in order to put the bodies of the leading female performers on display, the acceptance of cross-dressed women under these conditions apparently created an opening for other, less exploitative uses of this practice. In her recent study of this issue, Kristina Straub suggests that by the middle of the eighteenth century, most instances of female theatrical cross-dressing could be read as challenges to the process by which the masculinist specular economy came to be established as a social and aesthetic norm (127–35).

It took the two Restoration companies three years to determine how the king's decree should be applied to *Epicoene*, but they finally decided that the title character should be played exclusively by women, and the play was cast that way between 1663 and 1776 (Noyes 177). As a result—and here we return at last to the species of engulfment mentioned earlier in this section—the gestus described earlier was emptied of its original contents and invested with a significance which ran directly counter to the one it had offered Jonson's audience. Instead of showing the audience that Epicoene and the other female characters shared a common and somewhat suspect means of production, the Restoration and eighteenth-century versions of the play separated Epicoene from her onstage sisters, thereby allowing the hostility toward Mrs. Otter and the "collegiate" ladies (her colleagues in shrewishness) to continue unabated. By pretending briefly that one of the female actors on stage was a male character, the eighteenth-century productions of *The Silent Woman* also avoided the male-to-female cross-dressing of an earlier era. But where the supposed maleness of the new Epicoenes helped to clear them of the charge of violating standards of feminine decorum and virtue, no such license was extended to the actors playing Mrs. Otter and the collegiates, because in those cases the correspondence between the sex of the actors and the gender of the characters directed the audience's attention away from the act of impersonation and toward each character's unseemly language and behavior.

This effect was heightened by certain circumstances connected with the Drury Lane actors' rebellion. By the 1730s, cross-dressing in either or both directions was a staple of farces and other kinds of experimental drama, and theatrical travesties of this sort coexisted with more traditional deployments of the breeches part. At the same time, however, such travesty performances were generally the province of the more marginal companies, and the Drury Lane rebels did not wish to be mistaken for a second-class troupe. Judith Milhous has argued that throughout the Restoration era, the use of breeches parts and other gender-bending theatrical tricks had been used as a cost-cutting measure by companies who could not hope to lure spectators into the boxes and galleries with the promise of more extravagant visual effects (93). Given this tendency, the fact that the newspaper and poster advertising for the rebel company announced that the audience at the Haymarket would see "All the Characters entirely new drest. With new Scenes and Decorations" (Scouten, ed., *London Stage* 3:321) can be read as a signal that these plays would *not* challenge conventional assumptions about how men and women should dress and behave. To the extent that the rebels succeeded in presenting themselves as the true guardians of the English theatrical tradition—and they succeeded so well that when they returned to Drury Lane in the spring of 1734, Highmore was forced to sell his patent, and many of the rebels had their salaries increased—they also succeeded in presenting the gender transgressors played by Charke as safely marginalized figures. This tendency presumably held true regardless of whether a particular transgressor appeared on stage in breeches or simply misbehaved; Mrs. Otter, who apparently wore some sort of "Chinese" costume, could be included under either category. Stigmatized by the mainstream ideology to which Theophilus had pledged his allegiance, and (unlike her Renaissance predecessors in the role) denied the recuperative influence of Jonson's original gestus, the eighteenth-century Mrs. Otter became more monstrous as the performance itself became more respectable.

*   *   *

Because many Restoration and eighteenth-century spectators apparently believed that the onstage world could, should, and did in fact mirror some offstage reality in a simple and straightforward manner,[13] female performers of this era often found themselves characterized by the characters they enacted. In Charke's case, she had been driven off the stage as Mother Lupine, but allowed to remain a part of the company as Mrs. Otter—an altogether less threatening presence. That she had also lost a degree of power in her professional life was made evident by her struggles when the rebel company returned to Drury Lane in the spring of 1734. Despite her successes at the Haymarket, Charke soon found herself competing with two or three other actors for roles she considered to be hers alone. She blamed her brother and the new Drury Lane manager, Charles Fleetwood, for the apparent demotion, and she tried to fight them that summer by ridiculing both men with a company of her own at the Haymarket.[14] With some assistance from her usually negligent father, she returned to Drury Lane in September of 1734, but the following summer she was on her own again. Then it was back again to Drury Lane, and finally, in the spring of 1736, back to the Haymarket, where the Great Mogul's Company had just struck it rich with *Pasquin*. The company's manager, Henry Fielding, hired Charke at a good salary to play Lord Place—a parody of the poet laureate and former Drury Lane patent holder who also happened to be her father.

Lord Place was only one of a number of male characters Charke played for Fielding at the Haymarket; the list also included Mr. Hen (a caricature of high-society auctioneer Christopher Cock) in *The Historical Register* (1737), Spatter (one of Fielding's ubiquitous broken-down author figures) in *Eurydice Hissed* (1737), and a minor role or two in *The Tragedy of Tragedies* (1731) and other, more ephemeral pieces. These roles are much different from the kind of breeches roles Charke had played with the

Drury Lane company, where female characters adopted masculine costumes and identities temporarily, only to be returned to their original gender shortly before the curtain fell. In "Performative Acts and Gender
Constitution," Judith Butler compares the experience of seeing a transvestite onstage to that of sitting next to a transvestite on a bus, and asserts
that the second experience "becomes dangerous, if it does, precisely because there are no theatrical conventions to delimit the purely imaginary
character of the act" (278). Breeches roles like those of Clarinda or Silvia
are doubly insulated from offstage reality, because in each case the rein-
scription of gendered normalcy at the end of the play suggests that such
transformations are inherently unstable (and therefore less threatening)
even within the imaginary world on stage. The new characters in Charke's
repertoire could not be dismissed so easily, although they of course were
still circumscribed by the limits of the stage itself.

From Charke's perspective, the shift from Mrs. Otter to Mr. Hen
allowed her to regain some measure of control over her public identity;
playing masculine roles emphasized her skills as a performer and reduced
the risk that she would be identified with the characters she portrayed. At
the same time, this greater freedom carried with it an explicit challenge to
the conventional equivalence of gender with sex, which meant that the
body of the actor was still an issue. In a 1989 essay, Joseph Roach uses
the examples of castrati opera singers and acting virtuosos to argue that
"the history of performance since the eighteenth century is the history
of the ever more rigorous subjection of the body to forms of internalized
control" (101–2). Although I believe that this claim is generally valid, I
also believe that it is somewhat misleading with respect to the phenomenon of theatrical cross-dressing, if only because it suggests that the exercise
of that control was invariably approved by London theater audiences.
Charlotte Charke's success with Fielding at the Haymarket (like her later
offstage successes) suggests that an actor who portrayed a character of the
opposite sex could achieve the same level of self-mastery that was attributed to the castrati and the acting virtuosos of her era. Her fate, however,
suggests that the response to that mastery could sometimes be determined
not by what was displayed, but rather by what was masked.

At least one of the roles Fielding wrote for Charke seems to have been
designed to emphasize this difference; even the name of Mr. Hen is calculated to focus the attention of the Haymarket audience on the phallus
she did not possess, and the impersonation itself clearly showcased her

ability to reproduce masculinity without maleness.[15] As Roach points out, the self-mastery displayed by the castrati was an easily recognizable product of an elaborate training regimen (109), but regardless of the aesthetic discourse that was invoked to justify this program, its effect was to produce an exterior that clearly identified the body in question as that of a castrated male. On the other hand, transvestite portrayals demonstrated that masculine and feminine behaviors were every bit as stylized and artificial as the vocabulary of gestures and inflections that identified the castrato, even as they challenged the hegemony of the "natural" that was apparently reinforced by the correspondence between the castrato's body and his style.

When Fielding integrated Charlotte Charke's talent for cross-gender impersonations into his social satires, he gave her access to a degree of social and financial stability that had been unavailable to her while she was working for more conventional companies. The Great Mogul's Company might have been marginal in an ideological and an aesthetic sense, but the taste of the town conferred a degree of legitimacy on the group in the form of cold hard cash. At the same time, however, he helped to create a rift between Charke and her father which was never mended. Before she joined the Great Mogul's Company, she had developed a reputation as an eccentric; she had not, however, dared to confront her father openly.[16] The authorization she had achieved at this point in her career was effectively revoked by the provisions of the Stage Licensing Act. Perhaps in an effort to add insult to injury, the stage historians of the following decade even managed to impose a kind of retroactive engulfment on her performances with the Great Mogul's Company. Apparently as a result of her association with Fielding, Charke was disowned by her father in the spring of 1736.[17] Then, in May 1737, the passage of the Stage Licensing Act recapitulated her family situation on an institutional level.

The success of both Charke and Fielding had depended entirely on the openness of the London stage during the mid-1730s, when actors had more freedom to move, playwrights had more opportunities for getting their works produced, and audiences had more choices available to them than at any previous point in English theater history. All this was brought to an end by the Licensing Act, which not only created a system of state-sponsored censorship, but also closed down the innovative alternative theaters at Goodman's Fields, Lincoln's Inn Field, and the Haymarket, thereby throwing the entire weight of the government behind the management and repertory practices of the two patent theaters at Covent Garden and Drury Lane. On a more personal level, it could be said that the authorization Charlotte Charke had achieved by this point in her career was essentially revoked by the Licensing Act. Because her father was no longer willing to mend fences for her at Drury Lane, she was thrown suddenly into unemployment and poverty. For reasons that will be addressed shortly, she began appearing in men's clothes on the streets of London soon after the public stage was closed to her. As soon as contemporary stage historians and controversialists connected this fact with her onstage breeches roles and with the well-known antagonism between Fielding and Cibber, they began to cite her in print as an eccentric, rebellious child whose primary goal was to embarrass her father.

In 1742, for example, an anonymous pamphlet titled *Sawney and Colley* attempted to embarrass Cibber by describing a blustering "Daughter CHARK" who had been "celebrated for her Performances in the Hay-Market Theatre, where, in the Farce of *Pasquin*, the *Historical Register* &c. she play'd off her Father and Brother with surprising Humour" (4, 4n). Five years later, John Mottley asserted in his *List of Dramatic Authors* that Charke had opened *The Historical Register* with a parody of Cibber's most recent New Year's Ode, delivered in her father's "own Character" (qtd. in Battestin *HFL* 219). There is only one problem with these summaries: the first is only half-true, and the second is not true at all. In fact, although *The Historical Register* contains at least three distinct Cibber parodies, none of them was enacted by his daughter.[18] Despite its shaky grasp of the facts, Mottley's account encapsulated what was to become the general perception of Charke's role in Fielding's company; it serves, in other words, as the imaginary gestus that might have defined that largely imaginary role. These accounts imply that Charke joined Fielding's company in order to ridicule her father, and that she also chose her roles with that goal in mind. In fact, however, the first claim must be viewed as partially true but probably misleading, while the second can be disproved simply by looking at *The Historical Register*.

In essence, Mottley's anecdote shows us that the sudden passage of the Stage Licensing Act allowed other writers to define her work with Fielding solely in terms of Lord Place. Her skill as a performer was obscured by an exaggerated public interest in the challenge to her father's authority, and the issues raised by her transvestite stage portrayals were subsumed under the same heading. Her time with the Drury Lane rebels had cast her as an ambiguously gendered monster—as an eccentric but not (given the fate of characters like Mrs. Otter) a dangerous figure. On the other hand, the standard summaries of her time with Fielding presented her as openly antagonistic, not only to (usually unspecified) standards of public decency, but also, and more importantly, to her father. In a recent study titled *Vested Interests*, Marjorie Garber suggests that mainstream commentators often distort the contents of narratives about transvestites by trying to normalize the phenomenon (68–69). When Mottley and his anonymous colleague present Charke's cross-dressing as though it were undertaken merely for the purpose of offending her father, they provide a striking example of this tendency. As Garber points out, if these commentators can explain Charke's cross-dressing exclusively in terms of her family conflicts, they can avoid the social and ideological issues raised both by that behavior and by the public response to it. By the time she undertook her *Narrative*, Charke herself was not above attempting to normalize her own activities in this fashion, but her family seems to have been convinced that there was something more going on; as Charke herself acknowledges, "my being in Breeches [off stage] has been alleged to me as a very great Error" by family members who sought to keep her and her father apart (139).

As a general proposition, we might suggest that when the public and private aspects of the actor's personality interpenetrate each other like this, the audience will have difficulty distinguishing between the performer's self-fashioning and the shape imposed on the performer from outside. Under these circumstances, we can discuss the figure of the performer in the same terms applied by Roland Barthes and Michel Foucault to the figure of the author;[19] that is, we can argue that beyond a certain point, the performer's name refers not to an individual human being, but rather to a matrix of attitudes, motives, and gestures attached to the name through various means, for various reasons, by various individuals and institutions. There are a number of plausible explanations for the distortions connected with Charke's celebrity status: they range from deliberate malice on the part of the authors toward Charke or her father or both, to an innocent confusion of *The Historical Register* with *Pasquin*. It is also possible either that these authors knew Cibber had disowned Charke and were therefore predisposed to accept his version of events, or that they had been offended by one or both of them in the past. By the 1740s, Charke herself was certainly in no position to retaliate. In a sense, it made no difference why her past had been rewritten by other people; what mattered was that her challenge to her father's authority had become the primary "fact" that defined her public persona.

*   *   *

Charlotte Charke apparently began wearing men's clothes in the streets of London shortly after the Licensing Act was passed, and the *Narrative* implies that she impersonated a man almost continuously while she was gone from London between 1746 and 1753. There are a number of reasons why Charke might have chosen this particular course of action: [20] as an actor seeking employment, she needed to be able to walk the streets after dark; as a debtor, she needed a way to throw the bailiffs off her trail; as a sometime street peddler or tavern-keeper, she needed to be able to protect herself. Finally, as a woman who for a number of years shared her life and ill fortunes with another woman (known in the *Narrative* only as "Mrs. Brown"), she needed a way to protect herself and her family (in addition to "Mrs. Brown," she kept her daughter with her until the latter married and emigrated to America in 1751) not only from all the difficulties already mentioned, but also from the prying eyes of moral authorities, self-appointed and otherwise.

By the time Charlotte Charke reappeared in London in 1754, virtually every source of authorization had been taken from her. Her father had disowned her, and her mother was long dead; two marriages had gone terribly wrong, and her longtime companion Mrs. Brown had died a few years earlier, shortly before Charke's daughter had set sail for America, never to return. She had tried and failed to earn a living in several different ways, and the profession at which she excelled was closed to her by a combination of her father's estrangement and the government's decree. Given this extraordinarily difficult set of circumstances, it should perhaps come as no surprise that Charke was at least temporarily willing to renounce any and all parts of her past life if that meant she could at last come in from the cold. Although Charke makes no effort in the *Narrative* to deny her cross-dressing—the publicity she had garnered in better times would have made that impossible in any case—she does try to achieve a reconciliation with her father by presenting herself as both misunderstood and repentant. As part of this effort, she concocts a small fable, set during the seven-year period when she was wandering the English countryside as

a strolling player, which comments explicitly on her sense of the relationship between role-playing and identity.

Charke writes that shortly after she left the city to join one of the
strolling companies, she found herself on a ramshackle stage in a town just
outside of London. In the audience for this unnamed production is "an
orphan Heiress" (106) who proceeds to fall desperately in love with the
dashing Mr. Brown. When Mr. Brown learns of this infatuation, he meets
with the heiress to apprise her of her error, eventually revealing to her that
he is not in fact a man. The wording of this announcement is particularly
significant; instead of identifying herself as a woman, an actor, or as
Mrs. Charke, she presents herself as "actually the youngest Daughter of
Mr. Cibber, and not the Person she conceived me!" (111). When Charke returns to her company, she continues to emphasize the distance between her
current surroundings and what she wishes to present as her essential self:

> On my Return Home, the Itinerant-Troop all assembled round me to hear
> what had passed between the Lady and me—when we were to celebrate the
> Nuptials?—Besides many other impertinent, stupid Questions; some offer-
> ing, agreeable to their villainous Dispositions, as the Marriage they supposed
> would be a Secret, to supply my Place in the Dark to conceal the Fraud: upon
> which I looked at them sternly and, with the Contempt they deserved, de-
> manded to know what Action of my Life had been so very monstrous, to
> excite them to think me capable of one so cruel and infamous? (112–13)

Then, for good measure, she also reveals her true identity to the townspeople in general—thereby insuring, she hopes, that "in Case [the heiress's
mistake] was spoke of, it might be regarded as an Impossibility" (113).

Like much else contained in the *Narrative*, this episode can be neither
verified nor disproven, but I am very much inclined to believe that it is
entirely fictional. Morgan could not find any trace of the incident Charke
describes, and it is at least conceivable that she had heard a story very
similar to this one told about Mademoiselle de Maupin, the seventeenth-
century French performer whose transvestism, like Charke's, was not limited to the stage. Also, the situation Charke describes could easily have
landed her in jail. Lillian Faderman has identified several female transvestites who were arrested, tried, and punished during this period for marrying or plotting to marry other women. Mademoiselle de Maupin, who
actually eloped with the girl in question, was arrested and briefly imprisoned under a sixteenth-century antisodomy law (57), while in England

Mary Hamilton had been whipped through four towns and sentenced to prison for marrying four different women. Hamilton's sensational trial prompted the publication of Fielding's *The Female Husband* in 1746; the chronology of the *Narrative* is generally very vague, but it is at least possible that Charke's placement of the orphan heiress episode was inspired by the author's hope that her readers would compare her to the well-known criminal and recognize her superior moral sense.

Finally, the basic situation seems to me to have obviously literary origins; many students of sixteenth-, seventeenth-, and eighteenth-century English literature could list two or three examples of women falling in love with women dressed as men without even getting around to less respectable genres like transvestite autobiography. It seems to me, moreover, that Charke's account of this particular incident is designed not to connect, but rather to distance herself—not only from that tradition, but also from the previous incarnations of herself that separated her from her father. Charlotte was the only one of Cibber's children who was born after he had made his fortune, and the first installment of the *Narrative* concludes with her blaming herself for falling in love with Richard Charke against her father's wishes (50). She also presented herself as a swashbuckling male figure on more than one occasion, and the fact that her desperate circumstances had forced her to go strolling was well known. These details suggest that the episode should be treated as a kind of private myth about fragmentation and recuperation: the foolish but tenderhearted heiress (Charlotte Cibber) falls in love with the dashing actor (Charles Brown) who does the honorable thing by abandoning both his persona and the loot, and by rejecting his disreputable companions (Charlotte Charke) as well. Finally, of course, the whole incident is organized around her hope of being reincarnated as Charlotte, the youngest daughter of Mr. Cibber.

Taken as a whole, the heiress anecdote sends a curiously mixed message. On the one hand, the story seems to celebrate once again her ability to create and sustain the image of masculinity; on the other hand, the position occupied by "Mr. Cibber's youngest daughter" suggests that Charke wanted to believe that family ties could be used to establish an identity that somehow transcended all this role-playing. At the same time, however, the passage begs the question of whether the situation can in fact be defused. Charke presents the father-daughter relation as an absolute, but Cibber's decision to disown her had already demonstrated that this, too, could be considered performative rather than essential; and if that were true, what could possibly make the identity defined by the phrase

"Mr. Cibber's youngest daughter" any more stable than any of the other identities presented and discarded in these few pages?

Ultimately, Charke's fable suggests that the morality of any specific impersonation depends not on the degree to which it conforms to a pre-determined natural order, but rather on the assumption that both the actor and the spectator understand exactly where the line is being drawn be-tween the onstage and offstage worlds. Her story defines four audiences and her relationship to each: the heiress is complimented and let down gently because she does not understand; the players are insulted and dis-missed because they do understand, and because they want to exploit their knowledge; the townspeople are told that the heiress is not at fault and are reassured; and her readers are invited to laugh, to share her righteous indignation, and to approve of her openness and gallantry. Presented with an ethically dubious and potentially dangerous situation, she extricates herself by establishing new boundaries for herself and for her audience.

In the terms established by Wilshire's model, both the heiress episode and Cibber's response to the *Narrative* demonstrate the principle that no character can stand in for either an actor or a spectator without the consent of both individuals: on the one hand, Charke does not have to be Charles Brown unless she chooses to be, and she doesn't have to define herself as a strolling player unless she chooses to do so; on the other hand, she needs to be absolved of blame by the heiress and the townspeople, and she can-not be Mr. Cibber's daughter unless he allows her to play that role. The wording of Charke's confession to the heiress is also suggestive in this respect, because it hints at a connection between an "actual" reality and an enacted role, and because the double meaning of the verb "conceived" can be construed as an allusion to the role played by an audience in creating and authorizing a particular identity.

＊   ＊   ＊

Charke's orphan heiress story appears at a crucial moment in her life as well as her text. While the early part of the *Narrative* was being written, she still believed in the possibility of a reconciliation with her father, and she tried to distance herself from the elements of her past that might have alarmed or offended him. Charke might very well be forgiven for believing that the old playwright would accept her apologies; Cibber's own dramas are full of last-minute reversals of this sort, and many of those are less convincing than his daughter's expressions of regret. At the same time, she should perhaps have recalled her father's comedy *The Provok'd Husband* (1728), which first appeared when she was only fifteen. In his introduction to the published version of the play, Cibber praises himself for having "preserved the . . . chastity" of the title character's wife, who provokes her husband by staying out all night in order to play cards. The playwright goes on to explain that he has avoided the issue of sexual misconduct in order to guarantee that "the sense of her errors might make a reconciliation not impracticable" (6). In Cibber's view, some reconciliations were practicable, and some were not.

Unfortunately for Charke—and, as it turned out, fortunately for her readers—Cibber was no more willing to forgive her in 1755 than he had been nearly twenty years earlier. Shortly after the heiress episode appears in the *Narrative*, Charke presents an intensely pathetic scene that radically alters the course of her tale. This incident revolves around a letter she sent to her father, begging him to forgive her and announcing her intention to "send again, to know if I may be admitted to throw myself at your Feet"; she goes on to explain that the letter had been returned to her enclosed in a blank sheet of paper (117). Finally convinced that her penitent stance was getting her nowhere, Charke gives it up, and sets about writing the fascinating and poignant tale of her adventures in London and elsewhere as "Mr. Charles Brown." It goes without saying that very few of these adventures could have met with the approval of Colley Cibber.

If the orphan heiress episode explained how Charke hoped to be recuperated as Mr. Cibber's youngest daughter, the account of Cibber's final rejection can be construed as a kind of elegy for that uselessly obsequious aspect of herself. She describes Colley Cibber as "forgetful of [the] TENDER NAME [of father] and the GENTLE TIES OF NATURE" (117) and goes on to note that "MERCY has even extended itself at the Place of Execution to notorious Malefactors," and to ask "what I have done so hateful! so very grievous to his Soul! so much beyond the Reach of Pardon! that nothing but MY LIFE COULD MAKE ATONE-MENT?" (121). There is more to these lines than melodramatic posturing; in a patriarchal society, the name of the father and the ties of nature determined the nomenclature and (at least in this one sense) the identity of the individual. To accuse her father of forgetting that fact is to say that a specific social contract has been broken, and that all bets are now off; if fathers will no longer behave like fathers, the filial obligations of daughters can easily be dispensed with. Similarly, the analogy to the condemned prisoner continues the motif of self-obliteration which is predicted in earlier passages even as it sets up yet another figurative equivalence between Charke's private quarrels and the sociopolitical conflicts of her era. She was not a willing martyr to the struggle of the marginalized. At her moment of crisis, she offered to conform as best she could to conventional expectations, to put on a command performance before her father and even perhaps to be willing to deny that it *was* a performance. When Cibber refused that offer, he returned her, metaphorically speaking, to the ranks of the strolling players; he refused to authorize her, as she wished to be authorized, in the narrative of the prodigal son, and he condemned her to search for that missing acceptance from any and every new audience she could find.[21]

In a sense, however, the heiress episode can be considered the imaginative counterpart to her decision to give up cross-dressing when she returned from her years in the western counties of England, while the incident with the letter, conversely, signals her refusal to continue in the role of the penitent daughter if there is nothing to be gained from it. The latter half of the *Narrative* offers Charke as a kind of picaresque hero. We see her as "Sir Charles," the well-known friend of many well-known London prostitutes; as a gentleman's valet, an inept grocer, an innkeeper; as a dashing actor singing airs from *The Beggar's Opera* in a country jail; as husband, father, and hapless breadwinner for Mrs. Brown and the teen-aged Kitty Charke; and even, in one of the variant forms of this last guise, as "Mr. Charles Brown, pastry-chef, from London." Confronted by such an astonishing variety of impersonations and situations, her readers may need to be reminded that the "Mrs. Charke" who had been celebrated and vilified in London during the late 1730s and early 1740s had for all intents and purposes disappeared for eight years. With the exception of the heiress episode—which I believe is fiction rather than fact—no one in the western counties knew that she was "actually the youngest Daughter of Mr. Cibber," or actually the notorious Mrs. Charke, or actually anyone other than the Mr. Brown she apparently claimed to be at the time.

The latter half of her autobiography brings the old troublemaker out of mothballs. Stringing this diverse group of identities and occupations together with nothing more than her own implicit assertion that she never accidentally blew her cover, she finally claims for herself the image of the subversive trickster she had tried to write out of existence earlier in the *Narrative*. As Patricia Meyer Spacks points out (82), one indication of this new attitude is Charke's "The Author to Herself," a written dedication that she added to the *Narrative* only after it had succeeded so well in serial form that plans had been made to republish it as a book. The doubled self in the title seems to me to be entirely appropriate, because it reflects her late discovery that the writer could authorize the actor even if her father would not authorize his daughter. The fact that Charke continued to struggle unsuccessfully against poverty and institutional resistance to her efforts to resume her stage career should not obscure the fact that the autobiography itself defiantly asserts her right to be whoever and whatever she needs to be in order to survive.

*   *   *

In the opening pages of this chapter, I suggested that actors were neither free agents nor puppets, but at that point I had established neither my interest in the consequences of performances nor the analogy between performers and individuals seeking authorization from the world at large. We can now develop the original point by suggesting that actors (and individuals) maintain their tenuous grasp on freedom only to the extent that they succeed in shaping and obtaining the authorizations they seek. If they fail to obtain those sanctions, they may find themselves constrained by circumstances and forced to serve as characters in a script authored by someone else. This is not to suggest that either performers or individuals do in fact become those characters; one of the defining characteristics of performance is the material presence of human beings who are clearly *not* who they pretend to be, and each individual's identity is always more than a simple conglomeration of the roles she or he is playing at a particular moment (see Wilshire 226–27). Performers and individuals can be distinguished in this respect from fictional characters and even from textual constructs of real people; to put it another way, there is no engulfment quite so complete as that of being absorbed into someone else's narrative.

With regard to Mother Lupine, Mrs. Otter, and Mr. Hen, our sense of what and how each character means must take into account the disjunction between the material presence of Charlotte Charke's female body and the character and behavior she enacted. However, when the Stage Licensing Act and her family situation conspired to deny her any further access to the London stage, Charke found herself unable to insist on that presence, that prior claim of shared humanity. On the printed page, the body becomes just another verbal construct; its undeniable significance on stage is easily engulfed by various units of symbolic discourse, including those that seek explicitly to devalue the physical aspect of human experience. When Charke was forced into the world of texts, her material presence was supplanted by the figure of her displeased father. It was her relation to Colley Cibber, not her enactments and critique of eighteenth-century masculinity, which in retrospect defined her time with the Great Mogul's Company, and it was the prospect of reconciliation with him that shaped or misshaped much of the *Narrative*.[22]

To finish this thought, we might look briefly at how Mother Lupine fared in her transition from the London stage to the pages of the eighteenth-century realistic novel. As I noted earlier, much of the plot of Richardson's *Clarissa* is taken from *Caelia*; in the novel, Mother Lupine becomes Mrs. Sinclair, and the animus generated against her on stage is worked out in the novel as one of the most lurid and overheated death scenes anywhere in English literature (1387–93).[23] I suggested earlier that Charke as Mother Lupine might have sought to implicate her audience in the exploitation of Johnson's innocent heroine. The Drury Lane audience refused to tolerate this implication, but they could not deny the material presence of the character; their only alternative was to stop the performance itself. During the sixteen years between the premiere of *Caelia* and the publication of *Clarissa*, the London stage had become increasingly respectable—that, in fact, was the stated goal of David Garrick, whose star rose so rapidly during the 1740s—and on that basis had become thoroughly inhospitable to the kind of gender-bending tricks that had been the stock in trade of the Great Mogul's Company. Mother Lupine's shift from the stage to the page suggests that, in the eyes of her eighteenth-century audience, her engulfment could not be accomplished until her physical presence had been completely expunged. And if that was indeed the case, the novelist's gleefully pornographic account of Mrs. Sinclair's inarticulate howls and the horror of her rapid physical deterioration might best be understood as the achievement of this long-deferred goal—that is, as a kind of ritual execution in prose, the justification for which had been shaped and reinforced over the previous two decades by the same social and institutional processes that had driven Charlotte Charke from the London stage, and placed her, like her literary descendant, forever on the wrong side of the spectator's controlling gaze.

4. "So much written about what deserves not the least consideration": Performance and Physical Experience in *Clarissa*

I want to begin my discussion of *Clarissa* by quoting two passages from the final volume of the novel. The first of these occurs shortly before the death of the heroine, when Lovelace returns to Mrs. Sinclair's brothel to upbraid her for her role as an accessory to the rape. In response, Mrs. Sinclair tries to mollify and distract Lovelace by offering to "show [him] a new face"—a prostitute she claims is "just in the trammels." Lovelace is thrown into turmoil by this offer; although he is eager to see the new arrival, he also claims that "I shall never see any face with pleasure but Miss Harlowe's." He is upset even further by the discovery that the supposedly new face belongs to Sally Martin, a well-known associate and accomplice of Mrs. Sinclair whom he had earlier refused to see, and by her strange attempt to court his favor:

> Come, said she, what will you give me, and I'll be virtuous for a quarter of an hour and mimic your Clarissa to the life.
> I was *Belforded* all over. I could not bear such an insult upon the dear creature (for I have a soft and generous nature in the main, whatever you think); and cursed her most devoutly for taking her name in her mouth in such a way. But the little devil was not to be balked; but fell a crying, sobbing, praying, begging, exclaiming, fainting, so that I never saw my lovely girl so well aped; and I was almost taken in; for I could have fancied I had her before me once more.
> Oh this sex! this artful sex! There's no minding them. At first, indeed, their grief and their concern may be real: but give way to the hurricane, and it will soon die away in soft murmurs, trilling upon your ears like the notes of a well-tuned viol. And, by Sally, one sees that art will generally so well supply the place of nature, that you shall not easily know the difference. Miss Harlowe, indeed, is the only woman in the world, I believe, that can say, in the words of her favourite Job . . . *But it is not so with me.* (L416, 1217)[1]

The second passage occurs shortly after Clarissa's death, when Jack Belford, Lovelace's rapidly reforming companion, returns likewise to the brothel, this time to witness some of the last hours accorded to Mrs. Sinclair, who has injured herself in a fall:

> The old wretch had once put her [broken] leg out [of its setting] by her rage and violence, and had been crying, scolding, cursing, ever since the preceding evening, [because] the surgeon had told her it was impossible to save her, and that a mortification had begun to show itself . . . her apprehensions of death and her antipathy to the thoughts of dying were so strong, that . . . she was raving, crying, cursing, and even howling, more like a wolf than a human creature, when I came; so that as I went upstairs, I said surely this noise, this howling, cannot be from the unhappy woman! Sally said it was, and assured me that it was nothing to the noise she had made all night; and stepping into her room before me, Dear *Madam* Sinclair, said she, forbear this noise! It is more like that of a bull than a woman! (L499, 1387)

Each of these episodes is organized around a male spectator/narrator and a female spectacle, and—as I will show later in this chapter—each one also serves to contrast the behavior of a specific fallen woman to the behavior of Richardson's virtuous heroine. At first glance, however, the differences between the two scenes may strike us as more prominent than their similarities. On the one hand, Sally Martin's impersonation is presented as a seductive illusion, the creation of an autonomous performer whose histrionic abilities are treated as both attractive and threatening. On the other hand, Mrs. Sinclair obviously has no control over her rapid disintegration; the scene demands our attention, but it is framed and constructed by Belford, who presents it as an appalling monitory fable, justified only by his desire to present Lovelace with a report that "will make thee seriously ponder and reflect, or nothing can" (L499, 1386). Perhaps more importantly, the first episode seems to be about performance, while the second seems to be about embodiment.

In the pages that follow, I will argue that these apparently disparate episodes and the apparently disparate themes they encompass are in fact inextricably linked by the plot of *Clarissa*. Simply put, Richardson mistrusts performance in general (and female performance in particular) because of the inherent duplicity involved in any impersonation, and he seeks to expose such deceptions by subjecting the deceivers to trials that are rooted in physical experience. At the same time, the novelist takes a rather naïvely Cartesian attitude toward the question of how the physical half of the mind/body duality should be valued. The plot of *Clarissa* suggests that although material reality will eventually win out over the instability of performance, that reality must itself be transcended before virtue can be properly rewarded. All of this is both illuminated and complicated by the connection I mentioned earlier between Charles Johnson's *Caelia* and Richardson's novel, primarily because any such discussion raises questions not only about the connections between particular works, but also about the general relationship between plays and novels, between performances and printed texts.

*   *   *

After three chapters in which my analyses have focused on the negotiations between the concrete materialities of performance and the determining abstractions of the script, we are now left alone with only the words on the page. The materiality of theatrical performance is incontrovertible; the body on stage, no matter what else it represents, still manifests itself as a body. The body in the text is naturally more difficult to locate, and the path to the discovery of the body in the text may not always pass by the theater. In this case, however, I think that it does. In the introduction to this study, I argued that the general incommensurability of texts and performances did not entirely rule out the possibility of connections between specific plays or performances and specific print narratives. My discussion of *Clarissa* is rooted in this sort of local connection.

To be more specific, I wish to make three fairly limited claims about the ways in which Richardson's *Clarissa* enters into a dialogue with Charles Johnson's *Caelia* and with the London stage in general. First, I will argue that in certain important respects the novel organizes the question of individual identity in a manner that is identifiably theatrical; in other words, it reproduces the structures of enactment, authorization, and engulfment which I explored in the previous chapter. The plot of the novel appropriates the theatrical model of identity primarily in order to condemn it. Generally speaking, the "theatrical" characters in *Clarissa*—Lovelace, Mrs. Sinclair, Sally Martin, and their associates—are morally dubious, while those characters whose sense of identity is rooted in narrative structures—Clarissa, Anna Howe, and, ultimately, Jack Belford—find their views and behavior validated to one degree or another by the end of the plot. Second, I will argue that the novel uses certain kinds of physical violence to expose the corruption and deception of the world created through performance. As we shall see below, Mrs. Sinclair's death is only the most striking instance of this paradigm.

Finally, I will show that, after using certain kinds of physical experience to expose certain theatrical falsehoods, the novel attempts at last to reject physical experience entirely in favor of the Christian transcendence exemplified by Clarissa's peaceful death. This last claim is complicated to some extent by an ending that vindicates Richardson's heroine by destroying her. Clarissa has herself been accused of theatricality by both Lovelace and her family, and it is only her response to the rape that convinces them that she was not merely impersonating a virtuous woman. Approximately a third of the way into the novel, Lovelace presents Belford with the question—"What must that virtue be which will not stand a trial?"—that provides the casuistical justification for his maltreatment of Clarissa (L110, 430). Ultimately, however, the deeper structure of Richardson's plot raises the unsettling possibility that, on this crucial point at least, the novelist shares the opinion of his archvillain.

✳   ✳   ✳

I noted in the previous chapter that much of the plot of *Clarissa* was appropriated directly from Johnson's *Caelia*. Despite Richardson's silence on this subject,[2] there are more than enough circumstantial similarities between the plots of the two works to justify this claim. Like Clarissa, Caelia is lured away from her parents' house—a country estate to which the playwright assigns the suggestive name of Clareville—by a notorious and unscrupulous rake. Both women are imprisoned in a London brothel by their seducers, and in both instances, the madam of the brothel plays a major role in terrorizing the helpless victim. In each case, the heroine is unjustly arrested and imprisoned; in each case, the rake's closest friend breaks with him and tries to help the innocent and long-suffering heroine; and in each case, the rake himself is killed in a duel with one of his victim's friends.[3]

There are also, of course, substantial differences between these two plots. Johnson's tragedy is set in London, and by the time it begins, his pathetic heroine has already left her home and lost her virginity to the by now entirely indifferent Wronglove. It ends in prison, with the death of Caelia, but not before she has been reunited with and forgiven by her father, and not before Wronglove has been killed in a duel. The novel begins at. Harlowe Place, and it takes a long time to get Clarissa to Mrs. Sinclair's brothel, and an even longer time before Lovelace commits the rape he has been meditating almost from the beginning; Clarissa dies peacefully in a private house, but she never achieves the hoped-for reconciliation with her family, while Lovelace goes the way of his predecessor. In Johnson's tragedy, Caelia is seduced, not raped, and Mother Lupine and her associates are cast into prison and forgotten—the better, one assumes, to focus on the heroine's reunion with her father and her pathetic demise. In *Clarissa*, the first half of Richardson's plot elaborates a sequence of events that is only summarized in the play (the family arguments, the elopement, the tricks used to force the victim to accept lodging in a brothel, the deteriorating relationship between the rake and his victim), while the latter half spins out the tale of the heroine's death, presented in this context as a triumph and accompanied by a number of less peaceful, less pious, and more graphically rendered exits.

The presence of the London stage in this novel is by no means limited to plot details and character types borrowed from Johnson's tragedy. In fact, the novelist's simultaneous distaste for and interest in the theater and theatrical conventions [4] is manifested in at least two significant ways. First, Richardson allows his correspondents to expend a great many words on the general subject of plays and playacting. Lovelace displays an extensive knowledge of seventeenth-century English drama, and he congratulates himself repeatedly on his ability to manipulate appearances to suit his needs. Meanwhile, Clarissa condemns Lovelace for his insincerity and machinations, and she and her allies seek continually to expose the performances he has arranged as falsehoods. Second, this series of theatrical references is complemented by an intermittent exploration of metatheatrical issues—the possibility and means of distinguishing between appearance and reality, the power dynamics of a specific specular economy, and so forth. The remainder of this section of my discussion will be concerned with the first of these tendencies, especially insofar as it is connected with the novelist's portrait of Sally Martin. The section that follows this one will focus on the second tendency in general, and on the portrait of Mrs. Sinclair in particular.

The novel opens with a letter from Anna Howe asking for Clarissa's version of the events that have mushroomed into full-scale "disturbances . . . in your family" (L1, 39). At Anna's request, Clarissa begins with an often comic account of Lovelace's aborted courtship of Arabella, who had thought to pique his interest by playing hard to get. Though Clarissa condemns Arabella for her foolish hopes and misperceptions, she also tells Anna that she did not intend to reflect badly on her sister,

> for what can any young creature in the like circumstances say, when she is not sure but a too ready consent may subject her to the slights of a sex that generally values a blessing either more or less as it is obtained with difficulty or ease? Miss Biddulph's answer to a copy of verses from a gentleman, reproaching our sex as acting in disguise, is not a bad one, although you perhaps may think it too acknowledging for the female character.

> > Ungen'rous sex!—To scorn us, if we're *kind*;
> >   And yet upbraid us, if we seem *severe!*
> > Do *You*, t'encourage us to tell our mind,
> >   Yourselves put off disguise, and be sincere.
> > You talk of coquetry!—Your own false hearts
> > *Compel* our sex to act dissembling parts.   (L2, 44)

Clarissa's equivocal endorsement of a poem by her imaginary acquaintance suggests a degree of ambivalence on this subject. On the one hand, she recognizes that men frequently force women into this position, and on the other, she also recognizes the potential in this sort of situation for losing one's dignity and reputation.

Unfortunately for Clarissa, the risks of involving herself in the social world of Harlowe Place are not limited to those that might be generated by her own insincerity. This is chiefly because the Harlowes think of Clarissa as a performer even when she is not performing. Thus her frank expressions of her distaste for Solmes are received as cryptic indications of her supposed interest in Lovelace, and the esteem she earned (to say nothing of the estate she is expected to inherit) from her grandfather is classified by Bella as the result of Clarissa's "blandishing ways" and "little, whining tricks" (L42, 195). In terms of the critical vocabulary developed in the previous chapter, Clarissa is experiencing the same combination of engulfment and refusal experienced by Charlotte Charke; like the youngest daughter of Mr. Cibber, the younger daughter of Mr. Harlowe discovers to her cost that no one will allow her to be the person she wishes to be.

In contrast to Clarissa, who is immersed against her will in these theatrical negotiations, Lovelace throws himself into both acting and stage managing with undisguised glee. Clarissa assumes from the beginning that Lovelace is not being honest with Arabella or the family as a whole (L3, 44), and the rake's skill in conceiving and orchestrating various confrontations is evident throughout the early volumes of the novel. The novelist also establishes a more explicit connection between his villain and the London stage in Lovelace's first letter, which establishes a recurring pattern by presenting us with a half-dozen quotations from seventeenth-century English plays (L31, 143–47); he also makes a great point of taking Clarissa herself to the theater after they get to London (L195, 620). The sad irony in this latter detail is that by this time Clarissa is inhabiting a world which is as illusory as any that could be presented on stage. As Terry Castle points out (*CC*, 96–97), Lovelace peoples Clarissa's London world with imposters, including not only the infamous "Mother" Sinclair and her "nieces," but also "Captain Tomlinson," "Miss Partington," "Mrs. Fretchville," and a number of other bit players. He also forces Clarissa herself to assume a false identity on several occasions. In one respect, Clarissa's situation in London reproduces her situation in Harlowe Place; she wishes to be authorized as a virtuous woman in difficult circumstances, but Lovelace's theatrical maneuvers and counternarrative deny her that wish. Instead, she is cast as his mistress or his wife in the eyes of the world and as a proud and overscrupulous prisoner in the eyes of her captor.

The fragmentation of Clarissa's identity is reflected in the novelist's reimagining of the London brothel that provided the setting for much of Johnson's *Caelia*. As we have already seen, Johnson's theater audience was deeply offended by his decision to place even Caelia's already compromised innocence in the presence of known prostitutes. Richardson's solution is the ingenious (if highly improbable) house that Anna Howe describes as actually "two houses; the one, in which all decent appearances were preserved, and guests rarely admitted; the other, the receptacle of those who were absolutely engaged, and broken to the vile yoke" (L229.1, 745).

We have seen this tension before, most obviously perhaps at Harlowe Place, where Clarissa's family insists that she allow herself to be sold to Solmes because that is the only way she can show a younger daughter's proper deference to the wishes of her parents and older siblings. This grotesque parody of family obligation becomes literalized as a species of theater when Clarissa is tricked into taking up lodging at Mrs. Sinclair's brothel. The mother who loves Clarissa but cannot help her is replaced by a corrupt monster who has difficulty even pretending to be virtuous, and the unnatural siblings who hope to see their sister brought low are replaced by the two nieces (Sally Martin and Polly Horton), both of whom are jealous of Clarissa because of their past relationships with Lovelace, and both of whom are as eager to see her ruined as James and Arabella are to see her married to the repulsive Solmes. To continue the parallel, we need only note that Mrs. Sinclair and her two nieces urge Lovelace repeatedly to turn Clarissa over to them when he is finished with her, because they (like the Harlowes) hope to grow rich themselves by selling her (L154, 522).

Taken in aggregate, the illusions constructed by Lovelace provide the reader with a vision of a transitional phase between the apparent comfort of Clarissa's childhood and the sordid reality of her physical violation—transitional because the illusions, like the unstable identities of both the heroine and Lovelace's role-players, are constantly at risk of being exposed and resolved by the ordering processes of narrative. On a purely textual level, Lovelace's inveterate tendency to boast about his stratagems in his letters serves the double purpose of keeping us informed about the real state of things and, on a more abstract level, suggesting to us that theatrical performance in general is a problem that is somehow solved by narrative. In a more activist strain, both Clarissa and Anna Howe are fond of certain kinds of detective work; they are attempting to construct a narrative of Clarissa's flight and captivity which will reveal the machinations that Lovelace hopes to obscure. Only the rake's intermittent ability to keep Anna's letters from Clarissa prevents them from discovering his various misdeeds and deceptions in time to avoid the rape.

Of the many London imposters controlled by Lovelace, Mrs. Sinclair's two nieces are unique, because they are presented as transitional in not one but two distinct senses. Like their employer and their supposed friends and relations, Sally Martin and Polly Horton are always in danger of being exposed for what they really are; unlike these cohorts, Sally and Polly are given real histories—histories that trace their incomplete progress toward complete debauchery—to go along with their aliases. Richardson's editorial persona summarizes Lovelace's character sketch of the two women by describing them as "[c]reatures who, brought up too high for their fortunes, and to a taste of pleasure and the public diversions, had fallen an easy prey to his seducing arts; and for some time past had been associates with Mrs. Sinclair"; then the text quotes Lovelace himself, who claims that Sally and Polly

> had not yet got over that distinction in their love which makes a woman prefer one man to another.
> How difficult it is, *says he*, to make a woman subscribe to a preference against herself, though ever so visible; especially where love is concerned? This violent, this partial little devil, Sally, has the insolence to compare herself with an angel—yet owns her to be an angel. I charge you, Mr. Lovelace, said

she, show none of your extravagant acts of kindness before me, to this sullen, this gloomy beauty!—I cannot bear it—Then her first sacrifices were remembered—What a rout do these women make about nothing at all! (L157.1, 534)

Sally and Polly have not yet fully accepted their status as prostitutes; each still hopes that Lovelace will return to her, and neither one is entirely comfortable with the "trammels" Mrs. Sinclair mentions in the episode cited at the beginning of this chapter.

In his first novel, Richardson had invented a character named Sally Godfrey who had been seduced and not quite abandoned by Squire B——before he met and fell in love with Pamela. Margaret Doody describes this brief interpolated tale as "a compressed thematic subplot to Pamela's own story; this is what happened in the case of a girl who did *not* preserve her virtue when attempted by Mr. B——" (66). In *Clarissa*, Sally Martin starts out as the same sort of character, but she eventually contributes to the thematic development of the novel in a much more complicated way than her eponymous predecessor. This is primarily because Sally Martin has had the bad taste to remain alive and in London after being ruined (the similarly disgraced Sally Godfrey had emigrated to the West Indies), and because she "has the insolence to compare herself with an angel." Despite Lovelace's early assertions to the contrary, the comparison is by no means inappropriate. As the London charade continues, the two nieces attempt to ingratiate themselves with Clarissa by asking her advice. Sally, who has pretended to be engaged to a tradesman, makes that engagement the subject of her inquiry, and Lovelace thinks he sees some irony in Clarissa's response:

> *Sally* has had a quarrel with her woollen draper; and made my beloved lady chancellor in it. She blamed Sally for behaving tyrannically to a man who loves her. Dear creature! to stand against a glass, and to shut her eyes because she will not see her face in it! (L194, 617)

Lovelace's claim that Sally is holding a glass to Clarissa here is dubious on several counts; however, what stays with the reader on this occasion is the idea that Sally is once again being compared to his supposedly beloved lady. As we find out more about Sally's past and about Lovelace's plans and impulses, we discover that the rake is trying to drive Clarissa along the same path that Sally traveled before her. For example, Lovelace's first sketch of Sally suggests that she was seduced, but he later acknowledges—in a letter that alludes to his plan to rape Clarissa—that his "first attempts" on both Sally and Polly also involved the use of force (L198, 633).

The climax of this series of comparisons is of course the passage I cited (L416, 1217) at the beginning of this chapter. By the time Sally launches into her full-scale impersonation of Clarissa, Clarissa herself lies dying elsewhere, out of Lovelace's reach. Since Sally's jealousy of Clarissa and her interest in Lovelace and in performance have not wavered from the first,[5] her tactics should come as no surprise; what should surprise us, however, is her relative success. Lovelace is so impressed by the performance that he finally accepts the claim of resemblance he had initially denounced: "I never saw my lovely girl so well aped; and I was almost taken in; for I could have fancied I had her before me once more." Perhaps more importantly, he presents the incident in a manner that encourages a similar confusion in the reader. When he describes Sally's first reference to Clarissa as "taking her name in her mouth," the momentary confusion over the antecedent of the first possessive links the two women together; when Sally goes on to lay claim to Clarissa's ineffectual modes of resistance, the connection is further strengthened, so that Lovelace's "there's no minding them" applies, again only momentarily, to both.

The repeated comparisons between Sally and Clarissa emphasize the difference between the heroine's principled resistance and what we are supposed to perceive as the feigned reluctance of the once-innocent Sally, but the similarities between the two women—their intermittently shared status as unauthorized performers—complicates what seems at first to be a fairly straightforward value judgment. Lovelace's anecdote concludes with two remarks. The first of these—"by Sally, one sees that art will generally so well supply the place of nature, that you shall not easily know the difference"—is oddly anticlimactic; both the insecurity reflected in the shift to second person and the vagueness of the second clause create the impression that Sally's impersonation has raised a question that Lovelace still cannot answer. The second remark is the obligatory exemption of Clarissa from this whole discussion. If Clarissa has convinced Lovelace at last that she is indeed more natural than artful, Sally Martin's final performance continues to insist that there is both a need for and a difficulty in knowing the difference.

*   *   *

How does Clarissa herself transcend the difficulty of distinguishing between art and nature? We can begin to answer this question by returning to the crucial difference between Clarissa and Sally Martin. We do not know enough about Sally's past to know whether she ever believed herself to be virtuous, but we do know that Lovelace used flattery, trickery, and ultimately force to subdue her. Whether she regrets this chain of events is unclear. In any case, she continued on her downward course of her own accord and managed even to thrive for a brief period in her new station. Clarissa, on the other hand, never recovers from the rape, but neither Lovelace nor her family take her reaction seriously—both parties think she is still posturing—until she dies.

In *Reading for the Plot*, Peter Brooks points out that while the crucial events of any narrative must seem to follow logically from the episodes that occur earlier in the text, such events also have the effect of revaluing all that preceded them. As he puts it, "prior events, causes, are so only retrospectively, in a reading back from the end" (28). If we look at the plot of *Clarissa* from this perspective, we might conclude first, that the rape defines (or at least confirms the definition of) Lovelace as evil, and second, that her peaceful death defines (or at least confirms the definition of) Clarissa as ultimately inviolate. Both events validate claims that have been made by Clarissa and her allies elsewhere in her text, but the general direction of Richardson's plot seems to prove Lovelace's claim that virtue must be tested and proven before it is honored. It also seems, given the novel's series of implicit and explicit comparisons to Lovelace's theatrical tricks and Sally Martin's impersonations, to suggest that moral truths must be accompanied by deeply embodied events before they can be distinguished from mere "decent appearances." In this section of my discussion, I will examine how the novelist treats the phenomenon of physical experience in his text, and how that treatment might connect with the theatrical origins of *Clarissa*, and with the epistemological question raised by Sally Martin's playacting (and, for Richardson at least, by performance in general).

In my discussion of Charlotte Charke, I suggested that her performance as Johnson's evil Mother Lupine might have implicated her audience in the exploitation of an innocent heroine, and that the Drury Lane audience stopped the show because they refused to tolerate this implication. Like the violent response of the theater audience, Johnson's statement that he wished he had left Mother Lupine and her prostitutes out of his play reflects not so much a wish to engulf the character in an agenda that knew less of horse-coursers as a hope of expunging her completely. When Richardson created his own version of the brothel madam character, the shift in medium made it possible for him to achieve both the engulfment the theater audience could not manage and the expungement they apparently hoped for.

In *Clarissa*, the character is destroyed in a way that determines not only her silence but her thematic significance. The novel accomplishes this by casting Mrs. Sinclair first as a spectator—thereby establishing the link to Johnson's Mother Lupine—and later as a spectacle. When she is first introduced to Dorcas and Mrs. Sinclair at the London brothel, Clarissa writes to Anna Howe that the first has "a strange sly eye—half-confident, I think," and the second "an odd winking eye"; the mildly ironic pun contained in her apologetic comment that "people can't help their looks" (L155, 524–25) only serves to reinforce the connection between Mrs. Sinclair's behavior and Mother Lupine's gaze. By the end of the novel, the madam has followed the example of her most virtuous victim, not only by dying, but also by falling—as Clarissa does when she is raped—into a species of embodiment so extreme that it could not possibly have been enacted on the eighteenth-century London stage:

> Her misfortune has not at all sunk but rather, as I thought, increased her flesh; rage and violence perhaps swelling her muscly features. Behold her then, spreading the whole tumbled bed with her huge quaggy carcase: her mill-post arms held up, her broad hands clenched with violence; her big eyes goggling and flaming-red as we may suppose those of the salamander; her matted grizzly hair made irreverend by her wickedness (her clouted head-dress being half off) spread about her fat ears and brawny neck; her livid lips parched, and working violently; her broad chin in convulsive motion; her wide mouth by reason of the contraction of her forehead (which seemed to be half-lost in its own frightful furrows) splitting her face, as it were, into two parts; and her huge tongue hideously rolling in it; heaving, puffing as if for breath, her bellows-shaped and various coloured breasts ascending by turns to her chin and descending out of sight with the violence of her gaspings. (L499, 1388)

The gasps could not be more violent than the description. As Terry Castle has pointed out (*CC*, 32–33), the primary recurring motif in this passage is rupture; Mrs. Sinclair's leg is broken by her fall (and later threatened with amputation), her face broken by her mouth, her pleas for relief and reassurance broken by her howls. Each of these fractures has a complicated sort of double agency, whereby a private experience is appropriated and transformed by an institutional voice for an institutional purpose.

On the one hand, Mrs. Sinclair broke her leg on the back stairway of her own house; the scene of the accident is thematically significant, because it implies that the injury is a just reward for the madam's attempts to yoke together the middle-class respectability of Clarissa's side of the house with the corruption of the brothel. On the other hand, the amputation is proposed by the surgeons not because they think it will help

Mrs. Sinclair, but merely because they wish to collect their fees, and to be perceived as doing something. The grimace creasing the face of the injured woman is a consequence of the extreme pain associated with a broken leg and with the gangrene ("mortification") that has set in. However, this private experience is converted to a shocking metaphor by Belford in order to impress Lovelace with the grotesquerie of the situation. Like the minute descriptions of her arms, hair, and skin, and like the surgeons' ostentatious discussion of the muscular and skeletal structure of the leg (L499, 1390), the description itself is rendered invasive and threatening by the attitude of the speakers.

The last of these three examples seems initially to depart from this pattern—where is the institutional sanction for Mrs. Sinclair's inarticulate groans?—but in fact it goes to the very heart of this matter. In *The Body in Pain*, Elaine Scarry describes a narrative paradigm in which the structure of political power is reproduced in the imagination of the material circumstances which would dramatize that power. More specifically, Scarry contends that those who are identified as powerless will usually be described in ways that emphasize their "deep embodiment," while those who wield power will be, as she puts it, "materially unrepresented" (207). Because all human bodies are vulnerable to pain, and because those in power naturally seek to reduce their own vulnerability, political authority frequently presents itself as a disembodied voice which directs a physical assault on the body of the victim without itself being attached to any material presence. This relationship between voice and material presence is inverted for the victim, whose ability to protest, to defend, or even to constitute a world through language becomes less and less available as the pain and terror increase. In Mrs. Sinclair's death scene, one position of authority is occupied by Belford, whose narrative is designed to reform Lovelace. Playing the objective reporter, Belford observes the scene silently for a brief period; when he does begin talking, he counsels patience and repentance, but his advice is lost amid the patient's howls and fragmented exclamations. Mrs. Sinclair is reduced to incoherent howling by either the internal conviction that she is going to hell or the external stimulus of the pain, or by both; since she herself describes her pain as "the torments of the damned" (L499, 1389), there is probably little point in distinguishing between the two. In any case, her howls can be read as a kind of institutional counterpoint—as a confirmation, against her own will but from her own mouth, that this pain is deserved—to her desperate but perfectly understandable pleas for relief. It is perhaps for this reason that Sally Martin seems to be more interested than Belford in putting a stop to the howling; she recognizes the voice of authority, and the threat it contains, when she hears it.

It could be argued that the inherent brutality of this narrative paradigm is symptomatic of the shifting of the plot from the stage to the page; one might contend, for example, that the absence of material signifiers (actors, scenery, props) might lead some prose writers to construct exaggerated descriptions of physical experiences to compensate for the more restricted mode of representation. In this particular case, however, the abuse of Mrs. Sinclair might well be considered something of a throwback to the theatrical origins of this particular novel. To explain this assertion, we will need to distinguish between the signifying bodies of stage performers, the imaginary bodies of fictional characters, and the real bodies of the performers themselves.

Even in the latter half of the twentieth century, when some performance artists have set out deliberately to transgress the boundaries that define what can be shown of or done to a human body before an audience,[6] the actor's body has continued to serve as an important practical and ideological limit on the literal contents of theatrical representation. In the eighteenth century, a more narrowly defined model of social propriety helped contribute to an atmosphere which dictated that Charlotte Charke's Mother Lupine could not be suffered to look at Jane Cibber's Caelia as a horse-courser looked at a filly. The audience might have been offended by the juxtaposition of the heroine's virtue and the madam's sinister mercantilism, or by the spectacle of a well-known troublemaker inspecting a popular and highly sympathetic female lead,[7] or by the implication that anyone watching the play was just as mercenary as Mother Lupine appeared to be on this occasion.

Remarkably enough, there is some circumstantial evidence to support the claim that this particular Drury Lane riot can be traced directly to the material representation of Johnson's tragedy by human performers. Although *Caelia* failed miserably on stage, it apparently enjoyed a certain amount of success as a "reading play"; booksellers' advertisements in a number of periodicals highlighted the title of the play at least to the mid-1730s. This fact suggests that the eventual members of Richardson's audience might have learned about Mother Lupine by attending the performance in 1732, by reading about the uproar created by that performance, or by reading the play itself. It also suggests that the anger directed at Charlotte Charke's enactment of Mother Lupine had more to do with the play-as-acted than it did with the play-as-written. Generally speaking, eighteenth-century theater audiences seem to have respected the signifying bodies of characters much more than they respected the real bodies of the individuals who enacted them. (The widespread assumption that actors were promiscuous could be construed as either a symptom or a proximate cause of this disrespect.) During the first half of the eighteenth century, London playgoers frequently expressed their displeasure by throwing fruit or other objects at the performers, and many actors of this era were forced by angry audiences to beg pardon on their knees at center stage for their perceived shortcomings.[8] This combination of circumstances created a rather odd situation; within the context of a given play, merely looking at a virtuous woman in a certain way could be condemned as the moral equivalent of an assault, but that condemnation carried with it a presumed right to carry out real assaults on the performer who had offended.

Richardson's portrait of Mrs. Sinclair provides justification for reading her death scene both in this general context, and also in the particular context of the uproar surrounding the single staging of Johnson's *Caelia*. On the one hand, Mrs. Sinclair has been presented throughout the London portion of the novel not only as an actor, but as a bad actor. Clarissa's distrust of her has already been noted, and Lovelace finds her impersonation of a virtuous widow to be patently ridiculous (see L158.1, 537). On the other hand, we can establish the connection between Mother Lupine and Mrs. Sinclair not only by citing the collection of circumstantial similarities I mentioned earlier, but also by pointing out Belford's comment that the howls sent up by the dying Mrs. Sinclair make her sound "more like a wolf than a human creature" (L499, 1387)—that is, more lupine than human. Reading in this double context, we might conclude that Mrs. Sinclair's death scene appropriates both the general threat of corporal punishment that hung over all eighteenth-century performers and the specific response that closed down the production of *Caelia* to assert a more general claim of the spectator's moral and physical authority over the spectacle of the dying madam. No longer bound by stage decorum, Richardson brings the full weight of his judgment to bear on the body that is no longer represented by a body. Freed of the restrictions associated with the signifying body of the performer, the novelist gleefully and confidently dissects the purely imaginary body of Mother Lupine's fictional successor.

*   *   *

The poles of Mrs. Sinclair's existence are defined by her attempt to pass herself off as a respectable middle-class widow and by the appalling spectacle of her final suffering. The detailed account of that suffering and Belford's rather extended transcription of his conversations with her at this time provide by far the fullest description of the character's thoughts and feelings (as well as her appearance). The fact that such an account arises only on this occasion suggests that we should view deeply embodied physical experience as the means by which her essential personality comes to light. This effect is underscored in Mrs. Sinclair's final scene by Belford's description of the disheveled prostitutes (L499, 1388) who have come to observe her in her illness. When he invokes Jonathan Swift's "The Lady's Dressing Room" (1730) as a model for understanding what he has seen, he implies that the exposure of Mrs. Sinclair is accompanied by an equally shocking exposure of the fallen women who had been disguising their corruption through various arts.

In a study entitled *The Absent Body*, philosopher Drew Leder has examined the Cartesian model of a mind/body duality by positing a paradoxical relationship between our physical embodiment and our mental operations. According to Leder, most people tend to be unaware of their own embodiment. Under normal circumstances, we do not think about our legs as they carry us down a sidewalk or up a flight of stairs; nor, when we look at an object, do we think about our eyes. Leder argues that when the body calls attention to itself, it usually does so by interrupting the individual's actions or contemplations with urgent messages prompted by any of a number of sensory or emotional phenomena. A brief list of these phenomena might include pain, illness, or hunger on one side, and extreme anger or fear on the other. Leder refers to this process as "dys-appearance" (83–92), and he argues that our unarticulated awareness of both the self-effacing tendencies of the healthy body and the disruptive effects of bodily dys-appearance have predisposed us to believe in a Cartesian model of human intellectual activity that claims "an association between corporeality and its dysfunctional modes" (108). In Leder's view, this association creates a "phenomenological vector" (150) which has led most Western intellectuals to assume that the intellectual and spiritual progress of both the individual human being and the species as a whole depends in some sense on our ability either to resist or to ignore our own embodiment.

The limitations of Richardson's education are well-known, and it seems unlikely that he would have encountered Descartes in his own reading. However, as Barbara Stafford has recently pointed out, certain crucial aspects of Descartes's phenomenology were reproduced or echoed in

England by both Newton and Locke (11, 35, 133), and the ideas articulated by all three philosophers would have been available to the novelist in one form or another from a variety of sources. For the purposes of the present discussion, I wish merely to assert that the latter half of *Clarissa* reflects an attitude toward physical experience which can be construed—at least in part—as a version of the kind of dualism described in Leder's treatise. This attitude is reflected both in the nature of the rewards and punishments meted out to the characters in the novel, and in the experiences and responses of Richardson's heroine. Generally speaking, the novelist's particular version of the mind/body duality suggests, first, that the human body is an unavoidable obstacle to enlightenment, and second, that those who are most deeply embodied will also be those who are most deeply mired in vice. Mrs. Sinclair's suffering is obviously the most extreme example of this latter paradigm, but the deaths of Thomas Belton (L424, 1240–43) and Lovelace (L537, 1486–88), and the final note on the fates of Sally Martin and Polly Horton (Conclusion, 1490–91) share the same basic structure.

The crucial exception to this generalization is of course Clarissa, who is deeply embodied by the rape, but who manages ultimately to transcend her embodiment and disprove Lovelace's endlessly repeated hypothesis that a woman who is once subdued will be always subdued. The recent attempts to present *Clarissa* as a protofeminist novel[9] have celebrated both Richardson's apparent rejection of Lovelace's claim and Clarissa's ability to transcend the rake's attempt to define her first and foremost as the inhabitant/possessor of a female body. Although I share the political interests of many of these critics, I am skeptical of this view of the novel. In this section of my discussion, I will argue that Clarissa's transcendence is constructed in a manner that fails to resolve the primary ideological issue raised both by Richardson's general treatment of the relationship between embodiment and spiritual progress, and—to ground the discussion in a more concrete social reality—by the rape itself.

Terry Castle has argued for certain connections between the ruptures and discontinuities of Mrs. Sinclair's final hours and those inflicted on Clarissa by her family and Lovelace (*CC*, 35). The critic uses this connection to contend that Richardson's regard for his heroine makes him more sympathetic to the plight of women in general than he sometimes realizes. It seems to me, however, that it is equally plausible to argue that the misogynistic horror that characterizes the novelist's treatment of Mrs. Sinclair and her associates changes the quality of his sympathy for Clarissa by leading him to value her only as an angel and not as a woman. In this section of my discussion, I will take up the general question of how Clarissa can or should be connected to the negative female exempla in the novel.

Earlier in this chapter, I argued that the duality of the world of *Clarissa* is created by performance and exposed by narrative; Lovelace in his role as stage manager (and braggart) explains each stratagem as it occurs, while Anna Howe and Clarissa herself recapitulate each of these explanations as more information comes to light. Significantly, however, none of this information becomes available to Clarissa until after she has been raped. Metaphorically speaking, it is the dys-appearance of Clarissa's body—the sudden and horrifying discovery that she is vulnerable to physical abuse—that somehow allows her to see through the deceptions Lovelace has laid in her path. To modern readers at least, the impossibility of the situation is both troubling and familiar. If Clarissa remains innocent, she will fall victim to Lovelace; however, if her ability to see through the world's corruption depends upon what is likely to be perceived as her own corruption, any effective resistance on her part will condemn her as somehow too knowledgeable about attitudes and practices that presumably should be mysterious to any virtuous woman. Throughout the novel, both Lovelace and the Harlowes assume that Clarissa's understanding is the result of her corruption. When she leaves Harlowe Place, both her abductor and her relatives conclude that such an action could result only from her unauthorized interest in the rake. Before the rape, Lovelace routinely discounts Clarissa's emotional outbursts on the grounds that they are motivated by wounded pride rather than any more legitimate sort of distress. After the rape, the Harlowes continue to believe that Clarissa got what she wanted—they are only too willing to believe the worst about her new friendship with Belford—and nothing short of her peaceful and penitent death will persuade them that she has been wronged.

Richardson's text does not overtly encourage us to accept this view of his heroine, but it does encourage us to think this way about every woman other than his heroine. Clarissa's behavior after the rape confirms the sincerity of her earlier outbursts, but Sally Martin's impersonation encourages both the rake and the reader to discount such utterances in every case but Clarissa's. The rhetorical goal of this episode is clearly to discredit Sally's "crying, sobbing, praying, begging, exclaiming, [and] fainting" (L416, 1217); the list foreshadows the parodic version of these utterances soon to be produced by Mrs. Sinclair, which Belford describes as "crying, scolding, cursing, . . . raving, crying, cursing, and even howling" (L499, 1387). In both cases, the female spectacle is framed and interpreted by an authoritarian male speaker. Although Clarissa's performances are finally accepted as sincere even by her greatest skeptic, and although her peaceful death in most respects could not be more different than that of Mrs. Sinclair, she is ultimately no more immune to such engulfment than either of her two disreputable attendants.

In *Pamela*, Richardson displayed a propensity for solving plot difficulties by shifting the vices or errors of his protagonist onto secondary characters. When the novelist realized that he needed to turn Mr. B——— and his innocent victim into a loving couple, he banished the rake from the text temporarily and assigned his worst traits—his class snobbery and his sexual aggressiveness—to Lady Davers and Mrs. Jewkes, respectively. By replacing Pamela's single male antagonist with two female antagonists, the novelist created a situation where Mr. B——— could enact his own reformation by lecturing two women who in each case were worse than he was in one important respect. In *Clarissa*, this effect is muted to some degree by the fact that neither Clarissa nor Lovelace has to change as much as B——— does, but it is still very much in evidence.

Although Lovelace is clearly the individual who is most responsible for the abduction and rape of Clarissa, the novelist did in fact go out of his way to emphasize the sinful nature of his female subordinates. When Belford first rises to Clarissa's defense, he attacks Lovelace for bringing her to a place where "the people . . . will too probably damp and suppress any honourable notion which may arise in her favor" (L143, 500). His fears are confirmed soon afterward, when Lovelace reports that "our mother and her daughters [have] been about me," urging him to turn Clarissa over to them when he is finished with her (L154, 522). After the rape, Mrs. Sinclair and Sally attempt to convince Lovelace that he should "leave the perverse beauty to their *breaking*, as they call it, for four or five days" (L264, 906)—a suggestion Lovelace angrily rejects. It should also perhaps be noted that in *Caelia* the plan to turn the heroine into a whore comes from the rake, not from the other prostitutes. In the novel, it is Mrs. Sinclair who persuades Lovelace to drug Clarissa before he rapes her, and it is Sally Martin, not Lovelace, who arranges to have Clarissa thrown into prison on trumped-up charges; in the play, Mother Lupine's house is raided by constables, and Caelia is simply dragged off to jail with everyone else.

Similarly, if we look closely at the implicit and explicit comparisons involving the female characters in *Clarissa*, we can trace yet another version of the pattern of displacement that determined the respective ill natures of

Mrs. Jewkes and Lady Davers in *Pamela*. On the one hand, Clarissa dem-onstrates the sincerity of her earlier performances by refusing to live in a body that has been violated; Sally Martin's attempt to please Lovelace by impersonating her absolves Clarissa of such motives even as it impugns the performances of every other distressed woman. On the other hand, if Clar-issa transcends the materiality of the fallen woman by dying a peaceful and pious death, Mrs. Sinclair's final submersion into bodily dys-appearance can be read as a displacement of the whole weight of both Clarissa's physi-cal experience and her own onto the figure of a single corrupt individual. Since both the need to perform and her deep embodiment are imposed upon Clarissa from without, the analogy between Clarissa and B——seems imperfect. At the same time, the plot of the later novel demands that the questions raised by Clarissa's (extremely limited) complicity with Lovelace and by the conventional judgments leveled against the fallen woman must be resolved before Richardson's heroine can be sanctified. And it is the nature of those two resolutions that ultimately calls the nature of Richardson's sympathy for Clarissa into question.

There are two basic problems here. First, both of these displacements serve to discredit every woman in the text who is driven by anything less than Lovelacian villainy either to perform her own victimization or to survive her own embodiment. Second, neither displacement helps Clarissa herself. She cannot disprove her family's accusation of insincerity unless she dies; nor can she prove herself to be an exception to Lovelace's rule of "once subdued, always subdued" without redefining "always" in terms of eternity. At the end of the novel, Clarissa abandons her physical self to obtain the purely figurative and explicitly phallogocentric reconciliation that is represented by her letter about returning to her father's house (L421.1, 1233).

The letter presents the reader with the notion of a metaphorical rather than a literal return; in a sense, this gesture recapitulates Richardson's en-tire plot by presenting us first with an unstable mixture of physical and abstract connections, then with a descent into deep embodiment, and fi-nally with a triumphant disembodiment. In terms of Clarissa's personal relationships, this arc is registered by her successive incarnations as daugh-ter, rape victim, and angel; the letter about her father's house traces roughly the same arc by moving from Harlowe Place to paradise. The first of these locations is rife with family conflicts pitting material against moral considerations. Although Clarissa does not refer to the middle step in her journey, Mrs. Sinclair's brothel is similar to Harlowe Place because it pro-vides a dark parody of middle-class respectability, accompanied by an even more extreme version of the money-for-sex equation that drove Clarissa into exile. In any case, the end of the letter shows both James Harlowe Sr. and Mrs. Sinclair being supplanted by a parent who will not demand that Clarissa dispose of her body to suit the whims or designs of the patriarch— unless, of course, one wishes to read the premature death of Richardson's heroine as yet another version of this trope.

Which I do. Before the rape, Clarissa's body provides the occasion for a variety of misjudgments and abuses deriving from a combination of greed and radical skepticism. Both her family and Lovelace think of her as a valuable possession to be assigned as they see fit, and both refuse to believe that any woman has either the right or the ability to resist such transactions. After the rape, the female body in general appears only as a means of deceiving men (Sally Martin), or as a source of sorrow that must ultimately be cast aside (Clarissa herself), or, finally, as a grotesque parody of itself (Mrs. Sinclair). It is thus disqualified from signifying, rendered irrelevant, and, finally, broken to pieces. Clarissa's willingness to die under these circumstances and in this manner ultimately obscures the moral issues raised by the rape and its aftermath. Regardless of whether she is perceived as guilty or innocent, there is no good reason why she should have to prove her virtue either to Lovelace or to her parents, either before or after the assault; nor is there any good reason why any woman, innocent or guilty, should suffer the social consequences Clarissa apparently accepts as a matter of course. In the final section of this chapter, I will argue that the ending of the novel obscures and circumvents these issues primarily by suggesting that literary survival is sometimes preferable to literal survival.

*   *   *

In *Factual Fictions*, Lennard J. Davis has observed that in the latter part of *Clarissa*, Richardson's heroine "literally becomes the sum and total of the written account that she herself actively pushed into publication" (186). The end of the novel entails not only Clarissa's physical deterioration and death, but also Belford's gradual accumulation of the letters that tell her story. The cumulative effect of these simultaneous developments is that Clarissa the character is gradually supplanted by *Clarissa* the text. Clarissa dies well before the novel itself actually ends, and the physical and textual gestures that occupy her at the end of her life seem to be concerned primarily with the task of consolidating the words of both her literal and her metaphorical fathers. I will cite only three details in connection with this point. First, when Clarissa chooses her coffin, she has her death date listed as April 10; this is months earlier than her actual death, but Clarissa explains this misleading designation to Belford by noting that April 10 was "the fatal day of her leaving her father's house" (L451, 1306). The impulse to obliterate the experience of her abduction and the rape is of course understandable, but the inscription on the coffin is disturbing, because it effectively places that impulse at the service of the Harlowes' wish to avoid public scandal.

The other two details come from Clarissa's will. First, her treatment of Anna Howe seems strangely ambivalent. Clarissa gives Anna a diamond ring and other personal effects, but she also asks her not to go into mourning, and she is quite insistent about her hopes that Anna will marry Mr. Hickman as soon as possible. Anna Howe had been Clarissa's only friend throughout her trials and the only one who offered to assist her. Clarissa turned down more than one such offer, and she generally disapproved of Anna's recurring battles with her mother over these and other issues. Given the outcome of Clarissa's own attempts to resist Lovelace, she might have used the occasion of her will to acknowledge in some fashion that Anna's more activist impulses might have led to a better ending than the one she actually endured. Instead, she uses the imprimatur of a martyr to deny Anna both the emotional release involved in mourning properly and the right to refuse a suitor who, whatever his other virtues, does not seem to inspire anything more than respect. In her explanation of this latter recommendation, Clarissa indicates that she understands exactly what she is asking for:

> I bequeath to the worthy Charles Hickman, Esq., the locket with the miniature picture which I have constantly worn, and shall continue to wear near my heart till the approach of my last hour, of the lady whom he best loves. It must be the most acceptable present that can be made him, next to the *hand* of the dear original. And oh my dear Miss Howe, let it not be long before you permit his claim to the *latter*—for indeed you know not the value of a virtuous mind in that sex; and how preferable such a mind is to one distinguished by the more dazzling flights of unruly wit; although the latter were to be joined by that specious outward appearance which is too, too often permitted to attract the hasty eye and susceptible heart. (L507, 1416)

Anna, it seems, should resist the evidence of her eyes and the impulses of her heart; she should give her hand to Hickman, whom she does not yet know how to value, but who (thanks to Clarissa) nonetheless already possesses her image.

Clarissa's bequest to Hickman casts the suitor's proprietary gaze as a prelude to the physical possession of the individual who is being looked at. In this respect at least, it provides a (supposedly) benign recapitulation of the plot against Clarissa by Mrs. Sinclair and her nieces. This connection is also implicitly part of Clarissa's interest in restricting access to both her image and her corpse. In her will, she leaves full-length portraits of herself only to Anna and her aunt (in trust for her bereaved mother),[10] and she insists that her body "shall not be touched but by those of my own sex" (L507, 1413). Then, after some directions about her burial, a fervent wish that Lovelace will not see her corpse, and a plea for her father's post mortem forgiveness, she concludes this section of the will with the apologetic note that gave this chapter its title:

> So much written about what deserves not the least consideration and about what will be nothing when this writing comes to be opened and read will be excused when my present unhappy circumstances and absence from all my natural friends are considered. (L507, 1413)

This remarkably compressed statement signals the final triumph of the text over the body in *Clarissa*. The last word of the sentence echoes the first epithet ("what deserves not the least consideration"), thereby contrasting the insubstantiality of the first expression to the relative specificity of the final clause. At the same time, the second epithet ("what will be nothing when this writing comes to be opened and read") alludes even more directly to the transformation of Clarissa into *Clarissa*. The second phrase also encapsulates Clarissa's vision, mentioned above, of Lovelace breaking in on the funeral to see her corpse, only to be "[given] a paper whilst he is viewing the ghastly spectacle" (L507, 1413) that prompts him to repentance.

But when the text triumphs over the body, it triumphs over the character as well. Presenting one's self as a ghastly spectacle may be an effective way of inspiring reformation in Belford (and perhaps even in Lovelace), but the ending of *Clarissa* suggests that the specular economy which empowers the male gaze can be challenged only by a pious death—a gesture, in other words, which precedes the sanctification of the individual with a rather convenient obliteration of her human presence.[11] I alluded earlier to the attempt on the part of several recent critics to present Richardson's masterpiece as a protofeminist work. I believe that the impression that

Clarissa is a radical text is derived primarily from the extremity of Richardson's commitment to an essentially Cartesian perspective on human experience. Although the novel is marked by a deeply felt sympathy for some women, that sympathy is rooted in a conceptual system that condemns any woman who (unlike Clarissa) is unwilling to sacrifice herself for the sake of an abstraction whose value and physical correlatives are determined by the system that oppresses her.

5. Who She Was and What She Was: Female Characters and Physical Experience in *Tom Jones*

Students of the eighteenth-century English novel have been debating the relative merits of Richardson and Fielding for almost two hundred and fifty years, and for the last half-century of that period, critics and historians have tried to link the respective political and economic backgrounds of the two writers to the ideological contents of their works. At least since the publication of Ian Watt's *The Rise of the Novel* in 1957, the critical consensus on these matters seems to have been that while Richardson's bourgeois sensibility manifests itself in his novels as an accent on individual virtue and a certain social aggressiveness, Fielding's connections to the upper-class gentry lead him to dismiss the concerns of the middle and lower classes and to assert certain aristocratic privileges and attitudes more or less without question.[1] Over the past two decades, the growing interest in feminist literary history has led several critics to examine the treatment of gender relations in these novels, but the assumptions about the liberal Richardson and the conservative Fielding have continued to hold sway, so that the author of *Tom Jones* is frequently cited as an irredeemable sexist. Thus Margaret Doody, in her book-length study of Richardson, accuses Fielding of "unconsciously uphold[ing] something of the *droit de seigneur*" (73), and Michael McKeon, in *The Origins of the English Novel*, maintains that Fielding, at least in his early, anti-Pamelist works, "slyly avoids all the social ramifications of female chastity" (399).[2] Christine van Boheemen takes this claim even further by suggesting that *Tom Jones* is not merely about avoiding such issues, but rather about the need for the male hero to reject femininity altogether in order to achieve his rightful place in the patriarchal order (78), while John Zomchick has claimed that the novel's treatment of "[Tom's] natural, internal conscience . . . validates the male's prerogative of judgment, which is first threatened and then confirmed by a succession of female encroachers upon it" (539).

I do not believe that this general line of argument provides an accurate picture of sex and gender relations in Fielding's masterpiece. In this chapter, I will contend that *Tom Jones*, like *Clarissa*, emphasizes the embodiment of certain characters and the histrionic abilities of certain other characters, and that the tension between text and performance is also woven into his plot. Fielding differs from his most famous rival in his willingness to present the material world in general and the human body in particular as something other than a source of pain and sorrow. If the body of Clarissa Harlowe is eventually—and, we are led to believe, happily—obscured by the text that bears her name, Fielding's more complicated attitude toward physical experience leads him to explore the ways in which a sense of individual virtue and an awareness of one's own embodiment might be brought into harmony with one another.

Before the wayward Tom Jones can attain the ultimate happiness that Fielding plans to bestow on him at the end of his journey, he must find a way to regain the lost approval of both Squire Allworthy and Sophia Western. Since Tom loses the approval of these two characters through his imprudence and infidelities, and since he is eventually treated to both Allworthy's lecture on prudence (XVIII.x.960)[3] and Sophia's lecture on fidelity (XVIII.xii.972), many critics have concluded that any character in the novel who is either demonstrably imprudent or demonstrably promiscuous is implicitly discredited by Fielding's happy ending. In fact, however, both of these crucial reconciliations require not only Tom's reformation, but also the timely assistance of characters who clearly have no place in such a moralistic universe. More specifically, the happy ending of the novel depends on the unlooked-for intervention of Jenny Waters, who explains at last the mystery of Tom's birth, and of Squire Western, who bullies his daughter out of her plan to impose an additional year's probation on Fielding's hero. In both cases, the shared destiny of two unmistakably virtuous characters is controlled at last by two characters whose personalities and behavior are just as unmistakably rooted in appetite rather than prudence, in desire rather than reason.

This is a long way from where the novel begins. The Somersetshire chapters of *Tom Jones* present the reader with a world where the concrete realm of the body and the abstract realm of the mind are as separate from one another as they can be. (In this context, the second term should be taken in its broadest sense, to encompass not merely intellectual activity in general but the social manifestations of that activity, including language, the law, and the printed text.) The two poles of this rather Manichean universe are Allworthy's Paradise Hall and Western's unnamed estate, and each estate reflects the characteristic preoccupations of its patriarch. Western's lands are used for hunting, and conversations at his table concern foxes, horses, and the begetting of bastards. As for the squire himself, he has been aptly described by Robert Alter as

> a center of continually detonating energy that can scarcely be contained in anything so conscious, so premeditated, as human language. Western's vocabulary consists of full-throated cries, half-growled snatches of dialect, hearty blows or handshakes, allusions to, and demonstrations of, the less polite functions of the body. (90)

By way of contrast, the vast majority of the business done at Paradise Hall would take place in either a classroom or a courthouse today. Most of the conversations at Allworthy's table involve abstract discussions of learning and public morality, and although many contributions to these conversations are little more than flimsy rationalizations for the self-interested schemes being pursued by the speakers, Allworthy himself takes them at face value. The mind/body duality is also reflected in the way that the novelist organizes his cast of secondary characters in Somersetshire. Western's estate has Black George Seagrim, the gamekeeper who is dismissed by Allworthy for a violation of the poaching laws, and Parson Supple, whose defining characteristic seems to be his hearty appetite (IV.x.187–88), while Paradise Hall has Square and Thwackum, whose professions identify them with intellectual endeavors of one sort or another. (Thwackum is of course a bully and a sadist, and Square later supplants Tom as Molly Seagrim's lover, but the public utterances of both are invariably directed toward the abstract rather than the concrete; they deny the body, in their rhetoric if not in their respective practices.) To some extent, Mrs. Honour and Mrs. Wilkins reproduce the same sort of distinction: the former cannot help talking at length about such matters as Molly Seagrim, the whiteness of Tom's skin, and "my lady's muff," while the latter is presented as a self-appointed guardian of public morality and as an enemy not only of sexual license but even of physical beauty (I.vi.49; viii.57).

The general outlines of this opposition are clear even to a first-time reader of the novel. What is less obvious, perhaps, is that the conflicts that surface during the Somersetshire chapters repeatedly reveal the inherent instability of this apparently rigid separation between mind and body.

Many of these conflicts involve characters who find themselves marooned in the wrong camp. Well before we learn that Bridget Allworthy is Tom's mother, we recognize that she is ruled by her sexual appetite, and Aunt Western's consuming interest in political scheming—the closest thing to an intellectual activity that takes place under her brother's roof—is likewise evident from her first appearance. Both sisters are somewhat unhappy in their brothers' households, but their presence provides Fielding with a host of opportunities to exploit the comic potential inherent in the enforced proximity of such disparate temperaments.

Perhaps more importantly, both Tom and Sophia seem also to have been set down in the wrong place. Tom hunts with Squire Western, and throughout the early part of the novel he emulates Western's behavior toward women; meanwhile, Sophia is underappreciated by her father (although he loves her very much, he apparently approves of her primarily because of her musicianship) and much better esteemed by Allworthy—presumably for the restraint and decorum displayed in her behavior and for her philanthropic gestures. From a thematic perspective, there are good reasons why each of the lovers is located in what amounts to an alien environment. Before they can live happily ever after, both Tom and Sophia need to learn to accept what their surroundings have to offer; Tom must learn to restrain his appetites, and Sophia must learn finally to recognize and to accept at least some of the risks connected with the emotional attachments of others and with her own impulses.

Essentially, then, the logic of Fielding's plot seems at first to be exclusionary but is revealed at last as dialectical. The separation of mind and body in the Somersetshire chapters is extreme; characters who violate conventional standards of sexual conduct—in the early chapters of the novel, this group would consist of Tom, Molly Seagrim, Bridget Allworthy, and (by mistake) both Jenny Jones and Partridge—are punished in one way or another for their real or imagined misdeeds. By the end of *Tom Jones*, all these characters have been rehabilitated or forgiven, so that the unmistakable condemnation of sexual incontinence in the Somersetshire section loses some of its clarity. In the pages that follow, I will argue that this loss of clarity reflects an increasingly complicated view of the problems raised (and solved) by these characters. Since Fielding, like many of his contemporaries, associated the feminine with the physical, this new complexity also suggests a deeper sympathy for his female characters—especially for those, like Bridget Allworthy and Jenny Waters, who had implicitly or explicitly violated the standards of public morality presented by Allworthy in his early pronouncements on this subject.

I also hope to show that villainy in *Tom Jones* is associated not with femininity or femaleness, but rather with with the sort of textuality that is presented in *Clarissa* as the only means of gaining ascendance over deceptive appearances. Clarissa herself is quite certain that her final vindication depends on the task she has assigned to Belford—that is, on the ordering and publication of more than four hundred individual texts into a coherent narrative (L387.1, 1173). In *Tom Jones*, however, the editor is the villain; where Lovelace had legions of impersonators and a dramatist's flair for manipulating the senses of his audience, Blifil has only lawyer Dowling and a certain skill at selecting and arranging the details of Tom's misadventures into the most incriminating pattern possible.

Where the continued deception of Clarissa depends at crucial moments on Lovelace's ability to intercept Anna Howe's letters to her, Allworthy's ignorance of Tom's origins stems not so much from the letter that Blifil destroys as it does from the inconvenient timing of Bridget's death, which comes while she was rushing back to see her ailing brother. Because both Allworthy and his sister fall ill at the same time, Bridget cannot speak with him, and she is forced to write a letter instead. The shift from oral to written communication effectively converts a physical fact and a performance (Tom's parentage and Bridget's eternally deferred confession) into a single legal document, thereby taking control of the information away from Bridget and assigning it to Blifil and Dowling. This interest in theatrical performance is reaffirmed by Jenny Waters's long-delayed revelation that she and Bridget conspired at first to obscure Tom's origins. Since Blifil has destroyed the letter, the unraveling of the mystery depends at last on Jenny's willingness to supplant her deceptive first performance with a truthful second one.

As this last statement suggests, *Tom Jones* contains more than one version of performance. In fact, the narrator presents us with a number of possibilities here: courtroom dramas and private confrontations, dinner conversations and roadside parleys, churchyard rescues and sickbed interviews. Fielding's treatment of embodiment is also multifaceted; *Tom Jones* deals explicitly not only with sexual desire, but also with the vulnerability of both male and female bodies to illness and violence. Unlike Richardson, however, Fielding acknowledges almost from the beginning that embodiment carries with it the potential not merely for suffering, but for gratification as well. In fact, *Tom Jones* eventually seems to suggest that the second possibility goes a long way to redeem the first. Because this perspective informs Fielding's treatment of the struggle between the word and the body, he ultimately seems to be much less of a Cartesian dualist than his great rival. Where *Clarissa* establishes the validity of the textual by invalidating performance and trivializing embodiment, *Tom Jones* eventually undermines the textual by celebrating both performance and embodiment. In order to develop this latter assertion, the next two sections of my argument will be organized around these two general topics. I will begin by focusing on Fielding's portrait of Sophia Western—that is, on the character in *Tom Jones* who has been most frequently accused of partaking too much of the ideal and too little of flesh-and-blood reality.

*   *   *

At the end of Book IV of *Tom Jones*, the teen-aged Sophia Western is thrown from her horse. Fortunately, Fielding's hero is nearby, and he catches her in his arms, breaking one in the process. In gratitude for his assistance, Squire Western arranges for medical care for both Tom and his daughter, and once it becomes apparent that Tom will be laid up for a while, Squire Allworthy begins to pay regular visits to his ward:

> *Tom Jones* had many Visitors during his Confinement, tho' some, perhaps, were not very agreeable to him. Mr. *Allworthy* saw him almost every Day; but tho' he pitied *Tom's* Sufferings, and greatly approved the gallant Behaviour which had occasioned them, yet he thought this was a favourable Opportunity to bring him to a sober Sense of his indiscreet Conduct; and that wholsome Advice for that Purpose, could never be applied at a more proper Season than at the present; when the Mind was softened by Pain and Sickness, and alarmed by Danger; and when its Attention was unembarrassed with those turbulent Passions, which engage us in the Pursuit of Pleasure.
>
> At all Seasons, therefore, [but] especially when [Tom] was totally at Ease, [Allworthy] took Occasion to remind him of his former Miscarriages, but in the mildest and tenderest Manner, and only in order to introduce the Caution, which he prescribed for his future Behavior . . .
>
> *Thwackum* was likewise pretty assiduous in his Visits; and he too considered a sick Bed to be a convenient Scene for Lectures. His Stile, however, was more severe than Mr. *Allworthy's* . . .   (V.ii.215–16)

The passage emphasizes what Fielding conceives as the conflicting demands of the human body and the human mind, but it also seems to be presented in a manner that may prompt the reader to doubt both the fairness and the utility of the effort to stage the contest in this particular

situation. The primary indication that Allworthy's behavior on these occasions may not be quite fair is that his gentle remonstrances are seconded
and imitated by the odious Thwackum. Even without that connection,
however, Allworthy's assumption about the salutary effects of a little softening by pain and sickness might seem a bit suspicious. Tom is in a sickbed
because he was injured while trying to protect another person; to use such
an event as an occasion for anything other than expressions of gratitude
and sympathy seems rather coldhearted and thus somewhat out of character for the patriarch of Paradise Hall.

The unspoken logic behind Allworthy's effort is interesting, if only
because it provides an eighteenth-century articulation of the train of
thought described by Drew Leder in *The Absent Body*. Hidden in the passive constructions at the end of the first paragraph is Tom's dys-appearing
body—the body, that is, which manifests itself only or primarily as a
source of pain. The "softening" Allworthy hopes for is the process that
Leder describes as turning against the body, because the mind begins to
associate an awareness of embodiment with its negative potentialities. Fortunately, what Tom and Sophia learn from this episode is not derived from
the bedside lectures provided by either of the two older men. Instead,
Sophia's fall and Tom's injury establish a physical connection between the
two lovers, not only because their accidental embrace predicts their eventual union, but also because they are placed under the care of the same
incompetent surgeon at Western's estate, and because their temporary
proximity to each other gives Fielding the opportunity to introduce Sophia's muff as a symbol of each lover's emotional and erotic interest in the
other.

Before the accident, Tom had been somewhat cool to Sophia because
of his ongoing affair with Molly Seagrim. Sophia first becomes aware of
the intensity of her own interest in Tom when he approaches her about
assisting Black George, and her response to his request prompts an effu-
sion of gratitude from Tom (IV.v.167–68). At this point in the narrative,
however, Tom is presented as having "no Design upon her Person"
(IV.v.166)—a circumstance which is explained shortly afterward as a consequence of his affair with the gamekeeper's daughter. Since that affair is
clearly based in mutual sexual attraction rather than in more abstract considerations, we might argue that Tom's situation reflects the unstable separation of mind and body that distinguishes the early chapters of the novel.
Before the accident, he has one woman he pursues to satisfy his sexual

appetites and another who attracts him, for the moment at least, for purely sentimental reasons. In a sense, Sophia's fall and Tom's injury can be said to begin the process of reconciling these two apparently distinct kinds of desire. The process itself is reflected in the way certain details that had been noted in connection with Tom's liaison with Molly are revised and reenacted in the later episode with Sophia.

To be more specific, Sophia's accident occurs soon after the narrator's mock-epic, blow-by-blow description of the churchyard brawl between Molly and several villagers. Tom eventually breaks up the battle with his horsewhip, but not before Molly has had her hair pulled, her dress torn off her back, and her nose bloodied (IV.viii.182). In the later episode, the novelist goes somewhat out of his way to make certain both that Sophia is bled following her fall, and that Tom is there to witness the event. As with many of Fielding's set pieces, the churchyard scene demands a kind of multilevel interpretation. On one level, it can be read as a predictable exposure of the relative merits of Tom's attachment to Sophia and his attachment to Molly. The poise and good humor of Sophia present a sharp contrast to the disheveled and bellicose Molly, and the narrator's rather laconic account of Tom's reaction—"when he saw the Blood springing from the lovely Arm of *Sophia*, he scarce thought of what had happened to himself" (IV.xiv.204)—invites comparison with the description of Tom's response to the attack against Molly, where he "raved like a Madman, beat his Breast, tore his Hair, stamped on the Ground, and vowed the utmost Vengeance on all who had been concerned" (IV.vii.183–84). From this angle, the contrast between mock-epic histrionics and more straightforward narration displays Sophia's temperament to good advantage, and suggests that Tom, like the male ingenues in any number of Shakespeare's plays, reveals the immaturity of his sensibility through the operatic extravagance of his actions and his declarations on Molly's behalf.

We can also, however, read the narrator's account of the churchyard brawl and the different medical treatments administered to Tom and Sophia as commentaries on the vulnerability of the human body in relation to both the official and unofficial representatives of social authority. In the churchyard scene, Molly Seagrim is attacked because she is both pregnant out of wedlock and better dressed than many of the parishioners. In the later scene, the lynch mob is replaced by the self-important surgeon, who is presented as an unmistakable threat to the health of both Tom and Sophia. When the surgeon supports the squire's assertion that Sophia should be bled, the narrator comments that this proposal was "entirely contrary to her own Inclinations: For she suspected, I believe, less Danger from the Fright, than either the Squire or the Surgeon" (IV.xiv.203). The syntax here is susceptible to two very different interpretations: does Sophia suspect less danger than her father and his surgeon suspect, or does she suspect that the fright was less dangerous than the two men might turn out to be? Luckily, her promise to forgive the surgeon even if he opens an artery reminds her father of what is at stake here, and his threats force the doctor to treat Sophia a bit more conservatively than he might have.

Tom is less fortunate. When Western first learned of his injury, he had promised to "get a Joiner to mend un again" (IV.xiii.201), and the surgeon does in fact treat Tom's broken arm as though it were a piece of furniture. He hurts Tom badly and unnecessarily, and he refuses even to acknowledge the existence of the pain he has caused (IV.xiv.204). Foucault has spoken and written about the crucial role played by doctors in the definition and enforcement of certain kinds of social control over the individual body.[4] Fielding's handling of this episode clearly demonstrates his awareness of this role and the power it conveys to the professional. Perhaps more importantly, by allowing Sophia to be first threatened by and then saved from the surgeon's incompetence, the novelist hints at the value of both Squire Western's anarchistic impulses and his extreme devotion to the physical well-being of his daughter. Similarly, by subjecting Tom to that incompetence, Fielding calls into question the wisdom of those who do not mistrust authority and dramatizes the fate of those who lack the social status that might protect them from officially sanctioned forms of physical abuse.

Nor is this connection the only important parallel between these two scenes. The churchyard brawl and the aftermath of Tom's accident are also linked by Fielding's distinctive and recurring tendency to punctuate every act of violence in the novel with a sudden and unexpected shift away from brutality and toward voyeurism. In the final stages of Molly's battle, after having been expected to absorb four pages of mock-epic head-knocking, the reader suddenly encounters two paragraphs of speculation about why women engaged in hand-to-hand combat allegedly do not "assail the Bosoms of each other," followed by the suggestion that Tom swoops down from his horse just in time to prevent the flat-chested and jealous Goody Brown from striking "a fatal Blow" at Molly's more substantial breasts (IV.viii.178–83). Since this kind of leering silliness seems to support the perception of Fielding as the eighteenth-century equivalent of a fraternity boy, it is something of a relief to discover in the later scene that this tendency is not limited to male narrators:

> Among the good Company which had attended in the Hall during [Tom's] Bone-setting, Mrs. *Honour* was one; who being summoned to her Mistress as soon as it was over, and asked by her how the young Gentleman did, presently launched into extravagant Praises on the *Magnimity*, as she called it, of his Behaviour, which, she said, 'was so charming in so pretty a Creature.' She then burst forth into much warmer Encomiums on the Beauty of his Person; enumerating many Particulars, and ending with the Whiteness of his Skin.
>
> This Discourse had an Effect on *Sophia's* Countenance, which would not perhaps have escaped the Observance of the sagacious Waiting-woman, had she once looked her Mistress in the Face, . . .   (IV.xiv.204–5)

Coming as it does immediately after the doctor's ill treatment of Tom's injury, Honour's innocent testimonial suggests that on some level Fielding conceives of sexual desire as a kind of saving grace or as compensation for the troubling susceptibility of the human body to physical damage and decay.

In the case of the attack on Molly Seagrim, this odd juxtaposition of sex and violence is part of an even more elemental opposition between love and death, with roughly the same type of woman occupying both poles of the comparison. By situating this episode in a churchyard, Fielding makes it seem barely plausible that his various combatants would have armed themselves with human skulls and bones to use as both weapons and props, and that his description of the terrain could include an open grave. As a result, there is no mistaking that the scene is designed to emphasize, however facetiously, the fact of human mortality. An assault on a pregnant woman under these circumstances suggests a deliberate attempt to stage a conflict between the opposite poles of physical existence; the human body's ability to create life is opposed directly to its vulnerability to physical force. Given this general context, the fact that Molly's chief antagonist is an Amazonian rabble-rouser seems like a typical case of conjuring up a female monster to distract attention from other kinds of oppression. It seems fairly obvious that this thumbnail sketch serves as the repository for whatever fears of female deviance Fielding may have harbored. Goody Brown's promiscuity, her maltreatment of her husband, her martial prowess, and even her bony figure recall many of the anxieties that surfaced in his treatment of castrati and transvestite performers on his own stage.[5] On some level, the implication here is that Molly, bare-breasted and pregnant, represents woman in her natural state, while her opponent, who claims to be the self-appointed champion of conventional morality, is in fact an avatar of the dreaded Woman Out of Control. The manner in which this particular conflict is worked out can hardly inspire confidence in Fielding's feelings or judgments on the part of feminist readers. It seems to me, however, that the evident misogyny of this passage[6] is gradually undermined by what happens in the later parts of the novel. I will have more to say on this point shortly.

Partly because of the treatment accorded in these early pages to characters like Molly and Goody Brown, Sophia seems at first to be more ideal than real. Obviously, her physical presence is treated much more gingerly than that of Tom or Molly; in fact, whatever humor there is in the scene with the surgeon stems primarily from the implied comparison between what happens to her and what happened to Molly. The crucial exception to this generalization is the series of scenes that focuses on Sophia's muff—scenes which, with their obvious double-entendres on the slang expression for female genitals, keep the issue of her sexuality clearly and more or less continuously before the reader.[7] In *Occasional Form*, J. Paul Hunter has noted that both the title character and the heroine of Fielding's *Joseph Andrews* appear at first to be "comic object[s]," but that they gradually develop into "flesh-and-blood character[s]" (105–6). Something like this process occurs with Sophia in *Tom Jones*, except of course that she does not appear at first as a comic object, but rather as an idealized (and hence disembodied) vision of a virtuous young woman. Where readers of the earlier novel must be taught to take Joseph and Fanny more seriously than they seem at first to deserve, readers of *Tom Jones* must be taught to think about Sophia in ways that have little to do with the platonic ideal she represents.

Book IV of the novel seems to be devoted primarily to this process. The author's customary introductory chapter leads in this instance to the announcement that "Our Intention, in short, is to introduce our Heroine with the utmost Solemnity in our Power, with an Elevation of Stile, and all other Circumstances proper to raise the Veneration of our Reader" (IV.i.154). This is followed by the "sublime" introduction to Sophia, which consists primarily of allusions to various beautiful women in history and literature, and of rather general comments about the perfections of both her mind and her body. And where does this book end? After Molly's churchyard battle and Sophia's fall from the horse, after the entrance and exit of Western's surgeon, the final incident in the book is Honour's tale

about Tom kissing Sophia's muff and praising her as a "Goddess"—all of
which leads to

> Here the Dinner-bell interrupted a Conversation which had wrought such
> an Effect on *Sophia*, that she was, perhaps, more obliged to her bleeding in
> the Morning, than she, at the time, had apprehended she should be. As to
> the present Situation of her Mind, I shall adhere to a Rule of *Horace*, by not
> attempting to describe it, from Despair of Success. Most of my Readers will
> suggest it easily to themselves, and the few who cannot, would not under-
> stand the Picture, or at least would deny it to be natural, if ever so well drawn.
> (IV.xiv.208)

The passage begins by once again contrasting the physical experiences of
pain and pleasure. Moreover, since the second and third sentences amount
to no more than an apology for what the narrator does *not* say at this
point, the earlier reference to his heroine's physical condition stands as the
final substantive word on this part of the novel. The respectful solemnity
reflected in the original description of Sophia has become the basis for a
joke. The stuffy syntax and the misleading reference to the treatment she
received from her father's hired quack prompt the reader to think of Sophia in terms which are at least somewhat more earthy than those allotted
to her by Fielding's narrator.

The muff joke works in much the same manner. The slang meaning
of the term intrudes continuously on the narrator's ostensibly symbolic
purpose, which is to establish the object for both Tom and Sophia as a
metonymic substitute for the absent lover. Honour's account of Tom's first
encounter with this article pretends to describe a fervent admirer's romantic gesture. Tom's words emphasize the distance between him and his
"Angel" or "Goddess," while the image conjured up by Honour's words
eradicates the metaphorical distance between them: "'La,' says I, 'Mr. *Jones*,
you will stretch my Lady's Muff and spoil it;' but he still kept his Hands
in it, and then he kissed it—to be sure, I hardly ever saw such a Kiss in
my Life as he gave it" (IV.xiv.206–7). In this scene, as well as in that where
Sophia rescues the muff from the fire (V.iv), the sentiments of the lovers
themselves are not in any way undermined by the double-entendres. For
the moment, at least, Tom's rhetoric counterbalances Honour's inadver-
tently ribald description, and there is nothing overtly sexual about Sophia's gesture in the latter case. In each case, the humor of the situation
stems from the artificial barrier between the sexual and the sentimental.

When the muff appears again amidst the chaos at Upton, Fielding

combines the sexual double-entendre and his thematic concerns to produce an elaborate literary joke that speaks directly to his sense of the relationship between lofty sentiments and the physical facts of human
experience. Although this joke is based on a well-known scene borrowed
from the eighteenth-century London stage, Fielding scholars have apparently failed to notice the connection. In order to correct this oversight, I
will digress briefly to provide the necessary background information.

When Sophia discovers that Tom has been staying in the inn at Upton, and that he has been to bed with Jenny Waters, she leaves quickly,
stopping only long enough to place her muff in the bed where Tom has
been sleeping. When Tom returns to his room and discovers the muff, he
exclaims "Oh Heavens! How came this muff here?" (X.vi.548) and decides
that from that moment forward he will devote his life to the pursuit of
Sophia. Tom's initial response alludes quite explicitly to a famous scene
from *The Careless Husband* (1704), a relatively well-known comedy written
by Colley Cibber. By the 1740s, a number of characters in Cibber's sentimental comedy had become bywords to the theater-going public, but the
play was best known for its "steinkirk scene." Supposedly based on a true
incident involving one of Cibber's acquaintances, this episode represents
the turning point in the marriage involving the philandering Sir Charles
Easy and his long-suffering wife. Their moment of crisis occurs a little way
into Act V, when Lady Easy discovers her husband asleep in a chair with
a maidservant in his lap. Instead of upbraiding him for this, she simply
places her handkerchief (her "steinkirk") on his head and leaves the scene.
When Sir Charles awakens, he finds his wife's handkerchief and exclaims
"How now! What's this? How came this here?" (V.v.38–39); soon afterward, his sense of the understated nobility of her gesture brings about his
rapid reformation.

Tom's situation at Upton is clearly analogous to that of Cibber's Sir
Charles, and his exclamation upon discovering the muff obviously alludes
to Sir Charles's comment in a similar situation. Given the relative popularity of *The Careless Husband*, it seems safe to assume that many of Fielding's readers would have recognized Tom's inadvertent obscenity as a
parody of a literary convention which had been promoted by Cibber and
other sentimentalist playwrights. Tom's words invoke this convention in
order to signal to Fielding's readers that his hero, like Sir Charles, is about
to commit himself to changing his ways. At the same time, they attack the
characteristically sudden reformations of sentimental stage comedies by
reminding Fielding's audience of the material dimension that Cibber left

out of his reckoning. For a variety of reasons, the rise of sentimentalism in the first half of the eighteenth century was associated with and accompanied by an increasing reserve about certain subjects, including that of the human body. We have seen the evidence of this in the outraged response to Mother Lupine's assessment of Caelia, and in Richardson's typography of women, which eventually divides female humanity into bad women, who have bodies, and good women, who do not. In the case of *The Careless Husband*, the sudden reformation of Sir Charles depends to a great extent on the assumption that an individual's physical attractions can and should be dictated by that individual's moral sensibility. Because Fielding's double-entendre relies once again on the safe assumption that his audience will read the muff as both a literal object and a reference to a woman's genitals, the passage may also lead his readers to concede that their own sexual interests are more difficult to ignore than Cibber's formulation implies.

Obviously, Tom's question refers not only to how the muff itself appeared in his bed, but also to how, in the light of his previous commitment to Sophia, he came to be sleeping with Mrs. Waters. The question hangs in the air until Tom's final conversation with Sophia, where she herself raises the issue in a more serious way and receives in return not one, but two very different responses. Tom's first answer is to show Sophia her own reflection in the mirror, and to argue that that image "would fix a *Dorimant*, a Lord *Rochester*" (XVIII.xii.973). Sophia responds to this claim by suggesting that images, like bodies, are impermanent: "'If I am to judge,' said she, 'of the future by the past, my Image will no more remain in your Heart, when I am out of your Sight, than it will in this Glass when I am out of the Room'" (XVIII.xii.972). In response to this, Tom apologizes to Sophia once more and tells her that "the Delicacy of your Sex cannot conceive of the Grossness of ours, nor how little one Sort of Amour has to do with the Heart." Sophia's rejoinder—"I will never marry a Man . . . who shall not learn Refinement enough to be as incapable as I am myself of making such a Distinction" (XVIII.xii.973)—does *not* suggest that she expects Tom to stifle his desires; instead, she demands that he recognize that the artificial separation between lust and sentiment is indeed artificial.

Tom tries to assert that one sort of "amour" has nothing to do with the other, but Sophia denies the distinction, and insists on a comprehensive connection between sentiment and behavior. Like any good hero, Fielding's protagonist promises to make such a connection: "the first

Moment of Hope that my *Sophia* might be my Wife taught . . . me [refine-ment] at once; and all the rest of her Sex from that Moment became as little the Objects of Desire to my Sense, as of Passion to my Heart" (XVIII.xii.973). Unfortunately, if this claim is examined in light of the plot up to this point, it must be considered extravagant. Flying in the face of Tom's past behavior and Sophia's better judgment, it asserts that the passions of the heart and the desires of the senses can be shaped and controlled by a conscious commitment to whatever transcendent principle Sophia is presumed to represent. Either Tom has changed or he has not. If he *has* changed, the probationary period that Sophia requests could be summarized in a sentence or two: the precedent for this sort of dismissal appears at the beginning of Book III, where Fielding's narrator quickly disposes of twelve years of Tom's childhood with the claim that "nothing happened worthy of being recorded in a Chronicle of this Kind" (116). If Fielding really wished merely to demonstrate the value of acquiring prudence, he did have this option available; when he brings in Squire Western instead, the marriage of Tom and Sophia suddenly takes on an impulsive aspect which in many respects is at odds with the cautious good sense of his heroine.

Readers may feel that Tom has indeed changed, but Sophia knows less about Tom than they do, and in that light her hesitation seems not only understandable but even reasonable. In point of fact, the ambivalence of both the character and the novelist is entirely justified. Sophia wants certainty, but the plot of the novel has demonstrated repeatedly the fallibility of good intentions and good nature, regardless of whether those traits are accompanied (as in Allworthy's case) by prudence or left (as in Tom's case) to fend for themselves. When Fielding presents Sophia's uncontrollable father as the solution to this problem, he effectively concedes the point that prudence alone is an inadequate guide for human behavior. Squire Western's impatient intervention reminds Fielding's readers that even where such paragons of virtue as Sophia and Squire Allworthy are concerned, every emotional commitment to another human being requires a leap of faith.

To the extent that the appetite attributed explicitly to Tom and at least implicitly to Sophia coincides with the political interests of both Western and Allworthy, this ending argues once again for the redemptive value of sexual appetite. Since the ending comes about despite, rather than because of, Sophia's expressed intentions, it cannot be viewed as feminist—at least, not to the point that it could constitute any sort of challenge to what was construed in the eighteenth century as the right of fathers to dispose of their daughters in almost any manner they thought fit. At the same time, it would be difficult to maintain that this ending is the unreflective and uncomplicated paean to patriarchy that some critics have seen here. Perhaps the most important detail with respect to this point is the fact that Fielding takes pains to separate Western's parental tyranny from Allworthy's more legitimate authority. Immediately before Tom's reunion with his uncle, Allworthy extracts a promise from Western not to bully his daughter into marrying Tom—a circumstance which elicits from Western the comment that "I don't know how 'tis, but d——n me, *Allworthy*, if you don't make me always do just as you please, and yet I have as good an Esteate as you, and am in the Commission of the Peace as well as yourself" (XVIII.ix.958). Of course, Western does end up doing what he pleases. This conversation simply indicates that he does so without Allworthy's support. The divided opinion of the two fathers suggests that it is not the voice of paternal authority, but rather the voice of sheer impulse that leads or forces Sophia to risk her happiness on Tom's promises.

Like Richardson's Clarissa, Sophia returns at the end of her life to her father's house. Of course, the crucial difference here is that Clarissa is speaking in allegory—her father's house is completely abstract and spiritual—while the literal reality of Squire Western's estate is as palpable and as earthy as ever. The squire will continue to hunt and get drunk, and Sophia will continue to accompany the latter activity on her harpsichord. Meanwhile, many of the characters who were condemned at earlier points in the text for various sins of the flesh—the two most important of these are Molly Seagrim and Jenny Waters—have been forgiven and even rewarded by the new bride and groom (XVIII. xiii.980–81). Most importantly, perhaps, Tom and Sophia have two children (a boy and a girl)—a demographic detail that indicates they have broken the sterile pattern of the previous generation, where no marriage produced more than one child who survived to adulthood.

Earlier in this discussion, I suggested that the rigid separation of mind and body in the Somersetshire section is abandoned by the end of the novel. This abandonment is manifested to some degree in Fielding's happy final portrait, but the shift in the case of Sophia was not extreme. The novelist treated her as an emblem only long enough to set up the series of comparisons which quickly established that she was meant ultimately to represent a human being. To arrive at a clear picture of Fielding's shift away from the naive Cartesianism of the early chapters, we need to focus not on Sophia or Molly, but rather on the previous generation of women—that is, on Bridget Allworthy and Jenny Waters.

*   *   *

In my discussion of *Clarissa*, I noted Peter Brooks's comment about the crucial process of "reading back from the end" in order to understand how the earlier events in a particular plot helped to shape and determine later ones. Sudden revelations like those made by and about Jenny Waters at the end of *Tom Jones* take this process to an extreme in two distinct ways. First, they force the reader to recognize that certain apparently random details from the earlier part of the text do in fact fit into a coherent pattern of development. Thus, for example, the news that Bridget Allworthy was Tom's mother provides a simple and straightforward explanation for her uncharacteristic willingness to approve her brother's lenient treatment of Jenny Jones (I.viii.56–57), and helps to explain why she loved Tom better than she loved Blifil (III.vi.139–40). The last-minute reversals also force readers to find new explanations for events that seemed perfectly under-standable but were in fact misinterpreted at the time. Thus, Allworthy's refusal to condemn Bridget's behavior with any degree of enthusiasm (XVIII.vii.942) forces the reader to reevaluate the occasional assaults on her character in the Somersetshire chapters. Similarly, the news that Jenny Jones and Mrs. Waters are the same person enables us to make sense of certain details linking the earlier descriptions of these two characters, but it also forces us to rethink the judgments that were based on what we thought we knew about them as separate individuals.

As Ian Watt has pointed out, the name of Fielding's hero is "made up of two of the most common names in the language" (272). Contrary, how-ever, to the impression created by this comment, the novel does provide specific sources for both Tom's surname and his Christian name. Both are assigned to the foundling infant by Allworthy, who gives him his own first name and the last name of Jenny Jones, the young woman who claims and is mistakenly assumed to be his mother. The connection between Field-ing's hero and Squire Allworthy is obvious from the beginning of the novel; the squire is a model of benevolence, and Tom is a fundamentally good man who, like his namesake, is metaphorically isolated among the self-interested villains who come and go at Paradise Hall. His connection to Jenny Jones is no less important, but it is perhaps less accessible to the first-time reader, because her character is so ambiguous at first and so pro-tean in retrospect.

From a feminist reader's perspective, the portrait of Jenny Jones which appears in the Somersetshire chapters of the novel is anything but promising. Fielding's narrator introduces her by noting that she

> was no very comely Girl, either in her Face or Person; but Nature had some-what compensated the Want of Beauty with what is generally more esteemed by those Ladies whose Judgment is arrived at Years of perfect Maturity; for she had given her a very uncommon Share of Understanding. This Gift *Jenny* had a good deal improved by Erudition. She had lived several Years a Servant with a Schoolmaster, who discovering a great Quickness of Parts in the Girl, and an extraordinary Desire of learning, . . . had the Good-nature, or Folly (just as the Reader pleases to call it,) to instruct her so far, that she obtained a competent Skill in the Latin Language, and was perhaps as good a Scholar as most of the young Men of Quality of the Age. (I.vi.48)

At its outset, the description seems fairly straightforward; in the narrator's eyes, Jenny is intelligent but not handsome. Once this contrast is established, however, the remainder of the passage tries very hard to subvert its original premises. Time and again, the narrator gives us what appears to be useful information concerning her education, only to force us upon further reflection to read each new detail as though it referred instead to a sexual liaison. Because Jenny's "Quickness of Parts" is discovered by the schoolmaster rather than being simply attributed to her by the narrator, the phrase (which is ambiguous to begin with) seems to hint at a physical rather than an intellectual relationship; likewise, the reader might be more willing to believe in her "extraordinary Desire of learning" if Fielding had capitalized the second noun as well as the first ("Learning" is capitalized twice on the two pages following this passage). Similarly, the question of whether her interest in books contributed in some way to her alleged incontinence is raised and dropped without an answer, and the compliment to her scholarship is deflated almost immediately by the novelist's ironic allusion to the educations received by contemporary young men of quality.

Jenny's appearance before Allworthy and her subsequent disappearance from the novel recapitulate this tension between what seem to be facetious tributes to her intelligence and disapproving references to her alleged sexual relationships. She listens patiently and silently to the squire's sermon about Chastity until he describes her unknown seducer as "a false, designing, treacherous, pretended Friend, who intend[ed] not only to debauch [your] Body, but [your] Understanding at the same Time"—at which point she displays so much "Concern" that Allworthy feels obliged to set off in a different and more reassuring vein (I.vii.53). After complimenting her "good Sense," the squire concludes by telling her that he will give her some money and send her away so that she can "avoid the Punishment which . . . is allotted to your Crime in this World" (I.vii.53). Given the fate she had been spared—Fielding reminds his audience repeatedly that Allworthy could have committed her to Bridewell—Jenny's final expression of gratitude is remarkable for what appears to be its misplaced emphasis:

> 'I beg leave to assure you, Sir, that I take your Advice much kinder, than your generous Offer with which you concluded it. For as you are pleased to say, Sir, it is an Instance of your Opinion of my Understanding—' Here her Tears flowing apace, she stopped a few Moments, and then proceeded thus, 'Indeed, Sir, your Kindness overcomes me, but I will endeavour to deserve this good Opinion; for if I have the Understanding you are so kindly pleased to allow me, such Advice cannot be thrown away upon me.'   (I.vii.54)

Although there is no reason to suspect her sincerity here, our next glimpse of Jenny shows her having apparently eloped with a recruiting officer (II.vi.101). As a result, the reader is apt to conclude that Allworthy's advice was indeed thrown away on her, and that her pretensions to "Understanding" were little more than that.

The early descriptions of Bridget, like those of Jenny Jones, do her very little credit. Like Jenny, Bridget is not considered to be physically attractive (I.ii.36–37), and like Deborah Wilkins, she is extremely jealous and censorious of those who are (I.viii.57). Bridget's intellectual pretensions, like those of Jenny Jones, are repeatedly revealed to be tinged with carnality. Alter has argued that the descriptions of Bridget's disputes with Captain Blifil about religious subjects can easily be read as oblique descriptions of a premarital sexual relationship (41–42). Her marriage to Blifil is an unmitigated disaster, a consequence of both her own confused motives and his purely mercenary approach to the union. As the narrator tells us,

> long before [Capt. Blifil] had discovered any flattering Symptoms in Miss *Bridget*, [he] had been greatly enamoured; that is to say, of Mr. *Allworthy's* House and Gardens, and of his Lands, Tenements, and Hereditaments; of all which the Captain was so passionately fond, that he would most probably have contracted Marriage with them, had he been obliged to have taken the Witch of *Endor* into the Bargain.   (I.xi.67)

The gratuitous swipe at Bridget in the final clause is in keeping with the way she is treated throughout these early books. Nothing about the character is remotely likable; even her single redeeming feature—her fondness for little Tommy—is presented at first as uncharacteristic and therefore

somewhat mysterious (I.v.44–45), and later as an accidental virtue growing out of her inveterate dislike of her detestable husband (II.vii.106).

A number of critics seem to have taken their cue from this early portrait and have joined the narrator in his derogatory assessment of Bridget's
character. When the narrator links her interest in religious controversies
to her namesake St. Brigid (the patron of Ireland who once conducted a
public argument with the pope himself), Martin Battestin, the editor of
the Wesleyan edition, adds a footnote that indicates that the name also
connected her to Bridewell and hence to loose women (I.x.62,n.). Van
Boheemen takes up an even more extreme position, arguing that young
Blifil's villainy is made possible only because his mother has concealed the
truth about Tom's origins, and that in Fielding's eyes it is Bridget and not
her scheming second son "whose dissembling hypocrisy is the origin of all
of Tom's troubles" (80). Although I wish neither to deny nor to defend
the misogyny inherent in these early characterizations of Bridget, I would
like to suggest that as Tom's story continues, the narrator's attitude toward
both Jenny and Bridget undergoes a radical change. This change can be
summarized by identifying three crucial differences between the world Sophia flees and from which Tom is banished and the world to which they
both return at the end of the novel. The first of these differences—the shift
of the center of the Somersetshire community from Paradise Hall to Western's unnamed estate—has already been mentioned. The second involves
the retroactive devaluation of paternal bloodlines, and the simultaneous
valorization of matrilineal connections.

When the dust finally settles at the end of the novel, it is not Tom's
father but his mother who connects him to Paradise Hall. When Jenny
Waters reveals the truth to Allworthy, her account begins with a clergyman
named Summer, who appears for the first time in the novel in her speech
and who disappears from the novel permanently long before she finishes
speaking. Allworthy, like Fielding's readers, must wait until Bridget is
named before he can make sense of the new information at his disposal
(XVIII.vii.942). The structure of Jenny's account emphasizes the irrele-
vance of Summer, who died before Tom was born and whose naming
solves nothing for anyone. Although Bridget apparently could have married him, she never did; thus it is only Tom's connection to Bridget,
coupled with the exposure and expulsion of his legitimate but undeserving
half-brother, that leads Allworthy to take the extraordinary step of naming
his sister's bastard as his chief beneficiary.

Of course, such an outcome cannot be completely unexpected. Before
the story ever begins, Fielding has arranged both the Allworthy and the

(rather loudly) that Fitzpatrick and his companion burst in on her while she was sleeping, and that Tom responded to her cries for help. Tom goes along with the ruse and escapes in the ensuing confusion, perhaps while the narrator was comparing Mrs. Waters to a stage actress and wondering aloud why all women seem to be able to act the part of virtue even when they do not possess the quality itself (X.ii.531–32). This snide remark suggests that the novelist is still wrestling with the question of this character's moral status, and with the more general question of whether virtue is something to be performed or simply a physical state. The question is of particular importance at this point in the text, because the portrait of Mrs. Waters presents her as deeply embodied and morally careless and, nevertheless, an attractive and amiable character.

Fielding's descriptions of Mrs. Waters seem calculated to establish her as the exemplar of sturdy feminine physicality. In the short time that she figures in this part of Fielding's plot, she walks several miles, fights off an attacker, takes part in a backroom brawl, and eats and makes love heroically. William Empson notes quite correctly that Fielding approves of her ability to walk about the countryside without tiring ("*TJ*" 51), and he might have added that the narrator at least approves of her willingness and ability to defend herself against Northerton's attack (IX.vii.521–22). Along these same lines, the eating scene which precedes her sexual encounter with Tom at Upton is drawn for the reader in loving detail. Notwithstanding the obvious relish with which Fielding recounts these events, critics have generally lumped Mrs. Waters in with Molly Seagrim and Lady Bellaston as part of a group of disreputable women whom Tom ought to have avoided. There are details in the text that seem to support this view. Fielding's narrator reports in disapproving tones the possibility that Mrs. Waters had been carrying on an adulterous affair with Ensign Northerton (IX.vi.514; vii.519), and her subsequent attachment to Mr. Fitzpatrick lends her little credit with the reader. In light of these circumstances, the summary of her character that precedes her appearance in Tom's prison cell in London—"who this Mrs. *Waters* was, the Reader pretty well knows; what she was he must be perfectly satisfied" (XVII.ix.909)—may seem only a little harsh.

In fact, however, anyone who knows how the story ends may be tempted to read this description ironically. After all, since at this point in the text we do *not* really know who Mrs. Waters is, we may also feel entitled to doubt the judgment put forth in the latter half of the sentence. The reader's sense of how to respond to Jenny Jones is undermined and reconstructed in much the same fashion. Earlier in the novel, when Allworthy discovers that she "had left her Habitation . . . with a recruiting Officer," he announces that "the evidence of such a Slut as she appeared to be, would have deserved no Credit" (II.vi.101). As it turns out, of course, Jenny is not the slut she appears to be, and her evidence is crucial.

Although the tolerance for harmless deviations from the straight and narrow is most obvious in the London chapters, it is clearly foreshadowed in the road section of the novel. Near the very center of the narrative, immediately after presenting his audience with two rather disapproving accounts of how Mrs. Waters came to be at the bottom of Mazard Hill, the narrator pauses to provide his audience with "a few wholesome Admonitions" concerning the proper way to respond to his novel. The last and most important of these admonitions is "not to condemn a Character as a bad one, because it is not perfectly a good one" (X.i.526). In the paragraph following this assertion, he continues to develop this point, this time in terms which refer equally to both Tom and Mrs. Waters:

> In Fact, if there be enough of Goodness in a Character to engage the Admiration and Affection of a well-disposed Mind, though there should appear some of those little Blemishes, *quas humana parum cavit natura*, they will raise our Compassion rather than our Abhorrence. (X.i.527)

The choice of the nouns "admiration" and "affection" allows for an attitude that encompasses not only ethical and emotional considerations, but erotic interests as well. In his explanation of why Tom and Mrs. Waters end up in bed together, the narrator discusses the carnal aspect of "affection" at some length, and although the passage as a whole is heavily laced with irony, he is careful to assert beforehand that "it will be a Mark more of Prudery than Candour to entertain a bad Opinion of [Mrs. Waters] because she conceived a very good Opinion of [Tom]" (IX.v.510). In any case, the point is simply that the tolerance and understanding advocated here, although it will be threatened by the incest scare in Book XVIII, is not simply a matter of last-minute generosity on the novelist's part. Rather, it is predicted at the center of the novel, and confirmed, not initiated, by the general amnesty extended in Fielding's final chapter.

*   *   *

Nothing about *Tom Jones* has generated so much controversy as Fielding's brief flirtation with the topic of incest at the end of the novel. For the most part, both supporters and detractors of the novelist have treated this episode as though Fielding expects his readers to take the possibility of incest very seriously. On the one hand, Fielding's supporters see this episode as a means of demonstrating his sincerity as a moralist without compromising his fundamentally comic vision of life; on the other, his detractors see it as a melodramatic trick.[9] Although I accept in principle the latter definition, I would also like to suggest that the purpose behind this trick has been generally misunderstood. Although the incest episode seems like a climax when it occurs, it is quickly exposed as a kind of false bottom to the novel. Ultimately, the whole incident serves as little more than a calculated feint in the direction of a rather Draconian morality—as what might be called, with apologies to Ronald S. Crane, the tragic analogue of the manner in which the novel is actually concluded.

This reading of the incest episode is supported in part by the fact that all this fuss is kicked up by Partridge, the superstitious Jacobite who up to this point in the novel has been wrong about *everything*. The narrator even reminds his readers of the little barber's absurd credulity by noting that when Partridge burst into Tom's prison cell, he "looked as he would have done had he seen a Spectre" (XVIII.ii.915). The letter Tom receives from Mrs. Waters shortly after Partridge's last and greatest error also hints that the situation is not what it seems. The letter itself is another of Fielding's small masterpieces of misdirection. As Empson points out, Jenny could not have known about Partridge's mistake when the letter was written (53), but Tom manages to read the letter entirely as though it did refer to their supposedly incestuous encounter. The reader may be no wiser in this regard than Fielding's hero, until the postscript, where Mrs. Waters attempts to reassure Tom by telling him that "whatever other grievous Crimes you may have to repent of, the Guilt of Blood is not among the Number" (XVIII.ii.917); the guilt she refers to is that of murder, but her word choice alludes to the alternate meaning of "blood" as kin and thus hints at the eventual resolution of this problem.

Of course, the impulse to treat the incest scare as a crisis seems to be supported by Tom himself (XVIII.ii.915–16), who uses Partridge's shocking news as an occasion for a kind of blanket self-recrimination ("why do I blame Fortune? I am myself the Cause of all my Misery"). This speech is generally perceived as an indication that Tom has at last achieved a degree of self-knowledge, but we need to be careful about taking it too literally. Fielding's hero might have been better off in the long run had he resisted the advances of Molly Seagrim, Jenny Waters, and Lady Bellaston, but blaming himself for *all* of his misery may seem a bit excessive in light of the incessant scheming produced by the competition to inherit Allworthy's

wealth. Even the squire himself recommends prudence to Tom not because it is inherently valuable, but rather because "when a Man lays the
Foundation of his own Ruin, others will, I am afraid, be too apt to build
upon it" (XVIII.x.960). Readers who know how the novel ends may also
connect Tom's self-accusation with Allworthy's lecture to Jenny Jones on
chastity; that is, they may recognize that although it is in certain respects
the right speech, it is (at least insofar as its central premise is concerned)
the wrong occasion. In any case, the second intervention of Jenny Waters
not only obviates any further speculation about incest, but also raises questions about the narrator's comment before her visit to Tom's prison cell,
about the innuendoes regarding her relationships with Ensign Northerton
and Captain Waters, and even about Allworthy's disgruntled remark following her elopement.

Early in the incest episode, the novelist alludes to the process Brooks
calls reading back from the ending. In the course of explaining how his
characters could accidentally commit incest, Fielding's narrator tells his
audience to review the Upton chapters in order to "admire the many
strange Accidents which unfortunately prevented any Interview between
Partridge and Mrs. *Waters*, when she spent a whole Day there with
Mr. *Jones*" (XVIII.ii.916). Of course, readers who know the story will recognize that the allusion to a possible reunion between Partridge and Jenny
Waters is simply a parodic foreshadowing of the reunion that actually did
have to occur before Tom could be saved—that, of course, being the reunion between the former Jenny Jones and Thomas Allworthy. The consequences of that reunion are clear. Although Jenny Waters could not have
been considered virtuous by any eighteenth-century standards, she is rewarded in the novel in both figurative and material terms for her fidelity
to Tom and for clearing the air with Allworthy. To be more specific, it is
Jenny Waters, not the squire, who first tells Tom who his parents really
were (XVIII.x.959), and (as I mentioned earlier) a note on the next to the
last page of the novel indicates that she "had a Pension of *60 l.* a Year
settled upon her by Mr. *Allworthy*, and is married to Parson *Supple*"
(XVIII.xiii.981). This last shift in fortunes is all the more remarkable because it amounts to a long-deferred fulfillment of the squire's original intentions regarding the virginal Jenny Jones (I.vi.50). Thus Allworthy's
largesse at the end of the novel can also be read as a reversal of his earlier
judgment.

In a sense, Tom is saved from himself by the protean nature of Jenny
Jones. As long as she is considered to be Tom's biological mother, Tom is

trapped in the legal schemes controlled and designed by Blifil and his allies. However, when she reappears in her guise as Mrs. Waters, and when her second personality is linked to her first, the eventual result is the rescue of Tom and the happy reordering of the Somersetshire community. This effect is heightened by the reader's awareness that the successive reincarnations of Jenny Waters seem to have been designed to bridge the differences between herself and at least three other major female characters in the novel. That she stands in for Bridget Allworthy at both the beginning and the end of the novel is obvious, but she is also linked by a number of details in the text to Molly Seagrim and Sophia Western. Tom's initial encounter with Mrs. Waters is connected to Molly's churchyard battle by Jenny's willingness to put up a fight, by her shirtlessness, and by Tom's role as the heroic rescuer. Jenny also shares with Molly a reputation for physical strength and a casual attitude toward her choice of bedfellows. She is linked to Sophia by the crucial muff episode—in fact, Jenny is one of the few characters in the novel who might actually laugh at the joke—and she and Sophia are also traveling the same road to London and displaying much the same stamina and fortitude as they proceed.

These doubling effects are of course only temporary and partial, but they do create opportunities for making certain useful comparisons and connections. For example, in the case of the two battlefield episodes involving Molly and Jenny, it is worth noting that the role occupied by Goody Brown in the first episode has been taken over by Tom's nemesis Ensign Northerton in the second. The substitution may suggest both a renunciation of the misogynistic fantasy lurking beneath the surface of the earlier incident, and, perhaps, a newfound willingness to explore the various forms of male misconduct enacted by Northerton, Fitzpatrick, Fellamar, Nightingale, Blifil, and of course Tom himself. More importantly, this series of connections suggests that in the view of the novelist, the frailties and virtues of the sometimes-reviled Jenny Waters are the frailties and virtues of womankind in general. Thus the happiness offered to her at the end of the novel is not only a victory for the individual character, but also a more general gesture of reconciliation.

Ultimately, of course, there is no way to escape the fact that the social order which is set right by Blifil's expulsion and Tom's recuperation is headed by Thomas Allworthy, not Bridget Allworthy or Jenny Waters. At the same time, however, Fielding's plot is constructed so that the recuperation of Tom Jones depends on the intervention and recuperation of Jenny Waters, and no critic who believes that the novel seeks to discredit or exclude the feminine can explain why Jenny's role in Tom's recovery should be so important and so positive. One of the most widely accepted interpretations of the thematic argument of *Tom Jones* is Battestin's view that "[i]n *Tom Jones* . . . Fielding's twin themes are Providence, the theological argument of the book's design, and Prudence, the moral doctrine of its fable" (*PW*, 164). In a sense, the greatest virtue of the recent, more theoretically informed treatments of the novel has been their willingness to pursue the political implications of this reading to their logical conclusion.[10] If the novel did in fact seek only to exalt the virtue of prudence and to exclude the elements that led Fielding's hero to behave imprudently, the oppressive force of the law and conventional morality would indeed exclude the feminine and the physical from the world defined by the novel's happy ending. I believe, however, that Fielding's moral and aesthetic vision is considerably more complicated than this.

In an earlier chapter, I alluded to Jill Campbell's argument that certain aspects of Fielding's plays reflect a tension between his belief in the value and importance of some rather conventional moral judgments, and his fascination with the ability of human beings (whether on- or offstage) to change their shape at will in order to evade, and sometimes even to modify, those judgments. The vision of Fielding put forth in Battestin's recent biography suggests that the plays were the product of an immature artistic sensibility, and implies that we might on that account expect that the maturity of *Tom Jones* would be reflected in part by a final resolution of the ambivalence Campbell sees in Fielding's stage pieces. In a sense, both van Boheemen and Battestin do read *Tom Jones* in this fashion, with the latter approving and the former disapproving the choice that Fielding has supposedly made. My own sense is that part of the vitality of Fielding's masterpiece derives from the manner in which the shape-shifting Jenny Waters successfully interferes—not only with the schemes of the lawyers and fortune-hunters who manage Allworthy so successfully in her absence, but also with the rather sterile tranquility of Paradise Hall.

Postscript

In an essay published in G. S. Rousseau's 1990 anthology *The Languages of Psyche*, Roy Porter denounces the misperception on the part of some cultural materialists that "the triumph of the bourgeoisie involved the disappearance of the body and its replacement by the book" (48). Although the argument presented in my study makes a claim which at times has resembled this one, I hope I have nonetheless avoided the kind of reductionism to which Porter properly objects. My primary defense against this criticism would be the narrow scope of my inquiry; I have focused not on bourgeois culture as a whole, but rather on the literary marketplace within that rising culture and on the ways in which that marketplace was shaped and disrupted by various extraliterary forces. I have argued that the presence of human performers invites, and in many cases requires, theater audiences to acknowledge the fundamental human connection between the character, the performer, and the spectator, and also that when these characters were shifted from the stage to the pages of the realist novel, the option of eliciting such an acknowledgment was left to the writers, who sometimes withheld that recognition to make or underscore a specific point. Obviously, the institutional forces that produced the change were not designed with this purpose in mind; the Stage Licensing Act was passed chiefly to prevent certain topical satirists from embarrassing the Ministry any further, and secondarily to reinforce the value of the patents held by the Drury Lane and Covent Garden theaters. I think it would be possible to argue that these goals somehow encompassed the goal of making the human body less prominent as an element of literary representation, but I have not attempted to work out the details of that position.

Furthermore, even within the narrow range of my own discussion, I would be unwilling to contend that either "the novel" or "the stage" spoke with one voice about the issue at hand. Instead, I have mapped out a dialectical pattern that retains at least its general shape even when it shifts from the medium of performance to that of print. I argued that *Clarissa* demonstrates one of the ways in which the medium of print can be used to defend an absolute rejection of the world of physical experience, but that in *Tom Jones* the novelist's sympathetic interest in physical experience generates a contrapuntal voice that resists a similar sort of totalizing abstraction. Likewise, it seems to me that *The Beggar's Opera* acknowledges both the risks and the pleasures of physical experience, while *The London Merchant* claims that failing to subordinate desire to reason and social convention will lead inevitably to social and personal catastrophe.

What I want to suggest at this point is first, that the authoritarian voice of the bourgeois culture of this era does seem to be interested in devaluing the human body as such; and second, that eighteenth-century English culture nevertheless included some voices that continued to resist the official line on these matters. I am thinking particularly here of Charlotte Charke, whose position in the heart of my discussion may still be in need of some defense. The structure of my argument presents a small group of canonical texts arrayed symmetrically around a marginalized figure. I have already explained her connection to *The London Merchant* and *Clarissa*, but I have not yet explored her position in relation to *The Beggar's Opera* and *Tom Jones*.

In my discussion of Gay's satire, I noted that *The Beggar's Opera* seems at times to stigmatize every woman who is not Polly as both mercenary and intolerant. The same sort of definition by negative example surfaces in the aftermath of the Stage Licensing Act, where the new legitimacy granted to the chosen few at Covent Garden and Drury Lane was matched by a new stigma attached to performers who could no longer find work at the non-patent-holding theaters. Lucy Lockit may sneak back into the dance, and Millwood's Lucy gets across the border between depravity and respectability just in time, but in the real world Charke herself was left on the outside while David Garrick began his campaign to make the theater world more respectable. This banishment led more or less inevitably to the series of disasters that make up the strolling part of her *Narrative*—the jail time, the poverty, and even the hashes the semi-professional actors made of the plays themselves. Many other performers were exiled along with Charke, but she was more resilient, more literate, and, perhaps, more willing to complain than most of her fellow expatriates. Because the riches-to-rags pattern traced by her life conflates the institutional forces that pushed her into exile with her self-obsessed authoritarian father, and because of the tone and content of the first half of the *Narrative*, most critics have quite properly focused on the family dynamic implicit in this model. (It is richly ironic that the works of Cibber himself—including several plays whose pious invocations of eighteenth-century "family values" were loudly praised at the time—may now be considered less valuable and less worthy of study than the autobiography of the daughter he disowned and disinherited.) At the same time, it would be a mistake to lose track of the institutional aspect of this struggle. Ultimately, her misfortunes and her astonishing ability to bounce back from them can be read not only in terms of her local resistance to a particularly egregious patriarch, but also in terms of the ways they reveal both the futility and the ferocity of the exclusionary efforts that had quietly victimized many less prominent individuals.

My attempt to imagine a connection between Charlotte Charke and *Tom Jones* has little more than a handful of interesting coincidences to lend it credence. There is, however, a remarkable string of similarities between what we know of the life of Charlotte Charke and Fielding's portrait of Jenny Jones. We first encounter Jenny Jones as a young woman who is scapegoated as the mother of an illegitimate child. Fielding's first contact with Charke may well have occurred in 1732, while she was playing Mother Lupine in Charles Johnson's *Caelia*. If so, what happened to Charke on this occasion might suggest the link between single motherhood and being condemned for one's sexual appetites which marks Jenny's first scenes in the novel. (Even the name Jenny Jones, with its alliteration and the echo of the first name in the second, seems on some level to recall that of Charlotte Charke.) Likewise, Jenny's second appearance, which culminates in her affair with Tom at Upton, might be construed as some sort of allusion to Charke's career as a strolling player. In this case, the connection rests upon the portrait of Jenny as a self-reliant female picaro wandering over the countryside of western England. Finally, in the London chapters of the novel, Jenny Waters appears in two more roles, the first as a violator of a fundamental sexual taboo, the second as the surprise witness who rescues the hero at the last minute by forcing the patriarch to listen to her side of the story—details that might (presumably without any conscious intention on the part of the novelist) allude to Charke's lesbianism and to her apparent willingness to make sure that all of her quarrels were put before the public.

Although Charke would not begin her *Narrative* until the mid-1750s, she was notorious in the mid-1740s for her efforts to circumvent the Stage Licensing Act with puppet shows, concerts, and so forth. Although I disagree with Jill Campbell's suggestion (80) that Fielding's knowledge of Charke provided him with some of the raw material for *The Female Husband*, I agree—not only with Campbell, but with Terry Castle ("MNF"

604) and with Kristina Straub (145) as well—that the portrayal of lesbian relationships in that pamphlet contains nearly equal degrees of revulsion at and fascination with what the writer is describing. The fact that Fielding interrupted his work on *Tom Jones* to produce *The Female Husband* underscores his interest in what he perceived as extreme forms of female sexual transgression during this period. If we suppose that the novelist's interest in lesbianism continues into the period when he constructed the incest episode in *Tom Jones*, we can read the recuperation of Jenny Waters from those charges as an attempt to deflate the sometimes operatic rhetoric used to condemn sexual deviance of this type. As usual, however, the gesture sends a mixed message. Jenny Waters is forgiven because she has *not* committed incest; if Charlotte Charke is also somehow forgiven here, on what terms is that forgiveness granted?

Obviously, too much can be made of this sort of speculation, and in any case it would be virtually impossible to defend the claim that Charke was in Fielding's mind when he was composing *Tom Jones*. There is no record of any contact between these individuals after the New Haymarket was closed in 1737, and Charke was out wandering the countryside while Fielding's masterpiece was being written and published. Furthermore, as I tried to suggest in my last chapter, the novelist's portrait of Jenny Waters is considerably more complicated than the previous paragraph seems to suggest. Although she shares with Charlotte Charke a certain flair for the transgressive and a remarkable ability to change her shape as circumstances warrant, Jenny Waters generally does not test the boundaries of gender. Nor is her eventual reward anything more than a reasonably comfortable middle-class existence. Still, by the time Charlotte Charke returned to London in 1754, she had given up cross-dressing, and middle-class security seemed to be all she aspired to. The fact that she could not achieve that security in her own life suggests that even the limited salvation granted by Fielding to his female rogues was a departure from social convention and a small step toward the ideal of accepting the notion of difference. The settling of Jenny Waters at Parson Supple's dinner table is one small detail in a large-scale transformation of Somersetshire society, but it has at least the virtue of suggesting that there is a place reserved in Fielding's reconstituted world for those—as he called them in the chapter heading attached to the crucial episode at Upton—"who have good Stomachs."

Notes

Introduction

1. This argument is worked out in detail in chapters 5 and 6 of Stone's study.

2. Stone disagrees with Laslett's belief that industrialization was the primary force for structural changes in the nature and function of the eighteenth-century family. He does not, however, deny that these changes took place.

3. One amusingly childish example of this tendency is Charles Gildon's "The Life and Strange Surprizing Adventures of Mr. D—— De F——" (1719). The general tone of the debate over the relative merits of Fielding and Richardson during the 1740s and 1750s is heavily laced with this sort of class-inflected commentary; for a summary of this pattern, see McKeon, 412, 416–17.

4. Perhaps the two most explicit examples of this phenomenon are Defoe's *Everybody's Business Is Nobody's Business* (1725), which denounces what the author presents as a new and dangerous solidarity among female servants, and the anonymous *A View of the Town* (1731), which levels the same charge at city apprentices.

5. The phrase was coined by Arthur Scouten in *The London Stage* (3.1.lii); more recently, it served as the title for Fidelis Morgan's 1988 biography of Charke.

6. For a more detailed treatment of this passage, see ch. 1 below.

7. For a valuable, if somewhat dated, survey of this community, see Charles H. Gray, *Theatrical Criticism in London to 1795*.

8. Additional examples of this kind of allusion might include Pope's *Imitations of Horace* (1737), which noted that while "our Wives read Milton, / our daughters [read] Plays" (II.i.172); James Miller's *The Modish Couple* (1732), a comedy which opens with a tired Lord Modely wondering whether a sermon or "one of the new Tragedies" would put him to sleep sooner; and William Chetwood's *General History of the Stage* (1749), in which the author claims to have taught Voltaire English by having "furnish'd him every Evening with the Play of the Night, which he took with him into the *Orchestre* (his accustom'd Seat)." In this last case, Chetwood adds that "in four or five Months he not only convers'd in elegant *English*, but wrote it with exact Propriety" (46–47).

9. Fielding was not the only author to abandon the stage for the page during the 1740s. Tobias Smollett, who had come to London in 1739 hoping to get a tragedy called *The Regicide* produced, turned to poetry and verse satire before achieving his first great success with *Roderick Random* in 1748; likewise, Eliza Haywood, who had written both plays and novels in the 1720s and who had supported herself as an actress throughout the 1730s until the Licensing Act was passed, re-

turned to novel-writing in 1741 with her *Anti-Pamela, or Feign'd Innocence Detected.*

10. The works I have in mind here would include Nancy Armstrong's *Desire and Domestic Fiction*, Jerry Beasley's *Novels of the 1740s*, Lennard J. Davis's *Factual Fictions*, J. Paul Hunter's *Before Novels*, Michael McKeon's *The Origins of the English Novel*, John Richetti's *Popular Fiction Before Richardson*, and, of course, Ian Watt's *The Rise of the Novel.* Although they have little to do with drama per se, Ronald Paulson's *Satire and the English Novel* and Terry Castle's *Masquerade and Civilization* might be considered exceptions to this general trend. For the purposes of this study, however, only Laura Brown's *English Dramatic Form* and John Bender's *Imagining the Penitentiary* take seriously the possibility that the reception and impact of stage plays in the first half of the eighteenth century might have helped to shape the rise of the novel. Both books will come up again in the later chapters of this study.

11. The term first appears in the title of Ira Konigsberg's 1969 study *Samuel Richardson and the Dramatic Novel.* Other works that examine the novelist's connection to stage plays and genres of his era include Mark Kinkead-Weekes's *Samuel Richardson: Dramatic Novelist*, and Margaret Doody's *A Natural Passion.*

12. This part of my discussion is intended partly as a response to the critical controversies over *Clarissa* which began with the publication of William Beatty Warner's *Reading Clarissa* in 1979. Warner argues that the struggle between Lovelace and Clarissa is purely a matter of language—that we have no access to any of the physical experiences represented in the novel. Within the next three years, both Terry Castle and Terry Eagleton published studies of the novel which attacked Warner directly and argued that Richardson's treatment of Clarissa's physical suffering reflects the novelist's deep sympathy for the position of women in his society. In response to the attacks by Castle and Eagleton, Warner published a review in *Diacritics* which asserted that the accounts of the rape in the novel cannot and should not be "assimilated to the crime of rape" (28).

13. According to T. C. Duncan Eaves and Ben Kimpel (Richardson's most recent biographers), the novelist disapproved of the women of his era because he considered them to be too vain of their appearances and too forward in courtship (556–58).

14. The source for this remark is a pamphlet called *Sawney and Colley* (1742), p. 4. This work dredges up several stories calculated to embarrass both Pope (Sawney) and Cibber (Colley); the ostensible goal was to convince them to end their undignified attacks on each other by showing them that neither could endure a public airing of their personal lives.

Chapter 1: Life Among the "Otamys": Gender and Demography in The Beggar's Opera

1. All citations will list act, scene, and line numbers as they appear in John Gay, *Dramatic Works*, ed. John Fuller (New York: Oxford University Press, 1983).

2. For a detailed examination of this phenomenon, see Linebaugh.

3. At least one critical examination of Enlightenment intellectual history

has asserted that eighteenth-century anatomists were trying to arrive at a "universal" understanding of the human body which achieved its universal status by eliminating the untidy physical differences which distinguish one human body from another. In *Body Criticism*, Barbara Stafford notes that during the 1720s, the Leiden anatomist Bernard Albinus had been attempting "to establish a universally representative, or average, [body] type free from abnormalities. This artificial, or codified, *homo perfectus* was deduced from a heterogeneous collection of specimens taken from different bodies" (112). Stafford devotes a large section of her study to the use of dissection as a metaphor for certain artistic and scientific activities in Enlightenment cultures.

4. For example, see Empson, *SVP* 217, 220–21; Denning, 35–36.

5. This may be as close as Gay gets to referring to the primary source of Jack Sheppard's fame (see below), and it could be argued that the device of stealing the keys is designed to trivialize the physical obstacles that had to be overcome in order to break out of Newgate, and hence to deflate Sheppard's legendary status. It is also possible that Gay's purpose here is not (or not only) to deflate the legend of Jack Sheppard, but rather to mock the sometimes baroque complexity of the system exploited by Peachum, Lockit, and their historical antecedents.

6. For a full description of the pamphlet war between Wild and Hitchen, see Howson 100–112; this episode is occasionally read as an allusion to a specific disagreement between Walpole and Lord Townsend (see Gay, vol. 2:381n), but that quarrel did not take place until 1729—that is, not until after the play was written.

7. Defoe's biography of Wild is currently available as an appendix to the Penguin edition of Fielding's satire on the same subject; for the passage discussing Wild's circumspection, see 236–40. For excellent discussions of the differences between Defoe's Wild and Fielding's Wild, see Denning, 36–37, and Bender, 150–54.

8. The *O.E.D.* cites the idiom "to burst one's heart" as obsolete, and refers the reader to nothing later than Shakespeare's *1 Henry VI*; the catch here is that Gay apparently borrows the expression "shotten herring" (III.iii; see above) from exactly that play, so it is conceivable that Lucy's line is no more than another such echo. I base my own judgment primarily on the *O.E.D.*'s indication that both the medical idiom of "to burst a blood vessel" and the quasi-medical idiom of "to burst one's buttons" were current in the early eighteenth century.

9. The scene might be traced to any number of possible literary antecedents, ranging from the Gethsemane episode in the gospels to a number of prison scenes in seventeenth-century heroic dramas. I have not dwelt on this point here because I agree with John Bender's argument that, generally speaking, Gay's use of such sources does not initiate a dialogue between the new form and the genres that preceded it; rather, it seems to loosen the older forms from their moorings, "to reformulate them in self-conscious, artificial ways" (104–5).

10. Gay's personal and literary interest in strong drink is evident in his biography, as are his struggles against what would now be characterized as bouts of clinical depression. I am not aware of any analysis of *The Beggar's Opera* which attempts to connect the events of Gay's own life to his characterization of Macheath, and considerations of space prevent me from pursuing the issue here; nevertheless, I think this scene might be a good place to begin such an inquiry.

11. For a dated and somewhat eccentric summary of these two aspects of Polly's reputation, see Charles Pearce, *Polly Peachum* 203–24, 280–83.

Chapter 2: *"The storm that lust began must end in blood"*: The Physical Economy of The London Merchant

1. For a summary of the relationship between Fielding and Lillo, see Battestin, *HFL* 204–7.

2. The phrase appears as a subtitle to Scarry's *Literature and the Body*.

3. All citations will list act, scene, and line numbers as they appear in George Lillo, *The London Merchant*, ed. William H. McBurney (Lincoln: University of Nebraska Press, 1965).

4. One version of this ballad appears as Appendix C to the McBurney edition of the play.

5. The standard authority regarding eighteenth-century apprentices and apprenticeship is M. Dorothy George, *London Life in the XVIIIth Century*; see esp. chs. 5 and 6 (213–312). First published in 1926, George's carefully documented study has yet to show its age, and more recent studies of this period have tended to confirm the accuracy of her claims and descriptions; see Sharpe 103–4, and Malcolmson 64.

6. Poor girls were indentured along with poor boys throughout this period (see George 221). However, it was the unruly mobs of male apprentices that frightened the London populace, and Barnwell's situation would not have been available to a young girl (daughters of the parish would not have been so well placed, and middle-class girls were almost never indentured). Because the existence of female apprentices has no bearing on the current discussion, I have used the male singular pronoun throughout this chapter.

7. Given Lillo's professed aims, it is somewhat ironic that the popularity of *The London Merchant* seems to have depended on an audience that did not include the group it was intended to reform. Ernest Bernbaum has asserted that *The London Merchant* owed its success to "influential citizens" who helped to finance performances "not because they enjoyed them, but because they thought young people should" (158). A number of the performances recorded in *The London Stage* throughout the 1740s indicate that the play had been staged "by desire"—that is, through the intervention of an individual who was wealthy enough to underwrite a performance—and both Lillo's preface and Richardson's decision to praise the play in *The Apprentice's Vade Mecum* support the claim that influential citizens thought the play might be good for apprentices. On the other hand, the idea that Fielding, Garrick, or any other London theater manager of the 1730s and 1740s could afford to keep an unpopular play in his repertory merely because he considered it part of his civic duty to keep the city's apprentices properly indoctrinated seems dubious at best. It seems safe to assume both that there *was* a small but significant audience willing to pay to see the play, and that that audience did not include many of the "City-Youth" for whom it was avowedly intended.

8. Laura Brown has summarized the relevant critical statements on this point (*EDF* 162).

9. The best recent essays on this subject are Laura Brown's "Reading Race and Gender: Jonathan Swift" and Laura Mandell's "Bawds and Merchants" (see esp. 119 n. 6).

10. For a discussion of this idea in relation to Pope's poem, see Susan Gubar, "The Female Monster in Augustan Satire," 391.

11. For a good brief summary of this argument (including bibliographical references), see the appendix to James Twitchell's *Forbidden Partners: The Incest Taboo in Modern Culture*.

12. The McBurney edition of the play includes a "Scene the Last" (Appendix B) which was apparently added to one of a Lillo's later editions in order to discourage those who were printing unauthorized editions of *The London Merchant*. Although the playwright claimed that this scene was part of his original plan, and that some friends had persuaded him not to make it part of "the representation" (Appendix A; p. 82), it is the model "representation," now generally called the playtext, and not the printed script which provides the basis for my analysis.

Chapter 3: "Not the Person she conceived me": The Public Identities of Charlotte Charke

1. See, for example, Sidonie Smith's chapter-length discussion in *A Poetics of Women's Autobiography* (102–22) and Patricia Meyer Spacks's brief but valuable commentary in *Imagining a Self* (75–77). Felicity Nussbaum's essay on scandalous memoirs helps to place Charke's autobiography in its generic context, and a new biography by Fidelis Morgan reproduces Charke's *Narrative* side by side with the author's attempts to document the details of her account. For an opinionated summary of many earlier references to and comments on Charke, see Morgan 205–12; see also her bibliography (218–19). Kristina Straub's *Sexual Suspects*, which was published after the initial work on this chapter was completed, represents a significant exception to the generalization in my text; although her study focuses exclusively on Charke's print narratives, she does read Charke's efforts at self-fashioning and her depictions of homosexual characters in her novels in terms of their respective relationships to various eighteenth-century examinations of theatrical cross-dressing.

2. Smith contends that Charke is torn between the transgressive and the penitent mode throughout the *Narrative* (104). Although I accept the claim that these two modes interpenetrate each other to some degree, I would also contend that the first half of the *Narrative* (up to approximately p. 117 in the facsimile edition, when she reports that her letter begging an audience with her father has been returned to her unmarked and presumably unread) consistently offers up apologies for Charke's past behavior, while the latter half treats her adventures in male drag both much more explicitly and much less apologetically than anything Charke has presented before that crucial turning point.

3. On the whole, I believe that Morgan's biography is a valuable addition to the body of work on Charlotte Charke, because it adds significantly to what

we know about this fascinating woman. However, I also think that Morgan is somewhat more credulous than she should be about some of the material in the *Narrative*; she seems at times to be willing to accept every detail in the autobiography as factual unless and until it is explicitly contradicted by specific external evidence. She also seems unwilling to consider seriously the possibility that Charke was a lesbian.

4. Wilshire's assertions seem to imply that Brecht's notion of the Verfremdungseffekt—a crucial element of the gestus (see Diamond 84–85)—is wrong in some sense, but in fact this contradiction is more apparent than real. Despite Brecht's assertions to the contrary, there is no logical reason that the spectator's identification with a character should cease merely because the mechanisms employed to construct that character are brought into the open (see also Wilshire 14, 14n).

5. The standard edition of Charke's *Narrative* is the facsimile reprint edited by Leonard R. N. Ashley (Gainesville: Scholars' Facsimiles and Reprints, 1966).

6. In its entry on Charlotte Charke, the *Biographical Dictionary of Actors, Actresses, etc.* claims erroneously that she played Mustacha in Fielding's *Tom Thumb* on 1 May 1730 (Highfill et al., eds., III:167). However, an examination of the primary sources by William Burling and Robert Hume has since confirmed the *London Stage* attribution of this part to a Mrs. Clark or Clarke (115 n. 43).

7. With the exception of court masques and other private entertainments, English women had not been allowed on English stages before the Restoration; this is perhaps the primary reason that the voyeuristic elements of the theatrical experience were especially prominent during the late seventeenth and early eighteenth centuries. Many seventeenth- and early eighteenth-century playwrights took pains to provide their audiences with female characters in men's clothes; John Harold Wilson has estimated that nearly a quarter of the plays first performed between 1660 and 1700 provided occasions for actresses to dress up in this fashion (73). It is possible that Charke wanted to perform in breeches from the very beginning, and that her status as a novice performer prevented her from getting the roles she wanted during those early years, but there is nothing in either the *Narrative* or the public record that would support this claim.

8. She had married Richard Charke two months after her seventeenth birthday, and he abandoned her less than a year later. A musician employed by the Drury Lane company, he had been introduced to her by Theophilus when Charlotte Cibber was only sixteen; he apparently married her only because he thought she would help him gain the approval and assistance of the influential Colley Cibber (see Charke 50). The failure of the marriage forced her to appeal frequently to her father and her brother for help, with predictably disappointing results.

9. Although Katharine Eisamann Maus has argued that "Restoration theater . . . provided, at least for the leading players, manifold opportunities for self-expression" (599), it would be unwise to apply this generalization either to Charke or to secondary roles like that of Mrs. Otter. Charlotte Charke was not a Restoration but an eighteenth-century actor. In his essay on eighteenth-century performance styles, Joseph Roach has noted the astonishing proliferation of what he calls "'how-to' manuals on the mastery of bodily expression" during the period in which she lived and worked (100). To obtain an impression of exactly how

prescriptive and restrictive these manuals could be—how much they might do to forestall any attempt on the part of the performer to express him- or herself—see Roach 109–15.

10. There is no way to tell whether the increasing number of breeches roles reflected a conscious choice on Charke's part; it is at least possible that she stumbled onto this specialty accidentally, because the actors who had performed these roles for the Drury Lane company in the early 1730s (Theodosia Mills, Sarah Thurmond, and Elizabeth Wetherilt) had died or moved on to other venues before the actors' revolt.

11. In *The Tender Husband*, Lucy Fainlove disguises herself as a man in order to assist one of the male leads with the project of reforming his wife; at the end of the play, she is married off to a country bumpkin. In *Oroonoko*, Charlotte Weldon marries a wealthy widow for her money and allows a male accomplice to take her place on the wedding night, but she eventually resumes her female identity and marries her accomplice's older brother; in *The Recruiting Officer*, Silvia disguises herself as a man so that she can evade her father and keep tabs on Captain Plume during their apparent separation.

12. Although Phyllis Rackin makes a persuasive case for the claim that the thematic argument of *Epicoene* is fundamentally misogynist (33, 36–37), I would still argue that the oddly aggressive ending of the play subverts the argument of the text to some degree. We might even speculate that Jonson's eventual decision to abandon the public theater for more easily controlled contexts reflected his awareness that stage mechanisms like these tended to undermine the hierarchies he sought to establish in his scripts—an argument whose general shape has been recently advanced by Herbert Blau (215–17).

13. For an extended discussion of this point insofar as it pertains to female performers of this period, see Ferris 72–74.

14. Judging from the tone and content of the puffs and other publicity Charke provided for her summer season at the Haymarket in 1734 (see Morgan 54–58), the roles she had played with the Drury Lane rebels during the 1733–34 season had earned her a reputation for eccentric tastes and behavior. There is, however, no way to determine whether this image reflected her offstage behavior at this point in her life, primarily because the *Narrative* is (rather uncharacteristically) silent on the subject. In any case, I do not believe that her willingness to capitalize on this reputation necessarily indicates that she accepted the characterization.

15. For a more detailed analysis of Mr. Hen, see Campbell 66–67, 74–77.

16. Before she joined Fielding, Charke had imitated her father only once, on 19 June 1735, when she had played Lord Foppington in Cibber's *The Careless Husband* (1704); certain circumstances connected with that performance suggest she was angry with her father at that point, but either the difference was patched up quickly or Cibber himself was angry enough to insist that Charke give up the role immediately. Since both Charke and Fielding had good reasons to be displeased with Cibber, it is impossible to determine whether he sought her out in order to exploit her private conflicts for his own purposes, or whether she was drawn to the Great Mogul's Company by the prospect of striking back at her father for his years of neglect. Since Charke was definitely a cut above the other actors in the company (see Hume, *HFT* 207–8), it is also just barely possible that both she and

Fielding looked on the change merely as a matter of professional advancement—a way to get her better roles, and to improve the level of acting in his plays.

17. According to the *Narrative*, Colley Cibber summoned his daughter to a family meeting that quickly degenerated into a shouting match; the conference ended with the old actor's announcement that he was cutting her off completely (124–25). A letter from Cibber to Charke which is now generally believed to deal with her connection with Fielding tells her in so many words that she will receive nothing from her father as long as she refuses to "dissociate [her]self from that worthless scoundrel" (qtd. in Morgan 87).

18. Fielding's cast includes a playwright named Ground-Ivy who satirizes Cibber's revision of Shakespeare, a blustering actor named Pistol who obviously caricatures Theophilus, and a playwright named Medley who presents an imitation of Colley Cibber's poetry. This last is written ostensibly as a prologue for his new production (*The Historical Register* is a rehearsal play) and delivered in full before the play is five minutes old. All three roles were played by men.

19. See Barthes, "The Death of the Author" (142–48 in *Image/Music/Text*), and Foucault, "What Is an Author?" (141–60 in Harari, *Textual Strategies*).

20. There is no adequate psychoanalytical explanation for female transvestism (Stoller 194–205); Garber points out quite rightly that this silence probably says more about psychoanalysts and sex researchers than it does about women who cross-dress (44–45, 94–99). Historical studies by Kathleen Crawford, Lillian Faderman, and Lynn Friedli have indicated that some "female soldiers" dressed up in order to be near their (male) lovers, while others were apparently male-identified individuals who sought to emulate the swashbuckling rakes who served as role models for numbers of men throughout this period. Nor should it be assumed that the motive for female cross-dressing was always predominantly a matter of sexual identity and appetite. Even if such information were available, it would have to be weighed in each case against the possibility that a decision to adopt a male identity was based on material considerations rather than sexual preferences; impersonating a man would invariably grant the woman involved higher wages, greater mobility, and a degree of immunity from certain kinds of persecution.

21. For an alternative reading of this passage, see Smith, 114–15.

22. In the early part of the *Narrative*, Charke presents herself as a four-year-old who cross-dresses in her father's wig and brother's waistcoat; the episode is presented as comic, the result of an innocent child's wish to emulate her famous father (17–18). As Straub argues, this episode loses some of its innocence in the context of the autobiography, because it held Cibber up to ridicule by reminding Charke's readers that her father's trademark periwig could be read as a signal that his masculinity was somehow suspect (139–40). At the same time, Charke's willingness to present her cross-dressing as the misguided escapade of a small child can be viewed as another version of the normalizing tendency reflected in the accounts that described her behavior as an attempt to embarrass her father. And as I suggested earlier, Charke's pursuit of this trope is only temporary; when she finally concludes, midway through the *Narrative*, that Cibber will not in fact respond to her overtures, her accounts of her adventures in men's clothes become more obtrusive and more obviously aggressive—as, for example, when she re-

counts the story that she had, while disguised as a (male) fishmonger, come upon her father in the streets of London and slapped his face with a flounder (141).

23. For a detailed treatment of this scene, see Chapter 4 below.

Chapter 4: "So much written about what deserves not the least consideration": Performance and Physical Experience in Clarissa

1. At the time of this writing, there are two widely available editions of the unabridged *Clarissa*: the 1932 Everyman edition, which is based on Richardson's final revision; and the 1985 Penguin edition, which is based on the first published version of the novel. Unless otherwise specified, the quotations and citations in this chapter are taken from the more recent of these editions. The number preceded by the "L" is the number assigned to the letter by Angus Ross, who edited the Penguin volume; it is included partly for the convenience of those readers who may be working with the Everyman text. The second number refers to the page(s) in the Penguin edition where the quotation appears.

2. As McKillop notes, the novelist "preferred to discuss his work in terms of the tragedies of the two preceding generations" (145)—that is, in relation to the tragedies of Nicholas Rowe, Thomas Otway, John Dryden, Joseph Addison, and others. In *Clarissa* itself, Belford explicitly compares Richardson's story to Rowe's *The Fair Penitent*; Belford of course finds Clarissa to be infinitely superior to the heroine of the earlier work, on the grounds that unlike her adulterous predecessor, Clarissa is "a penitent without a fault" (L413, 1205). The novelist may have believed that the older tragedies were more respectable than their successors and that by comparing his novel to more established works he was staking a claim to artistic legitimacy that might have been less well served by allusions to more recent works. McKillop also suggests that Richardson might have considered the social context of *Clarissa* to be closer to those of Rowe and Otway than it was to that of *The London Merchant*.

3. For a more detailed summary of the similarities between the two works, see Brown, *EDF*, 195–96. Given the extent of these parallels, it seems unnecessary to indulge in the excessive caution displayed by Richardson's most recent biographers, who say only that *Caelia* "may conceivably" provide the source for the novel (Eaves and Kimpel 235).

4. For a discussion of Richardson's attitude toward English drama and toward the London stage, see Eaves and Kimpel, 54, 582–83.

5. In addition to the passages quoted above, see also L209, 674, where Lovelace complains of Sally's attempts to use "trite and vulgar artifices" against Clarissa. It may also be worth noting that in later editions of the novel, Richardson placed even greater emphasis on Sally's histrionics. The final edition of *Clarissa*, a version of which is still available under the Modern Library imprint, adds the following paragraph to Lovelace's introductory description of the two nieces:

Here this little devil Sally, not being able, as she told me, to support life under my displeasure, was going into a fit: but when I saw her *preparing* for it, I went out of the room; and so she thought it would not be worth her while to show away. (II: 209)

Both the precise nature of the "fit" and the occasion for it foreshadow Sally's final scene.

6. For a discussion of these experiments and their significance in relation to performance theory, see Blau's ch. 4, "Repression, Pain, and the Participation Mystique," esp. pp. 165–66.

7. Since Charke was not especially well-known at this point, and since the "victim" of her specular aggression was her own sister-in-law, I think this possibility is unlikely; I raise it here only to indicate the difference between a response which focuses on signifying bodies, and a response which focuses on actors' bodies.

8. For a more extended discussion of this phenomenon, see ch. 7 of Straub's *Sexual Suspects*.

9. These would include studies by Terry Castle, Margaret Doody, and Terry Eagleton, among others.

10. She also leaves a miniature of herself to her cousin Col. Morden, but this is a special case that foreshadows the bequest of Anna's miniature to Hickman and establishes a kind of symmetry between the dead and living. Clarissa's symbolic commitment of herself to a cousin whose name is etymologically connected to death is counterbalanced by an analogous gesture which emphasizes her prescription for a happy life for Anna. Clarissa herself spins out a version of this parallel in L465, 1339.

11. To be fair, it should be noted that Johnson's *Caelia* shows no more willingness to confront the radical implications of forgiving a fallen women. In the play, the heroine's death guarantees that her father will have *only* to forgive her—that he will not have to take her back into his house. Richardson masks the convenience of his ending more effectively by allowing Lovelace a measure of remorse, and by suggesting repeatedly that society as a whole would be better off if Clarissa forgave him and accepted his now sincere offer of marriage. To the extent that we take these possibilities seriously (as several of Richardson's correspondents did), Clarissa's death in the novel seems less like the easiest way out.

Chapter 5: Who She Was and What She Was: Female Characters and Physical Experience in Tom Jones

1. For Watt's defense of these generalizations, see ch. 6, "Private Experience and the Novel," and ch. 9, "Fielding as Novelist: *Tom Jones*."

2. Later in his study, McKeon does suggest that *Tom Jones* is less conservative than Fielding's earlier works (418), but this claim is apparently based primarily on Tom's status as a bastard, and not on anything having to do with the novelist's treatment of gender relations.

3. All quotations and citations of *Tom Jones* refer to the 1975 edition published by the Wesleyan University Press and edited by Martin Battestin and Fredson Bowers. The novel is divided into eighteen books; the citations identify the book number, the chapter within the book, and the page(s) from which the quotation is taken.

4. See, for example, "Body/Power" (pp. 55–62) and "The Politics of Health in the Eighteenth Century" (pp. 166–82) in *PK*.

5. For a discussion of these issues, see Jill Campbell, "'When Men Women Turn,'" in *The New Eighteenth Century*; see also Terry Castle, "MNF."

6. Certain circumstances outside the novel itself suggest that this interest in female monsters may reflect some unspecified and temporary disturbance in Fielding's private life. It might be interesting to try to place the composition of the churchyard scene during the winter of 1746–47—a period when Fielding's work on *Tom Jones* was interrupted by only two other writing projects: *The Female Husband* and a prose paraphrase of Ovid's *Ars Amatoria* (see Battestin, *HFL* 411–12). There is an interesting essay to be written considering the portraits of the women in these pieces—both of which are blatantly misogynistic—in relation to what is happening at this point in *Tom Jones*.

7. For an extended discussion of this subject, see Maurice Johnson, "The Device of Sophia's Muff in *Tom Jones*."

8. See esp. IV.vi.175, V.v.228–29.

9. In the course of an essay that repeatedly praises Richardson at Fielding's expense, Frank Kermode condemns the use of the incest motif in *Tom Jones* because this possibility turns out to have been illusory (109); Kermode believes that Fielding cannot be taken seriously as a moralist because Tom's errors do not finally have consequences. In a more recent essay, Michael Hall attempts to salvage Fielding the moralist by suggesting that this episode shocks the reader as much as it shocks Tom. Hall argues that "it really makes no difference that Tom is finally relieved of guilt; the contrivance of the plot, the mere hint of incest, is enough to make the [immoral nature of casual sexual encounters] manifest" (104). Van Boheemen's approach, though it is more theoretically sophisticated, echoes this latter position; in her view, "while incest as an act does not, and cannot, take place in the comic structure of the fiction, the anxiety itself is sufficient to communicate Fielding's meaning" (79). For further summaries of this ongoing discussion, see Empson "*TJ*," 47; Battestin "SI," 7; Hall 101.

10. Van Boheemen is one of many recent critics who acknowledges her debt to Battestin (51n).

Works Cited

Alter, Robert. *Fielding and the Nature of the Novel*. Cambridge, Mass.: Harvard University Press, 1968.

Armstrong, Nancy. *Desire and Domestic Fiction: A Political History of the Novel*. New York: Oxford University Press, 1987.

Barthes, Roland. *Image/Music/Text*. Trans. Stephen Heath. New York: Hill and Wang, 1977.

Battestin, Martin. *Henry Fielding: A Life*. London: Routledge, 1990.

———. "Henry Fielding, Sarah Fielding, and 'the dreadful Sin of Incest.' " *Novel: A Forum on Fiction* 13 (1979): 6–18.

———. *The Providence of Wit*. New York: Oxford University Press, 1974.

———, ed. *Twentieth-Century Interpretations of Tom Jones*. Englewood Cliffs, N.J.: Prentice-Hall, 1968.

Beasley, Jerry. *Novels of the 1740s*. Athens: University of Georgia Press, 1983.

Bender, John. *Imagining the Penitentiary*. Chicago: University of Chicago Press, 1987.

Bernbaum, Ernest. *The Drama of Sensibility*. Boston: Ginn and Company, 1915.

Blau, Herbert. *The Audience*. Baltimore, Md.: Johns Hopkins University Press, 1990.

Boswell, James. *Boswell's London Journal: 1762–1763*. Ed. Frederick Pottle. New Haven, Conn.: Yale University Press, 1950.

Boucé, Paul-Gabriel. "Sex, amours, and love in *Tom Jones*." *Studies in Voltaire and the Eighteenth Century* (1984): 25–38.

Brooks, Peter. *Reading for the Plot*. New York: Random House, 1984.

Brown, Laura. *English Dramatic Form, 1660–1760*. New Haven, Conn.: Yale University Press, 1981.

———. "Reading Race and Gender: Jonathan Swift." *Eighteenth-Century Studies* 23 (1990): 424–43.

Brown, Laura, and Felicity Nussbaum, eds. *The New Eighteenth Century*. New York: Methuen, 1987.

Bullock, Christopher. *A Match in Newgate*. London, 1715. Rpt. in Guerinot and Jilg, 10–18.

Burling, William J., and Robert Hume. "Theatrical Companies at the Little Haymarket, 1720–1737." *Essays in Theatre* 4:2 (May 1986): 98–118.

Butler, Judith. "Performative Acts and Gender Constitution: An Essay in Phenomenology and Feminist Theory." In Case, 270–82.

Campbell, Jill. " 'When Men Women Turn': Gender Reversals in Fielding's Plays." In Brown and Nussbaum, 62–83.

Case, Sue-Ellen, ed. *Performing Feminisms*. Baltimore, Md.: Johns Hopkins University Press, 1990.

Castle, Terry. *Clarissa's Ciphers*. Ithaca, N.Y.: Cornell University Press, 1982.

———. *Masquerade and Civilization*. Stanford, Calif.: Stanford University Press, 1986.

———. "Matters Not Fit to be Mentioned: Fielding's *The Female Husband*." *English Literary History* 49 (1982): 602–22.

Charke, Charlotte. *A Narrative of the Life of Mrs. Charlotte Charke*. London, 1755. Fac. ed. Leonard R. N. Ashley. Gainesville: Scholars' Facsimiles and Reprints, 1969.

Chetwood, William. *A General History of the English Stage*. London: W. Owen, 1749.

Cibber, Colley. *An Apology for the Life of Colley Cibber*. Ed. B. R. S. Fone. Ann Arbor: University of Michigan Press, 1968.

———. *The Careless Husband*. Ed. William Appleton. Lincoln: University of Nebraska Press, 1966.

Conolly, L. W. *The Censorship of English Drama, 1737–1824*. San Marino, Calif.: Huntington Library, 1976.

Cooke, Thomas. *The Comedian*. London: J. Roberts, 1732.

Crane, Ronald S. "The Plot of *Tom Jones*." In Battestin, *TCI*, 68–93.

Crawford, Kathleen. *The Transvestite Heroine in Seventeenth-Century Popular Literature*. Unpublished dissertation. Cambridge, Mass.: Harvard University, 1984.

Davis, Lennard J. *Factual Fictions*. New York: Columbia University Press, 1983.

Defoe, Daniel. "Everybody's Business Is Nobody's Business." London, 1725. Rpt. London: Warner, Dodd, and Nutt, 1960.

———. "The True and Genuine Account of the Life and Actions of the Late Jonathan Wild." London, 1725. Rpt. in Henry Fielding, *Jonathan Wild*, ed. David Nokes. New York: Penguin, 1982.

Denning, Michael. "Beggars and Thieves: *The Beggar's Opera* as Crime Drama." In Humm et al., 29–47.

Derrida, Jacques. *Writing and Difference*. Trans. and intro. by Alan Bass. Chicago: University of Chicago Press, 1978.

Diamond, Elin. "Brechtian Theory/Feminist Theory: Toward a Gestic Feminist Criticism." *The Drama Review* 32:1 (Spring 1988): 82–94.

Dollimore, Jonathan, and Alan Sinfield, eds. *Political Shakespeare*. Ithaca, N.Y.: Cornell University Press, 1985.

Doody, Margaret. *A Natural Passion*. Oxford, U.K.: Clarendon Press, 1974.

Eagleton, Terry. *The Rape of Clarissa*. Minneapolis: University of Minnesota Press, 1982.

Eaves, T. C. Duncan, and Ben Kimpel. *Samuel Richardson*. Oxford, U.K.: Clarendon Press, 1971.

Empson, William. *Some Versions of Pastoral*. New York: New Directions, 1974.

———. "*Tom Jones*." In Battestin, *TCI*, 33–55.

Faderman, Lillian. *Surpassing the Love of Men*. New York: William Morrow, 1981.

Ferris, Lesley. *Acting Women: Images of Women in Theatre*. New York: New York University Press, 1989.

Fielding, Henry. *The Female Husband*. London, 1746. Rpt. ed. Claude E. Jones. Liverpool, U.K.: Liverpool University Press (English Reprints Series), 1960.

———. *The Historical Register for the Year 1736*. Ed. William W. Appleton. Lincoln: University of Nebraska Press, 1967.

———. *Jonathan Wild*. Ed. David Nokes. New York: Penguin, 1982.

———. *Tom Jones*. Ed. Martin Battestin and Fredson Bowers. Middletown, Conn.: Wesleyan University Press, 1975.

Foucault, Michel. *Discipline and Punish*. Trans. Alan Sheridan. New York: Vintage, 1979.

———. *Power/Knowledge*. Ed. Colin Gordon. New York: Harvester Press, 1980.

———. "What Is an Author?" In Harari, 141–60.

Friedman, Michael. "He Was Just a Macheath: Boswell and *The Beggar's Opera*." *The Age of Johnson* 4 (1991): 97–114.

Fuller, John. Introduction to John Gay, *Dramatic Works*. New York: Oxford University Press, 1983.

Garber, Marjorie. *Vested Interests: Cross-Dressing and Cultural Anxiety*. New York: Routledge, 1992.

Gay, John. *Dramatic Works* (2 vols.). Ed. John Fuller. New York: Oxford University Press, 1983.

George, M. Dorothy. *London Life in the XVIIIth Century*. 1926. Rpt., Chicago: Academy Chicago, 1984.

Gildon, Charles. "The Life and Strange Surprizing Adventures of Mr. D—— De F——." London, 1719. Rpt. in Daniel Defoe, *Robinson Crusoe*, ed. Michael Shinagel. New York: Norton, 1975.

Gray, Charles H. *Theatrical Criticism in London to 1795*. New York: Benjamin Blom, 1964.

Gubar, Susan. "The Female Monster in Augustan Satire." *Signs* 3 (1977): 380–94.

Guerinot, J. V., and Rodney D. Jilg. *Contexts 1: The Beggar's Opera*. Hamden, Conn.: Archon, 1976.

Hall, Michael. "Incest and Morality in *Tom Jones*." *The South Central Bulletin* (1981): 101–4.

Harari, Josue, ed. *Textual Strategies*. Ithaca, N.Y.: Cornell University Press, 1979.

Hay, Douglas, Peter Linebaugh, and E. P. Thompson, eds. *Albion's Fatal Tree*. New York: Penguin, 1977.

Hibbert, Christopher. *The Road to Tyburn*. Cleveland, Ohio: World Publishing Company, 1957.

Highfill, Philip, Kalman Burnim, and Edward Langhans, eds. *A Biographical Dictionary of Actors, Actresses, Musicians, Dancers, Managers, and Other Stage Personnel in London, 1660–1800*. Carbondale: Southern Illinois University Press, 1975–.

The History Of the remarkable Life of John Sheppard. London, 1724. Rpt. in Rawlings, 47–75.

Howson, Gerald. *Thief-Taker General*. New York: St. Martin's Press, 1970.

Hume, Robert. *Henry Fielding and the London Theatre, 1728–1737*. Oxford, U.K.: Clarendon Press, 1988.

———. *The Rakish Stage*. Carbondale: Southern Illinois University Press, 1983.

———, ed. *The London Theatre World, 1660–1800*. Carbondale: Southern Illinois University Press, 1983.

Humm, Peter, Paul Stigant, and Peter Widdowson, eds. *Popular Fictions*. New York: Methuen, 1986.

Hunter, J. Paul. *Before Novels*. New York: Norton, 1990.

———. *Occasional Form*. Baltimore, Md.: Johns Hopkins University Press, 1975.

Johnson, Charles. *Caelia, or the Perjured Lover*. London: J. Watts, 1733.

Johnson, Maurice. "The Device of Sophia's Muff in *Tom Jones*." *Modern Language Notes* 74 (1959): 685–90.

Jonson, Ben. *Epicoene, or the Silent Woman*. Ed. L. A. Beaurline. Lincoln: University of Nebraska Press, 1966.

Kenny, Shirley Strum. "The Publication of Plays." In Hume, *LT*, 309–36.

Kermode, Frank. "Richardson and Fielding." *Cambridge Journal* 4 (1950): 106–14.

Kinkead-Weekes, Mark. *Samuel Richardson: Dramatic Novelist*. London: Methuen, 1973.

Knoll, Robert E. *Ben Jonson's Plays: An Introduction*. Lincoln: University of Nebraska Press, 1964.

Konigsberg, Ira. *Samuel Richardson and the Dramatic Novel*. Lexington: University of Kentucky Press, 1969.

Laslett, Peter. *The World We Have Lost*. New York: Charles Scribner's Sons, 1971.

Leder, Drew. *The Absent Body*. Chicago: University of Chicago Press, 1990.

Linebaugh, Peter. "The Tyburn Riot Against the Surgeons." In Hay et al., 65–117.

Lillo, George. *The London Merchant*. Ed. William H. McBurney. Lincoln: University of Nebraska Press, 1965.

Malcolmson, R. W. *Life and Labour in England, 1700–1780*. London: Hutchinson and Co., 1980.

Mandell, Laura. "Bawds and Merchants: Engendering Capitalist Desires." *English Literary History* 59 (1992): 107–23.

Markley, Robert. "Sentimentality as Performance: Shaftesbury, Sterne, and the Theatrics of Virtue." In Brown and Nussbaum, 210–30.

Maus, Katharine Eisamann. "Playhouse Flesh and Blood: Sexual Ideology and the Restoration Actress." *English Literary History* 46 (1979): 595–617.

McBurney, William H. Introduction to George Lillo, *The London Merchant*. Lincoln: University of Nebraska Press, 1965.

McConachie, Bruce A., and Thomas Postlewait, eds. *Interpreting the Theatrical Past*. Iowa City: University of Iowa Press, 1989.

McKeon, Michael. *The Origins of the English Novel*. Baltimore, Md.: Johns Hopkins University Press, 1987.

McKillop, Alan D. *Samuel Richardson*. Chapel Hill: University of North Carolina Press, 1936.

McLynn, Frank. *Crime and Punishment in Eighteenth-Century England*. New York: Oxford University Press, 1991.

Milhous, Judith. *Thomas Betterton and the Management of Lincoln's Inn Fields, 1695–1707*. Carbondale: Southern Illinois University Press, 1979.

Miller, James. *The Modish Couple*. London: J. Watts, 1732.

Morgan, Fidelis. *The Well-Known Troublemaker*. London: Faber and Faber, 1988.

Noyes, Robert Gale. *Ben Jonson on the English Stage, 1660–1776*. New York: Benjamin Blom, 1935.

Nussbaum, Felicity. "Heteroclites: The Gender of Character in the Scandalous Memoirs." In Brown and Nussbaum, 144–67.

Paulson, Ronald. *Satire and the English Novel*. New Haven, Conn.: Yale University Press, 1967.

Pearce, Charles E. *Polly Peachum*. New York: Benjamin Blom, 1968.

Pope, Alexander. *The Poems of Alexander Pope*. Ed. John Butt. New Haven, Conn.: Yale University Press, 1963.

Porter, Roy. "Barely Touching: A Social Perspective on Mind and Body." In Rousseau, 45–80.

Rackin, Phyllis. "Androgyny, Mimesis, and the Marriage of the Boy Heroine on the English Renaissance Stage." *PMLA* 102:1 (Jan. 1987): 29–41.

Ravenscroft, Edward. *The London Cuckolds*. London, 1681. Rpt., London: W. Feals, 1737.

Rawlings, Philip, ed. *Drunks, Whores and Idle Apprentices*. London: Routledge, 1992.

Richardson, Samuel. *The Apprentice's Vade Mecum*. London, 1734. Rpt., New York: Garland, 1974.

———. *Clarissa*. Ed. Angus Ross. New York: Penguin Books, 1985.

———. *Pamela*. Ed. William M. Sale. New York: Norton, 1958.

Richetti, John. *Popular Fiction Before Richardson*. Oxford, U.K.: Clarendon Press, 1969.

Roach, Joseph. "Power's Body: The Inscription of Morality as Style." In McConachie and Postlewait, 99–118.

Rousseau, G. S., ed. *The Languages of Psyche*. Berkeley: University of California Press, 1990.

Sawney and Colley. 1742. Rpt. ed. W. Powell Jones. Los Angeles: Clark Memorial Library (Augustan Reprint Society Publication No. 83), 1960.

Scarry, Elaine. *The Body in Pain*. New York: Oxford University Press, 1985.

———, ed. *Literature and the Body*. Baltimore, Md.: Johns Hopkins University Press, 1990.

Scouten, Arthur H., ed. *The London Stage: 1660–1800*, Pt. 3 (1729–1747). 2 vols. Carbondale: Southern Illinois University Press, 1961.

Sharpe, J. A. *Crime in Early Modern England, 1550–1750*. New York: Longmans, 1984.

Smith, Sidonie. *A Poetics of Women's Autobiography*. Bloomington: Indiana University Press, 1987.

Spacks, Patricia Meyer. *Imagining a Self*. Cambridge, Mass.: Harvard University Press, 1976.

Stallybrass, Peter, and Allon White. *The Politics and Poetics of Transgression*. Ithaca, N.Y.: Cornell University Press, 1986.

Stafford, Barbara. *Body Criticism: Imaging the Unseen in Enlightenment Art and Medicine*. Chicago: University of Chicago Press, 1992.

Stoller, Robert J. *Sex and Gender*. New York: Science House, 1968.

Stone, Lawrence. *The Family, Sex, and Marriage in England, 1500–1800*. London: Weidenfeld and Nicolson, 1977.

Straub, Kristina. *Sexual Suspects*. Princeton, N.J.: Princeton University Press, 1992.

Swift, Jonathan. *Gulliver's Travels and Other Writings*. Ed. Louis Landa. New York: Houghton Mifflin, 1960.

Thompson, E. P. "Patrician Society, Plebeian Culture." *Journal of Social History* 7 (1974): 382–405.

Thurmond, John. *Harlequin Sheppard*. London, 1724. Rpt. in Guerinot and Jilg, 19–31.

Twitchell, James B. *Forbidden Partners: The Incest Taboo in Modern Culture*. New York: Columbia University Press, 1987.

Van Boheemen, Christine. *The Novel as Family Romance*. Ithaca, N.Y.: Cornell University Press, 1987.

A View of the Town: or, Memoirs of London. London, 1731.

Warner, William Beatty. *Reading Clarissa*. New Haven, Conn.: Yale University Press, 1979.

———. "Reading Rape: Marxist-Feminist Figurations of the Literal." *Diacritics* 13 (1983): 12–32.

Watt, Ian, *The Rise of the Novel*. London: Chatto and Windus, 1957.

Wilshire, Bruce. *Role Playing and Identity*. Bloomington: Indiana University Press, 1982.

Wilson, John Harold. *All the King's Ladies*. Chicago: University of Chicago Press, 1958.

Wrigley, E. A. "A Simple Model of London's Importance in Changing English Society and Economy, 1650–1750." *Past and Present* 37 (1967): 44–70.

Zomchick, John P. "A Penetration which Nothing Can Deceive: Gender and Juridical Discourse in Some Eighteenth-Century Narratives." *Studies in English Literature* 29 (1989): 535–61.

Index

Numbers in bold face indicate sections where topic is treated at length.

University of Pennsylvania Press
NEW CULTURAL STUDIES
*Joan DeJean, Carroll Smith-Rosenberg,
and Peter Stallybrass, Editors*

Jonathan Arac and Harriet Ritvo, editors. *Macropolitics of Nineteenth-Century Literature: Nationalism, Exoticism, Imperialism.* 1991

John Barrell. *The Birth of Pandora and the Division of Knowledge.* 1992

Bruce Thomas Boehrer. *Monarchy and Incest in Renaissance England: Literature, Culture, Kinship, and Kingship.* 1992

Carol Breckenridge and Peter van der Veer, editors. *Orientalism and the Postcolonial Predicament: Perspectives on South Asia.* 1993

E. Jane Burns. *Bodytalk: When Women Speak in Old French Literature.* 1993

Jones DeRitter. *The Embodiment of Characters: The Representation of Physical Experience on Stage and in Print, 1728–1749.* 1994

Julia V. Douthwaite. *Exotic Women: Literary Heroines and Cultural Strategies in Ancien Régime France.* 1992

Barbara J. Eckstein. *The Language of Fiction in a World of Pain: Reading Politics as Paradox.* 1990

Katherine Gravdal. *Ravishing Maidens: Writing Rape in Medieval French Literature and Law.* 1991

Jayne Ann Krentz, editor. *Dangerous Men and Adventurous Women: Romance Writers on the Appeal of the Romance.* 1992

Carole Levin. *The Heart and Stomach of a King: Elizabeth I and the Politics of Sex and Power.* 1994

Linda Lomperis and Sarah Stanbury, editors. *Feminist Approaches to the Body in Medieval Literature.* 1993

Karma Lochrie. *Margery Kempe and Translations of the Flesh.* 1991

Alex Owen. *The Darkened Room: Women, Power and Spiritualism in Late Victorian England.* 1990

Jacqueline Rose. *The Case of Peter Pan or The Impossibility of Children's Fiction.* 1992

Alan Sinfield. *Cultural Politics—Queer Reading.* 1994

This book has been set in Linotron Galliard. Galliard was designed for Mergenthaler in 1978 by Matthew Carter. Galliard retains many of the features of a sixteenth-century typeface cut by Robert Granjon but has some modifications that give it a more contemporary look.

Printed on acid-free paper.